T0305352

MONEY AND MONETARY SYSTEMS

Money and Monetary Systems

Selected Essays of Filippo Cesarano

Filippo Cesarano

Bank of Italy

Edward Elgar

Cheltenham, UK • Northampton, MA, USA

© Filippo Cesarano 2008

Published by
Edward Elgar Publishing Limited
The Lypiatts
15 Lansdown Road
Cheltenham
Glos GL50 2JA
UK

Edward Elgar Publishing, Inc.
William Pratt House
9 Dewey Court
Northampton
Massachusetts 01060
USA

A catalogue record for this book
is available from the British Library

Library of Congress Cataloguing in Publication Data
Cesarano, Filippo
    Money and monetary systems : selected essays of Filippo Cesarano / Filippo Cesarano.
        p. cm.
    Includes bibliographical references and index.
    1. Money—History. 2. Monetary policy—History. 3. Monetary unions—History. I. Title.
    HG231.C43 2008
    332.4—dc22

2008023876

ISBN 978 1 84720 519 3

Printed and bound in Great Britain by MPG Books Ltd, Bodmin, Cornwall

Contents

PART IV   MONETARY UNIONS

PART V   ECONOMICS AS A SOCIAL SCIENCE

Acknowledgements

The author and the publisher wish to thank the following who have kindly given permission for the use of copyright material.

Ashgate Publishing for 'The Bretton Woods Agreements: A Monetary Theory Perspective', in Philip L. Cottrell, Gérassimos Notaras and Gabriel Tortella (eds), *From the Athenian Tetradrachm to the Euro: Studies in European Monetary Integration*, Aldershot: Ashgate, 2007, pp. 113–35.

'Monetary Union: A Theoretical Perspective', *Banca Nazionale del Lavoro Quarterly Review*, **45**, September 1992, pp. 349–61; 'Money and Quasi-Money', Translated from *Moneta e Credito*, **38**, June 1985, pp. 219–29, reset; 'The Equilibrium Approach to Optimum Currency Areas', *Banca Nazionale del Lavoro Quarterly Review*, **59**, June 2006, pp. 193–209; 'Optimum Currency Areas: A Policy View', *Banca Nazionale del Lavoro Quarterly Review*, **59**, December 2006, pp. 317–32 all by kind permission of the Editor.

Blackwell Publishing for 'Legal Restrictions Theory and the Rate-of-Return Dominance of Money', *Manchester School of Economic and Social Studies*, **62**, June 1994, pp. 199–208.

Duncker & Humblot for 'Monetary Systems and Monetary Theory', *Kredit und Kapital*, **32** (2), 1999, pp. 192–208.

Elsevier for 'On the Viability of Monetary Unions', *Journal of International Economics*, **19**, November 1985, pp. 367–74; 'The New Monetary Economics and the Theory of Money', *Journal of Economic Behavior and Organization*, **26**, May 1995, pp. 445–55.

MCB University Press for 'The New Monetary Economics and Keynes' Theory of Money', *Journal of Economic Studies*, **21** (3), 1994, pp. 39–53; 'Providing for the Optimum Quantity of Money', *Journal of Economic Studies*, **25** (6), 1998, pp. 441–49; 'Competitive Money Supply: The International Monetary System in Perspective', *Journal of Economic Studies*, **26** (3), 1999, 188–200.

Springer Science and Business Media for 'Currency Areas and Equilibrium', *Open Economies Review*, **8**, January 1997, pp. 51–59.

Taylor and Francis for 'Financial Innovation and Demand for Money: Some Empirical Evidence', *Applied Economics*, **22**, October 1990, pp. 1437–42; 'Demand for Money and Expected Inflation', *Applied Economics*, **23**, October 1991, pp. 1649–53; 'Economic History and Economic Theory', *Journal of Economic Methodology*, **13**, December 2006, pp. 447–67.

Foreword
David Laidler

The study of monetary issues has always been difficult, but these days it presents particular problems, because many of them are not very amenable to the standard analytic approach of the now dominant neo-classical tradition in economics. Usually, we can safely proceed first of all to analyse the individual experiments to which the choices that face the typical economic agent give rise, and then to aggregate up to the market experiments through which those individual decisions, and the activities to which they give rise, are coordinated. But we don't get very far when we try to analyse the monetary system this way.

To be sure, we can and do discuss the factors that underlie, say, an individual agent's demand for money, as one step towards market experiments that determine the level of prices (if we lean towards monetarism), or of income and employment (if we are of a more 'Keynesian' bent), but this is at best a short cut and often a dangerous one; because our individual monetary experiments only make sense if they already presuppose the existence of arrangements through which that agent interacts with others. We can analyse Robinson Crusoe's demand for consumer goods, and his activities in producing them; and when Friday comes on the scene, we can analyse a two-agent economy that relies on barter to coordinate activity. But before we can sensibly discuss Crusoe and Friday's use of money, we need to add at least one more agent to their economy (and make sure that it is endowed with at least three goods as well). The outcome of some sort of market experiment is, that is to say, logically prior to individual experiments in monetary economics in a way that has no precise parallels elsewhere in the subject.

Of course, we can always ask awkward questions about the nature and origins, not to mention the ethical basis, of the property rights that make voluntary exchange feasible in the first place, but those who venture too close to such questions soon find themselves discussing awkward political, even ideological, issues that most economists prefer to avoid; and besides, in many contexts, the maximizing choices of individual agents can be analysed with impeccable logic without addressing them. However, there is no avoiding the fact that the monetary and financial system coordinates choices in the real world through the voluntary exchange of property rights, and the corollaries of this fact that the system's precise workings both depend upon how those rights are defined and affect their nature and security, too. These issues figure too prominently in the subject-matter of monetary economics to be ignored, so it is small wonder that this branch of economics is often controversial. It has to deal not only with questions about individual choices, but also with fundamental matters concerning how societies can, and even should, organize themselves.

To put this point another way, certain political, even ideological, fault lines, which usually lie deeply and safely buried beneath the landscape of economics, have long scarred the surface of its monetary region, nowadays as much as ever. At one edge of the region in question, we have a neo-classical tradition, closely associated with individualistic liberal politics. This tradition, particularly since the creation of its self-styled *new* classical manifestation in the early 1970s, has explicitly embraced the axioms that markets are always in equilibrium and that the expectations of the agents that operate within them rational. At its other edge is to be found post-Keynesian economics, which takes its lead from some of John Maynard Keynes's more radical writings of the late 1930s and whose political alliances are perhaps more collectivist. Exponents of this approach sometimes seem to argue that the differences between a monetary economy and one coordinated 'as if' by frictionless barter – even when that adjective is relaxed to accommodate a degree of contract-related price stickiness – are so fundamental as to render inherently nonsensical any conclusions derived from the logic of the latter about how any real-world economy might function.

Though future historians of economic thought will surely wonder whether the simultaneous rise of optimistic neo-classical ideas about the stability of capitalist economies and the politics of 'Ronald Thatcher' are manifestations of some altogether deeper seismic shift that took place in our society's intellectual bedrock about three decades ago, this important question, in the current context, should not be allowed to overshadow two more mundane considerations. First, economic models built upon the principles of equilibrium modelling, having assumed solved at the outset precisely those coordination problems with which the real-world monetary system exists to cope, can find no way of accommodating such a system within their structures; but second, these same models, awkwardly supplemented by a series of *ad hoc* monetary appendages – cash in advance, overlapping generations, the cashless economy, etc. – have nevertheless had enough success in explaining the time-series behaviour of such variables as output and the price level to provide an underpinning for the apparently successful conduct of monetary policy in many market economies during the relatively tranquil economic climate of the past few years.

Much as one may sympathize with the post-Keynesian critique of modern neo-classical orthodoxy's inability to come to grips with the fundamentals of monetary exchange, therefore, and admire its exponents' willingness to address rather than evade the issues it raises, it is difficult to concede the whole of even the economic debate about monetary questions to this school of thought, let alone the underlying political one. Today's neo-classical orthodoxy may be intellectually shaky, but it is too useful to be abandoned altogether; and besides, most of us do live in capitalist economies whose current policy problems cannot await the arrival of a more secure theoretical paradigm before they are addressed. We must rely on currently available ideas. Some of these are new, some old, and there are grounds for suspicion about the validity and even the mutual consistency of some of them, but they are all that we have. There is, then, a large, extremely untidy, and not very well mapped, territory lying between the two above-mentioned extremes of modern monetary economics, and it invites careful exploration.

Filippo Cesarano's stimulating collection of essays is a record of one thoughtful and scholarly economist's journeys into this country. He is much too wise to claim that he has a fully worked-out route through it to offer his readers, but all of the following essays, one way or another, do nevertheless relate to a single landmark:

namely, the idea that the monetary system exists to cope with fundamental problems in social and political organization having to do with the creation, preservation and dissemination of information in a decentralized environment. For Cesarano, such problems do not just impinge upon the decisions of individuals engaging in exchange with strangers – matters to which modern search theoretic approaches to monetary economics pay particular attention – though these are part of the story, but arise more broadly in any multi-agent economy based on voluntary exchange, where it is necessary both to keep track of who is entitled to what, from whom and when, and to ensure that such entitlements are enforced and fulfilled.

This insight, which Cesarano – at least as distinguished a historian of monetary thought as he is a contributor to it – traces back to the eighteenth-century Italian economist Ferdinando Galiani, turns up time and again in these essays. Most obviously it illuminates his critiques of the so-called 'new monetary economics' and its close intellectual relative the 'legal restrictions' theory of money. Here questions about the extent to which viable monetary institutions can arise spontaneously within an individualistic economic order loom large, and so do others about the extent to which the smooth functioning and continuing evolution of monetary arrangements require, or at least invite, some help from those other institutions to which the label 'the state' is usually attached. Cesarano offers nuanced and moderate answers to these questions, as befits an explorer of monetary economics' middle ground, and he then applies them to analysing relationships between the monetary order and the broader political order, both at the level of a stylized, closed economy and of the international monetary system, too. Here his explorations range through abstract monetary theory, to the practicalities of monetary unions and currency competition as they appear in today's world, using ideas about the interactions of individual behaviour and social institutions to illuminate important and pressing policy questions. And never far in the background of these discussions is that central idea about the informational function of the monetary system alluded to above.

There is no need to venture into a lengthy discussion of this book's contents, for its readers can gain immediate access to Cesarano's own ideas simply by turning a few pages. They are now urged to do just that, in the hope that they will find as much stimulation and even pleasure as has this writer in these imaginative and open-minded essays.

David Laidler
London, Ontario
December 2007

Introduction

In contrast with general equilibrium theory, monetary theory does not boast a well-grounded, widely shared body of knowledge. The multifaceted nature of money is a clear sign of its inherent complexity, defying an all-encompassing analysis. Money is a prismatic subject which, when looked at from different perspectives, reflects diverse images, each capturing only some of its main features. Alternative approaches, therefore, cannot provide but partial views, often leading to diametrically opposite results.

This should not be interpreted as a nihilistic vision. Notwithstanding the complexity of the subject and the lack of a commonly accepted paradigm, an understanding of the main approaches to the fundamentals of money and its effects on the economy is the starting-point for analysing institutional and policy issues. The basic principles underlying this relationship are examined in the opening chapter of this book, which serves as an introduction to the collection. In tackling a given problem, the decisive step is to identify the assumptions crucial to selecting the appropriate research strategy, whereas uncritically relying on settled ways of thinking may be highly misleading. Indeed, monetary history offers many examples of serious errors stemming from the failure to grasp the features specific to the issue at stake.

These difficulties emerge most clearly in the study of monetary arrangements. Theory obviously provides the box of tools to explain patterns of behaviour and the workings of monetary institutions (Parts I and II of the book), but it also contributes to shape the latter in an essential way (Parts III and IV). The informational role of money in removing 'frictions' naturally led to convergence on a single medium of exchange and unit of account. Market forces were momentous in triggering the spontaneous process that, subject to the state of technology, gave rise to monetary exchange and fostered the advancement of payment media through the development of the banking industry. Since the very beginning of coinage, however, the appropriation by the government of the issuing function and the related responsibility of managing the system gave theory a prominent place in the evolution of monetary institutions. In this regard, the alternation of contrasting views about the influence of money on the economy has been of paramount importance. The equilibrium approach of classical economics, that in recent decades has been rebuilt on more solid foundations, provides a theoretical benchmark against which the actual conditions of the economy must be set, helping to identify the assumptions most relevant to the problem at hand. This proposition does not exclusively relate to monetary theory and can be extended to other fields of economics, assigning a significant role to economic history (Part V).

The evolution of monetary arrangements has, therefore, been shaped by the interplay between diverse, heterogeneous factors – market forces, technological progress and dominant paradigms – apparently quite distinct from each other. Yet, a common thread runs through them: the concept of information. The availability of information about different behavioural variables and features of the economy is essential to account for both theoretical and policy issues: from the fundamentals of money to the effectiveness of monetary policy and the optimality of monetary institutions.

Throughout the centuries, the interaction between those factors was uneven. Theory often lagged behind major institutional transformations spurred by market forces while, in other instances, brilliant economists anticipated innovative forms of monetary organization. When the implications of this evolutionary process were not understood, disruptive imbalances broke out. The monetary history of the twentieth century, marking the epochal transition from commodity money to fiat money, is a glaring example. Nowadays, rapid advance in information technology is making tangible money obsolete, thus paving the way to the realization of the Wicksellian pure credit economy. This development poses new challenges to monetary theory that, by defying straightforward solutions on a par with previous experiences of institutional change, testify to the complexity and elusiveness of the subject.

The papers collected in this volume, except for the last one, deal with themes related to the workings of monetary systems. More than other topics in economics, the theory of money is closely intertwined with the institutional setting. Yet, monetary theory and monetary arrangements have mostly been kept in separate compartments, disregarding the interplay between them. The analysis of this relationship is the leitmotiv of the book. In the following pages, an outline of the collection tries to convey something of the flavour of the arguments but, needless to say, does not provide a summary of the papers.

The articles in Part I test some controversial hypotheses about the demand for money. The contrast between the classical and the Keynesian conceptions of money, underlying the development of clashing paradigms in macroeconomics, was hard to settle on theoretical grounds. Thus, the problem of the most appropriate definition of monetary aggregate was tackled by means of empirical analysis (Chapter 2). This issue was particularly conspicuous in Italy where, in response to high and variable inflation and an accelerating public deficit, the Treasury Bills market was established in the mid-1970s, bringing about a surge in short-term government debt. Hence, ascertaining the degree of substitutability of money with other assets was not only important *per se*, but also for assessing the impact of a fall in the average maturity of public debt, the effects of monetary policy and the overall economic policy strategy.

The case of Italy provided an *in vitro* experiment to study the implications of financial innovation, thought to undermine the effectiveness of monetary policy both by increasing the interest elasticity of money demand and impairing the stability of the money demand function (Chapter 3). Alvin Marty countered these propositions. First, the introduction of a money substitute flattens the money demand schedule for each individual and shifts each schedule to the left. However, since the latter effect is likely to be stronger for the more elastic schedules pertaining to agents that are highly sensitive to interest rate variations, the elasticity of the market schedule will decrease because the weight of agents whose demand is relatively inelastic will be greater. Second, the effectiveness of monetary policy is not impaired if the rate at which individuals learn to substitute new assets for money is stable. The empirical evidence relating to the introduction of Treasury Bills in Italy corroborates both Marty's hypotheses.

Lastly, an especially controversial issue concerned the role of expected inflation in the demand for money (Chapter 4). Most theoretical models offered convincing arguments for such a role, and yet no empirical evidence was found in the US case, which was puzzling. These discordant results can be accounted for by the efficiency of financial markets. In efficient markets all assets, including demand deposits, earn a competitive rate of interest that fully reflects expected inflation, thus reducing its impact on money demand. Vice versa in inefficient markets. An inverse relationship between the influence of expected inflation on money demand and financial market efficiency can, therefore, be conjectured. This hypothesis is corroborated by the Italian experience, particularly suited to the purpose because it exhibits different degrees of financial market efficiency in different periods.

Though concerning diverse problems, these empirical results delivered the same message, assigning a crucial role to money. This view was at the centre of a heated debate which, however, disregarded monetary arrangements. Only in the early 1980s was interest in this topic revived by various factors – the development of innovative payment media, the push for deregulation and the quest for rule-based monetary policy – bringing about an original strain of literature: the new monetary economics.

Part II critically assesses these contributions. The new approach emphasized the unit of account in an unregulated banking system devoid of tangible payment media in contrast with tangible money, considered a product of regulation (Chapter 5). Yet, the unit of account function is not essential to the concept of money; furthermore, the physical characteristic of money is entirely irrelevant to the properties of a monetary economy. Independently of its shape, tangible or not, money is not the creation of regulation. That money continued to be issued by the government from the very beginning of coinage is related to its informational role and the fiscal advantage of extracting seignorage, not to an interference with the functioning of markets. The phenomenon of money stems from efficient decentralized market behaviour, not from an imposition by the political authority. The smooth operation of monetary systems needs rules, but these are conceptually quite different from regulation.

A closely related doctrine is the legal restrictions theory, according to which the prohibition of private note issue accounts for the coexistence of non-interest bearing money and bonds as well as the effectiveness of monetary policy (Chapter 6). Given the similarity in approach, the legal restrictions theory is subject to the same criticisms levelled against the new monetary economics. The interest rate dominance of money is explained by the distinguishing features of a monetary economy as contrasted with a Walrasian economy. The government monopoly of currency issue can then be viewed within the framework of rules ensuring the viability of the monetary system, not as an instance of regulation.

Most of the criticisms of both the new monetary economics and the legal restrictions theory go back to the received view of monetary economics. Taking Keynes as a case study, the weaknesses of those approaches can be shown through his main works on money (Chapter 7).

Monetary economics obviously is a key tool for analysing monetary institutions; it is also a main factor in designing monetary arrangements. Part III examines several aspects of this proposition. In general, the government monopoly in money issue implied knowledge of the workings of the monetary system, and especially an understanding of the nature of money and the effects of changes in the money stock (Chapter 8). In the past century, in particular, the influence of theory on the evolution of the monetary system has been paramount. In the aftermath of the major shocks of the First World War and the Great Depression, the critique of the basic principles underlying the gold standard model – metallism and the equilibrium hypothesis of the economy – paved the way to the epochal transition from commodity money to fiat money. The prospective development of intangible money, however, may reinstate some of the characteristics of commodity standards. The solution of price level indeterminacy calls for a rule that, partaking of the nature of a technical device necessary for the system's viability, is not easily tampered with by political authorities. Furthermore, possible interferences would be immediately recognized. An advanced monetary setting is like the gold standard: both are characterized by highly credible rules.

In this connection, an accounting system of exchange provides a straightforward solution to the optimum quantity of money (Chapter 9). In the presence of currency, Friedman's proposition faces the problem of an equal rate of return on money and bonds, which makes the bond market disappear. Intangible money disposes of this problem, thus showing that the accomplishment of Wicksell's 'ideal banking system' squares with the optimality of monetary institutions.

This result also bears on international monetary arrangements (Chapter 10). Though often pictured as a 'non-system', after the inflationary surge of the 1970s the monetary environment displayed a relative degree of stability despite the absence of rules. Indeed, it represents the application of Benjamin Klein's model of competitive money supply since each country issues its own fiat instrument, distinguishable from the others and linked to them by floating exchange rates. Klein's hypothesis, unsuitable for a domestic set-up because it requires exchange rate flexibility between currencies in order to make Gresham's Law inoperative, well fits today's international set-up, whose performance compares favourably with the rules-based Bretton Woods monetary order. The substantial fall in inflation rates in the past decades stems from the countries' effort to maintain the brand name of their currencies in a competitive setting. The introduction of intangible money would be a further advance, connecting several apparently unrelated optimality principles.

On the other hand, the Bretton Woods monetary system was unique, in that it was designed at the drawing board (Chapter 11). The influence of theory was, therefore, crucial to its construction. The important contributions of the inter-war period did not lead to a widely shared paradigm, especially in regard to the institutional framework, and the Bretton Woods conference necessarily resulted in a compromise between different theoretical views and unequal political powers. The objective of reinstating fixed exchange rates clashed with the quest for activist economic policies grounded in the *General Theory*, producing a number of weaknesses – an inadequate adjustment mechanism, the adjustable peg and a perceived inconsistency between liquidity provision and gold convertibility – that eventually proved to be fatal. Bretton Woods represents the final stage of the transition towards fiat money, a last ephemeral attempt to maintain a link with a commodity standard while calling for full employment policy.

In this critical phase of the evolution of the monetary system there was a revival of interest in monetary unions, prodded by political developments in Europe. Part IV deals with several aspects of this subject. The viability of a common currency, a weaker notion than optimality, is analysed by applying Herbert Simon's approach to bounded rationality to a model of the economy under different exchange rate regimes (Chapter 12). Monetary union is a case study in the theory of money, and, as such, it is intimately related to the state of advancement of the field (Chapter 13). Mundell's paper on optimum currency areas was, therefore, grounded in the then dominant Keynesian model, assuming a very limited adjustment capacity that makes internal and external balance hard to achieve. Instead, the classical model, starting from the opposite assumption, arrives at altogether different results. Indeed, for the classics, the optimum currency area was the world because the circulation of many currencies impairs the transaction role of money while it yields no benefits in terms of activist monetary policy. The revivifying of the classical paradigm since the 1970s strengthened the case for monetary union, but did not displace the Keynesian approach.

The divergence in the state of the art was puzzling (Chapter 14). Many scholars lamented the weak foundations of the theory of optimum currency areas, witness the diversity of optimality criteria, and yet the received view prevailed until the mid-1990s when the development of the equilibrium approach belatedly brought the subject in line with the new classical macroeconomics. From an equilibrium viewpoint, the optimality criteria are not exogenous and unconnected features of the economy, but are endogenous and interrelated characteristics of adjustment. In particular, fixing the country borders can be viewed as a policy measure which, besides providing a common legal and institutional framework as well as an economic policy authority, impinges on agents' behaviour, enhancing adjustment inside the currency area. Political union thus plays a key role in the successful operation of monetary unions.

From a broader theoretical perspective, the traditional approach to optimum currency areas seems like a temporary detour from the dominant paradigm in economics based on the notion of equilibrium (Chapter 15). In fact, Mundell's optimality criterion of labour mobility and the other criteria as well were anticipated by several distinguished economists – Lerner, Friedman, Meade and Scitovsky – who, unlike Mundell, interpreted them as the outcome of domestic adjustment *vis-à-vis* international adjustment. The modern equilibrium approach built the argument for the endogeneity of optimality criteria on stronger theoretical foundations. That agents rationally respond to the extension of the currency area is simply an application of the Lucas critique. The equilibrium approach therefore turns the received view of optimum currency areas upside down. Optimality does not derive from pre-existent features, but is the result of an equilibrium process set off by the establishment of a common currency.

Albeit based on different hypotheses, the traditional approach and the equilibrium approach can both be useful in tackling different policy questions (Chapter 16). Equilibrium propositions relate to long-run adjustment and, thus, are not suitable to answer short-run problems characterized by frictions of various kinds and concerning highly differentiated economies. In this regard, the issues raised by the transition towards monetary union are distinct from those concerning its operation and require diverse models.

This proposition can be generalized to the realm of economics. In Part V the characteristics of economics as a social science are examined with a view to showing the usefulness of economic history for economic theory (Chapter 17). The inherent complexity of economic phenomena stems from the number of variables and interactions between them that potentially affect those phenomena with different intensity and timing. Hence, a hypothesis that is falsified under certain circumstances may not be falsified in other circumstances, independently of the historical setting. Hypotheses are therefore non-excludable, which makes the evolution of economic knowledge non-cumulative and assigns to economic history, and to the history of economic analysis, an important role in economic theorizing.

Excludability is a matter of degree not of kind and decreases with the complexity of the subject. Thus, also within the field of economics, abstract and less complex topics like price theory gain little from the contribution of history, and vice versa, for the most intricate ones like business cycles and economic growth. In this respect, the complexity of monetary theory and its consequent low degree of excludability render it most suitable to gain from the history of both facts and theories. The uneven performance of different monetary arrangements is a clear instance of historical experience that teaches a lot about the properties underlying their viability and optimality.

In tackling an intricate topic like the monetary system, sound judgement about the factors most relevant to the particular context is in order. In fact, a slight change in the key assumptions of a model can lead to quite different results, even within the same paradigm. In an equilibrium approach, diverse conjectures about the agents' information set or different institutional characteristics may well suggest contrasting policy recipes. An equilibrium model accordingly provides a benchmark against which the actual conditions of the economy must be set with a view to developing sound hypotheses.

My interest in monetary theory was first kindled while I was writing my undergraduate thesis on the optimum quantity of money. Friedman's seminal essay had just been published; it analysed the principles of money in depth, in a way that inspired further enquiries into the subject. The chance of continuing my studies at the University of Chicago offered a challenging and stimulating intellectual environment to pursue this objective.

Theoretical puzzles, policy issues and historical episodes provided various sources of inspiration. The variegated character of monetary theory poses a problem of choice among different research strategies which, in principle, could be solved in relation to the object of study. However, it is not always possible to keep the analysis within the boundaries of a given approach. In this regard, Keynes's example is quite telling, since each work of his trilogy – the *Tract*, the *Treatise* and the *General Theory* – stresses one of the three functions of money: medium of exchange, unit of account and store of value respectively. Indeed, the manifold nature of money makes the subject both intricate and elusive, so that embracing any particular school of thought inevitably proves limiting. The contrasting positions in Keynes's writings simply show his originality in setting forth diverse research paths.

Because of the complexity of the subject there is, of course, much to be gained from discussion with fellow economists. The opportunity to visit several academic centres – The Netherlands School of Economics, UCLA, Harvard University and the Hoover Institution – allowed me to have fruitful exchanges and stay in contact with many people. Their perceptive comments helped to improve the early drafts of my papers, as acknowledged in each chapter of the book.

I would like also to thank Alice Chambers, Daniel Dichter, Roger Meservey, John Smith and Christine Stone for revising my English, and Giuliana Ferretti and Antonella Pulimanti for superb research assistance.

The views expressed in this book are the author's own and not necessarily those of the Bank of Italy.

[1]

On money and monetary systems*

Monetary theory is a fascinating subject. The concept of money is apparently simple, and yet, when observed from different perspectives, it displays a variety of identities, a multifaceted nature. Its apparent simplicity therefore conceals an inherent complexity that defies a comprehensive view, making the subject rather elusive. This feature emerges from the textbook classification of the functions of money – unit of account, medium of exchange and store of value – which, though closely interrelated, suggest distinct roles for money. Indirect evidence of this proposition is provided by the diverse definitions of the price of money associated with the functions listed above.[1] Furthermore, alternative approaches and families of models originate from those functions, e.g. the new monetary economics, the cash-in-advance constraint model and the overlapping generations model respectively. In general, owing to the different emphasis laid on specific aspects of a manifold object of inquiry, the evolution of monetary theory has been characterised by contrasting currents of literature throughout the centuries. Thus, clarifying the distinctive features of money helps to avoid misconceptions about the workings of monetary systems.

1. The nature of money

The analysis of the essential properties of money dates back to the dawn of economics. Aristotle explained the emergence of money from the inconveniences of barter and singled out the medium of exchange function as the basic one, involving the others, a principle that has come down to the present intact (Aristotle 1924, 17, 26–9; Schumpeter 1954, 62–3). A medium of exchange naturally becomes the unit of account and, inasmuch as the disadvantages of barter imply sequential trade, it is necessarily a store of value. Since any commodity can act as a unit of account and any durable commodity is a store of value, these functions are not characteristic of money but are implicit in the medium of exchange, thus considered the primary, essential function of money (Wicksell 1906, 6–8).[2]

This theory is eminently correct, but was used to derive another principle, an incorrect principle: that in order to serve as a medium of exchange money must necessarily be a commodity. The doctrine of metallism, odd as it may seem today, held sway from Aristotle's time to the eve of World War I and even beyond. Since the eighteenth century, however, important contributions have shed light on the fundamentals of money. The analysis continued to be based on the lack of double coincidence of wants, suggesting the existence of 'frictions' in the market that were disposed of by the medium of exchange.

The theory of the origin of money is grounded in these tenets. The effectiveness of market forces triggers a spontaneous process that leads to the selection of goods with a high degree of saleability and certain market characteristics as commodity money (Menger 1892; Jones 1976). Numismatics has generally supported this hypothesis, although some scholars (Grierson 1977) attempted to build an argument for primitive money, as distinct from coined money, on the basis of the unit of account function. In ancient times, various kinds of partial money may well have performed only one or two functions, yet they can hardly be considered fully-fledged money because, in most instances, goods were still exchanged for goods. This is of course a matter of definition but, to the economist, the potential of efficiency gains generated by money is fulfilled by the introduction of a medium of exchange (Niehans 1978, 120–21).

The history of money has, in many instances, corroborated the theory of money and raised new theoretical issues as well. This relationship, however, is more complex, running also in the opposite direction. Indeed, monetary theory has also exerted a strong influence on the evolution of the monetary system, witness the lengthy dominance of the metallist doctrine. The complexity of the subject may induce emphasis on irrelevant or downright erroneous aspects, even starting from correct hypotheses. Thus the absence of double coincidence of wants, offering a sound rationale for the nature and origins of monetary exchange, maintained the focus on the need to resort to a commodity as a means of payment, which put off any substantial advancement for more than two thousand years.

In fact, research on the fundamentals of money gained momentum in the mid-1960s, when the problem of the lack of any meaningful role for money in general equilibrium theory was posed (Hahn 1965; Clower 1967). The Walrasian model solves the allocation problem by finding market-clearing prices, but not the problem of executing trade because individual excess demands and supplies are not known. Then, instead of cutting the knot by introducing a medium of exchange, the issue of the inconveniences of barter was effectively tackled by probing into the motivations underlying indirect exchange. Most modelling strategies were grounded in diverse costs – transaction, search, storage costs. Yet, these motivations boil down to one essential point: the recording of information about individual excess demands and supplies. The existence of 'frictions', therefore, should not be viewed as a consequence of physical obstacles to exchange commodities, but as a problem of insufficient knowledge to be solved by a record-keeping device (Ostroy 1973). Money is that device.

In their excellent survey, Ostroy and Starr (1990, 8–13) vividly illustrate this proposition in a series of parables. Two and a half centuries earlier, Ferdinando Galiani (1751, 67–71) told an original parable on the nature of money, highly suggestive of modern contributions. Observing that money is not used in small communities such as religious orders, he asked whether cities and kingdoms could also do away with it by communal living: each citizen would deposit the goods he produced in a public warehouse from which he could withdraw the goods supplied by others. However, since everybody would try to cheat by claiming more commodities than they were entitled to, the system would collapse. But there is a simple remedy: issuing notes certifying the quantity of goods deposited so that the holder of the notes can withdraw only an equal amount of other goods. In order to improve the efficiency of the system, a standard of value should be fixed and counterfeiting avoided, tasks which could be assigned to the prince, the sole issuer of notes. Yet these notes, Galiani concludes, actually are money, which thus represents a credit of the individual against society.[3]

Enquiring into the causes of the impossibility of eliminating money altogether, Galiani arrived at a modern conception of money as a means of recording the value of the goods that the individual wants to give up in order to acquire the goods he needs. This information is necessary to avoid inconsistent claims in executing trade. The inconsistency does not relate to relative prices (in Galiani's parable, they are fixed by the prince rather than the auctioneer) because it would be disposed of by arbitrage, but to individual excess demands and supplies. In a barter economy there is either direct exchange, where budget constraints hold, or no exchange at all. In a monetary economy, on the other hand, trade is always feasible because there is a record-keeping device which, by keeping track of individual excess demands and supplies, ensures the enforcement of budget constraints. This is a sufficient condition for monetary exchange.

Modern contributions, therefore, shifted the focus of analysis from the physical obstacles hindering direct exchange to the informational role of money in decentralising exchange. These theoretical developments have buttressed the classical principle of the primacy of the medium of exchange function[4] while rejecting the other classical principle, metallism. To provide money's information-producing mechanism there is of course no need for a commodity since any signalling contrivance will do, from cowrie shells to a system of electronic fund transfers. This clarification may seem belated and obvious, but it is important to restate it in the light of the ongoing evolution of monetary arrangements in the direction of non-tangible media of exchange. The analysis of the fundamentals of money enables us to map the structure of the monetary system onto the essential properties of a monetary economy. This relationship has far-reaching implications and disregard for it, tackling issues in monetary theory with the Walrasian model, may well lead astray (Laidler 1988, 689–93).

2.   Monetary systems

The early appropriation of the issuing function by the government may have been favoured by the political authority's role in certifying the weight and quality of the standard and fostered by the advantage of extracting seignorage. However, it also rested on theoretical principles in that the informational role of money makes the system converge on a single medium of exchange and unit of account. Government monopoly in money issue involved a volitional element or management responsibilities and thus the acquisition of knowledge, however rudimentary, of the monetary mechanism. Theory had therefore a strong influence on the shape of monetary arrangements.[5] Even though the fiduciary characteristic of money was clearly understood by brilliant economists like Galiani and Hume (1769), the dominance of metallism, viewed as a policy principle aimed at preventing currency manipulation, continued unabated.[6]

The evolutionary process that from the many forms of primitive money led to the use of metals and then of coined and paper money was conditioned by the state of technology. Hence, progress in metallurgy was essential to start coinage in the sixth century BC; the invention of paper, ink and printing fostered the issue of paper money in China in the ninth century AD; and the introduction of steam-powered stamping presses, by hampering counterfeiting, sustained the diffusion of the gold standard in England in the early 1800s (Redish 1990; 2000). This factor relates to the mere external aspect of money's signalling function and yet it had, and still has, important implications for the analysis of the monetary system. Even more important was the progress of payment media driven by resource savings and the profit motive underlying the growth of the banking industry. This advancement was propelled by market forces so that, rather than being influenced by theory, it raised new theoretical issues about the design and operation of monetary arrangements.

The evolution of the monetary system, therefore, is shaped by the interaction between several factors – market forces, technical progress and dominant paradigms. Nowadays, the quantum leap in information technology prefigures a world devoid of currency. From a theoretical point of view, however, this is a less dramatic change than the epoch-making transition from commodity money to fiat money, which marked a watershed in 2,500 years of monetary history. This transition, which began in the inter-war period and officially ended with the suspension of dollar convertibility, was the outcome of a major shift in the conception of the role of money in the economy, paving the way to managed money and modern monetary policy. On the other hand, the eventual disappearance of coins and notes only affects the physical aspect of fiat money, a relatively minor change in the evolution of monetary arrangements. Like the first experiments in paper money, this innovation raises delicate theoretical issues, some of them still unsettled. In fact, theory has sometimes been ill-equipped to tackle novel monetary institutions, with catastrophic consequences. The downfall of Law's System in early eighteenth century France is a glaring example. It testifies to the complex and elusive character of monetary theory which, by lending itself to be approached from different perspectives, may lead to serious errors.

In dealing with less abstract issues, the connection between money's informational role and monetary arrangements may not be immediate and yet, on closer examination, it quickly emerges. For instance, in his Nobel lecture Robert Mundell (2000) called for one world money in order to eliminate exchange rate volatility and restore a stable and integrated monetary order such as the gold standard.[7] Paradoxically, the quest for monetary stability also motivated the movement away from the gold standard a century earlier, but this involves no contradiction. Both positions stem from the quest for a reliable monetary meter and a steady monetary framework, viewed as the basis of economic stability. In the heyday of the gold standard, several distinguished economists, aware of the vagaries of gold mining and its effects on the price level, put forward various proposals to tame the variability of the money stock (Laidler 1991, Chapter 6; 2002). Together with the primacy of the medium of exchange function and the corollary that the means performing this function necessarily acts as the unit of account, the classics maintained an equilibrium approach, stressing the self-adjusting property of the economy. Monetary stability was therefore instrumental to economic stability and the structure of the monetary system had to be moulded to this principle with a view to improving on the gold standard and enhancing social welfare.[8]

In the inter-war years, these theoretical developments sowed the seeds of the transition from 'natural' to managed money. The price level was viewed as a policy target to be pursued by the central bank. Moreover, the disruptive shock of the Great Depression disparaged the equilibrium hypothesis of the economy, thus accelerating the process of abandoning commodity money. The impact on the rules of the game was substantial. In general, as the incentive of resource savings ushers in fiduciary elements into the system, the latter becomes more complex and the number of rules increases. Hence, while the purest forms of commodity money like the gold specie standard required only two rules – fixing the unit of account and free coinage (Niehans 1978, 141–2) – implicit rules featured prominently in the classical gold standard, providing the basis of its main properties (McKinnon 1993, 3–11; Cesarano 2006, Chapter 2). In particular, the restoration rule, stipulating the return to the gold parity after convertibility suspension, considerably stiffened policy-makers' discipline and heightened credibility. After the downfall of the gold standard, the reconstruction of the international monetary system was carried out through the lengthy negotiations culminating in the Bretton Woods agreements, a bold effort to reinstate a fixed exchange rate regime while allowing activist full employment policies. The inherent inconsistency between these objectives resulted in several weaknesses – inadequacies in the adjustment mechanism, the inconveniences of the adjustable peg, the implications of the Triffin dilemma – that eventually brought the post-war monetary order to an end.

In analysing these topics information is paramount, bearing not only on expectation formation (Fisher 1911, Chapter 13; Keynes 1923, Chapter 1) and credibility but also on the design of monetary arrangements. To give a cursory example, Mill (1848, 544–6) called for convertibility instead of stabilising the price of gold in the gold standard because, being a simpler rule, convertibility is more easily monitored by the public and thus discourages violations on the part of the monetary authority. The advancement of banking and technology then fosters innovation in payment media and feeds back into theory, which decisively influences the core of the monetary system, or the basic rules presiding over its operation.

Competition in supplying payment media, such as the free banking experience of eighteenth century Scotland, involved the issue of diverse inside monies (outside money being either gold or Bank of England notes); otherwise the efficiency of money as an information-producing mechanism would have been impaired. Furthermore, the circulation of various outside monies linked by fixed exchange rates would have triggered the effects of Gresham's Law and undermined the system. Instead, the hypothesis of competitive money supply, originally suggested for a domestic setting (Klein 1974), is applicable to today's international scenario: a flexible exchange rate regime in which each country issues its own fiat money and designs its economic policies with a view to keeping money's brand name (see Chapter 10 below). The decline in inflation rates in the past decades corroborates this hypothesis.

The one-country one-money configuration is, of course, related to political factors and yet it is grounded in theoretical principles. Notwithstanding Menger's (1892) widely accepted account of the development of money as a spontaneous process driven by market forces, the government has always maintained an important place in monetary affairs. This is no paradox: once the government came into the picture, it could hardly be removed, not because of its political power or certain features generating path-dependence, but simply for the informational role of currency and the huge costs of forsaking it. This concept links the various aspects of the analysis of monetary systems, both positive and normative. In a world of complete information money would not exist because its role of providing a record-keeping device would vanish. The notion of information explains what money is, but also what money does, or how it affects the economy, since the dimension of agents' information set is crucial for analysing a number of topics, ranging from the effectiveness of monetary policy to the optimality of international monetary institutions (Cesarano 1983; 2006, 71).

The theory of optimum currency areas is a case in point. While the received view considered the optimality criteria as pre-existing features of the economy and therefore exogenous, the equilibrium approach (see Chapters 14 and 15 below) emphasises the agents' response to the greater availability of information and effectiveness of adjustment inside countries, thus deeming those criteria endogenous. The notion of optimum currency areas is an application of the theory of monetary policy, in which equilibrium models can be viewed as an analytical benchmark to be compared with the actual conditions of the economy. Assessing this gap is essential for identifying the relevant assumptions and selecting a successful research strategy. Faced with pervasive uncertainty, in order to build a model with a high degree of explanatory and predictive power, policy-makers must rely on all sources of information, deriving not just from data and the prevailing paradigm but also from economic history (see Chapter 17 below) and the history of economic theory (Cesarano 2007).

In the end we have come full circle: the availability of information links theoretical foundations and institutional components of the monetary mechanism. On the one hand, information accounts for the nature of money as a record-keeping device of individual excess demands and supplies. On the other hand, the rules of the monetary system underlying its main properties, such as credibility, also build on information.[9] This link is essential to understanding the principles and the operation of monetary systems.

3. Intangible money

In a provocative paper, Fischer Black (1970) discussed an unregulated and competitive banking system, arguing that in this setting money would vanish. This proposition, which does not refer just to the physical aspects of money but also to its theoretical aspects,[10] entails a number of misconceptions.

The first misconception is to assess the existence of 'money' by focusing on the object playing that role, whereas the informational role of money is independent of its actual form, be it salt bars or electronic fund transfers. As the inconveniences of barter do not concern physical obstacles, likewise the physical characteristic of money is not essential to the existence of a monetary economy: an accounting system of exchange that provides very efficient transaction services clearly is a monetary economy.

The second misconception is to consider the unit of account in such a system as a mere numeraire instead of a means performing a truly monetary function, naturally entailed in the medium of exchange function. The point is simply that the theory of general equilibrium is fit for analysing the microeconomics of the banking industry, not a monetary economy. The informational role of money is embodied in its functions. In the Walrasian model, the numeraire plays no monetary functions and thus the existence of a stable equilibrium in a competitive unregulated banking system is irrelevant to the optimality and viability of the monetary set-up.

The third misconception is the need to impose regulations like reserve requirements in order to transform the numeraire into a fully fledged unit of account (Fama 1980, section 4). The tenets underlying a monetary economy have little to do with regulation and the microeconomics of banking, and it is indeed ironic that, after showing its inconveniences in the operation of the banking industry, regulation is resorted to for bringing about a monetary economy. The problem here is not one of regulation but of rules, or, more specifically, of defining the rules appropriate for an accounting system of exchange. In this connection, Mill (1848, 524) and Wicksell (1898, 62–80; 1906, 87–126) already envisaged a payment system devoid of currency and entirely based on bank accounts. Eager to supersede commodity money in order to pursue a stable price level, Wicksell analysed in detail this 'ideal banking system', drawing attention to the question of price level indeterminacy.[11]

These points are intimately connected since they arise from disregarding the distinction between a Walrasian economy, in which the actual execution of trade is not considered, and an exchange economy, in which individuals trade among themselves. Once again, the fundamentals of money are essential to understand the workings of monetary arrangements. Focusing on the numeraire to analyse an accounting system of exchange may be quite misleading, especially with respect to defining the rules of the system.

In the future, rapid progress in information technology may well render tangible currency obsolete and deregulation could go so far as to abolish all legal restrictions on banking activity.[12] The evolution of monetary institutions, however, is a continuous process, driven by the interplay of a variety of factors, partly spontaneous and partly planned. Bank clearing is but one among many examples of unplanned developments, initiated by commercial banks and later taken up by central banks. Certainly, discontinuities have been observed, mainly in the aftermath of disruptive shocks like major wars or crises, though their effects manifested themselves gradually, often without being fully perceived.

This sort of institutional hysteresis may accompany the spread of intangible media of exchange, but the survival of central banks need not depend on mere historical inertia. As long as there is a demand for central banking 'services', the role of central banks does not vanish. Consider the lender of last resort function. In an unregulated banking system *à la* Fama, banks pay depositors a return equivalent to that of the securities in which their deposits are invested less a competitively determined fee and manage their portfolio in a way that falls under the Modigliani-Miller theorem of the irrelevance of pure financing decisions. Thus banks are 'passive intermediaries' (Fama 1980, 48) that closely resemble open-end mutual funds, excluding a role for the lender of last resort. Instead, if banks guaranteed depositors in case of default on the part of borrowers as Black assumes (1970, 15), a lender of last resort would eventually emerge. Paradoxically, in an advanced and sophisticated financial environment, exacerbation of systemic risk in less frequent though more critical circumstances may well heighten the lender of last resort function (Goodhart 1999).

In the world envisaged by Fama, banks manage portfolios chosen by depositors. With regard to loans, however, whose pricing entails processing a great amount of information that depositors do not possess, asymmetric information raises serious problems since the risk of fluctuations in the market value of portfolio assets is entirely borne by depositors. Actually, banks differ from other middlemen, say real estate agents or money-changers, in that the pervasive uncertainty characterising the object of their trade requires the continuous gathering and monitoring of information. In particular, this privately-held information is instrumental to assessing the probability of repayment, a crucial dimension of banking. Absent this assessment, some of the most typical bank products would not exist, reducing welfare for society. However, since profit opportunities do not remain unexploited, markets for such products would eventually emerge. Thus, as long as information is incomplete and hard to gather, banks as 'active' intermediaries are unlikely to disappear and central banks are not likely to disappear either.

Incomplete information is central to the nature of banking and also to problems arising from unbalanced or downright fraudulent bank behaviour. As the Scottish experience of free banking shows (White 1984), solutions need not involve government intervention, though most of the conditions characterising that successful experience are unlikely to be realised nowadays.[13] Yet they indirectly suggest possible ways of avoiding resort to government, for instance by introducing an effective incentive mechanism, supported by severe penalties in terms of both pecuniary and reputation losses, able to prevent rather than contrast bank mismanagement. Designing such a mechanism, however, may prove awkward because the significant institutional changes in the past two centuries are almost certainly irreversible.

The role of central banks in ensuring the viability and optimality of monetary arrangements, then, is unlikely to vanish. Only the weight of some central bank functions could change compared to the traditional ones. In this regard, intangible money is a relatively simple system which, despite the advanced payment technology, resembles unsophisticated commodity money. As a pure commodity standard operates with very few rules, intangible money requires only a rule that makes the price level determinate. The inverse of the price level measures the value of money viewed as a medium of exchange, the function that is essential to defining a monetary economy. An indeterminate price level, therefore, is evidence of a deficiency in the rules of the monetary set-up.[14] Patinkin's solution was the exogenous fixing of a nominal quantity. Other solutions can of course be proposed like a claim to a good, say gold, or a bundle of goods, but some of them are foreign to an accounting system of exchange, like those suggested by Fama (1980, 49–53) – the introduction of currency or reserve requirements: currency would simply restore the traditional monetary setting; a reserve requirement is a type of regulation, a concept quite distinct from that of rules. Finally, an answer to price level indeterminacy has also been found in the impact of price expectations, a result, however, that holds only under certain assumptions (Woodford 2000, 256–9; 2003, 128–9).

The shift in emphasis from monetary aggregates to interest rates, though mainly related to the tactics of policy implementation, is intertwined with monetary policy strategy (B. Friedman 1990). In this connection, the argument for the optimum quantity of money advocated driving the nominal interest rate to zero through deflation in order to eliminate the discrepancy between the private cost and the social cost of holding cash balances (Friedman 1969). An accounting system of exchange solves the optimality problem more straightforwardly because currency disappears and interest is paid on bank 'deposits' (see Chapter 9 below). Without tangible currency, however, price level determinacy must be ensured, a requirement that is obviously satisfied in the presence of a central bank. This would vanish only under extreme assumptions – large availability of information, highly efficient markets and no interference with the equilibrium properties of the economy – akin to the scenario depicted by Fama in which banks are passive intermediaries so that risk is entirely borne by depositors. Yet, it is precisely because these assumptions seldom obtained that central bank functions emerged, at first performed by private agents. Hence, the further the actual conditions of the economy are removed from those extreme assumptions, the greater will be the role of the central bank. This gap could conceivably narrow, but it can hardly disappear except in a frictionless world with complete information like a Walrasian or non-monetary economy.

Finally, if, for the sake of argument, Fama's hypothetical scenario emerged, price level indeterminacy would still remain to be solved. A monetary authority could be created for this purpose, instructed to purchase a certain amount of government bonds. This measure is in the nature of a rule dictated by theory, analogous to establishing the gold parity in a pure gold standard, not of a regulation. Actually, any monetary system, including the most advanced, demands rules that provide for its viability. A well designed accounting system of exchange also makes for its optimality, therefore increasing the efficiency of monetary arrangements and the economy as a whole.

4. Conclusions

In the age of information technology, the idea of an advancement of monetary theory may arise naturally since the analysis of the subject is strictly connected to the notion and availability of information. The latter, however, does not merely relate to efficiency in gathering data but to knowledge of the essential properties of money and its influence on the economy. The quantum leap in technology, foreshadowing the emergence of a cashless economy, has raised novel and controversial issues, a recurring event in monetary history related to the elusive nature of monetary theory. The alternation of different paradigms and the coexistence of contrasting hypotheses for considerable periods[15] has sometimes led to misconceptions about policy implementation and institutional design, with serious consequences for social welfare. The Great Depression is a dramatic testimony of the effects of mishandling policy (Hawtrey 1932; Friedman and Schwartz 1963) and the malfunctioning of international monetary arrangements (Fisher 1934; Eichengreen 1992).

After the paradigm shift brought about by Keynes's *General Theory*, the pendulum has swung back to a classical research programme grounded in rational expectations.[16] On the other hand, microeconomic theory has exhibited a relatively greater degree of convergence. Hence, reforms aimed at eliminating price controls, regulations and other obstacles to the functioning of markets, would reduce frictions and, in principle, might narrow the gap with respect to the general equilibrium model. This would enhance the efficiency of the 'true' model and ultimately improve our knowledge about the economy's response to changes in monetary conditions. The achievement of this objective, however, requires a discontinuity in the progress of monetary theory, at odds with the complexity of structure characterising the subject.

Nowadays, the hectic development of modern finance and substantial advances in information technology have paralleled the contributions to the classical equilibrium approach, so that all three factors underlying the evolution of the monetary system are at work – market forces, technical progress and dominating paradigm. The outcome of the interaction between these factors will depend on their relative weight and the prevailing conditions. In an extreme scenario, close to a frictionless world devoid of tangible money, countries would fix the unit of account and provide for price level determinacy. Conditions of high flexibility in all markets would make fixed exchange rates a natural choice, allowing, as in the gold standard, some leeway in monetary policy. In a diametrically opposite setting in which regulation was diffuse and unemployment weighed highly in society's preferences, the monetary system would continue to be based on flexible exchange rates and maintain its present shape even without tangible money.

The former looks like a futuristic set-up, theoretically consistent but far removed from the prospective advance in both theory and institutions. Resorting to a metaphor, the economic body shows much greater complexity than the human body, certainly no simple organism, whose secrets, however, began to be unveiled after the breakthroughs of molecular biology in the past half century, with even more spectacular progress expected in the next hundred years. Economics does not enjoy the same successes of biology. Nonetheless, novel ideas emerge and, albeit with varying lags and effectiveness, influence policy and institutions. Since the late 1800s the call for managed money in order to stabilise the price level triggered a process that, in the course of the twentieth century, ultimately led to the epoch-making diffusion of fiat money (Cesarano 2006). Notwithstanding its limitations, therefore, monetary theory has exerted and will continue to exert a decisive influence on the shape of the monetary system. Incapable of delivering universal laws, the theory of money will maintain its elusive character. However, prevailing paradigms will play a paramount role in the design of monetary policy and institutions.

Notes

*   Thanks are due to Benjamin Friedman and David Laidler for their useful comments. The usual caveat applies.
1.   The exchange between Friedman and Tobin on monetarism vividly testifies to the importance of this issue. Friedman remarked: 'For the monetarist/non-monetarist dichotomy, I suspect that the simplest litmus test would be the conditioned reflex to the question, "What is the price of money?" The monetarist will answer, "The inverse of the price level"; the non-monetarist (Keynesian or central banker) will answer, "the interest rate". The key difference is whether the stress is on money viewed as an asset with special characteristics, or on credit and credit markets, which leads to the analysis of monetary policy and monetary change operating through organized "money", i.e., "credit", markets, rather than through actual and desired cash balances' (Friedman 1976, p.316). And Tobin countered: 'Friedman's own litmus paper test, "What is the price of money?" is fun at cocktail parties. But some of my friends are good enough capital theorists to question the question. They can recognize *both* the purchasing power value of a dollar bill and the per annum opportunity cost of holding a dollar bill rather than some other asset. Others are good enough Marshallians or Walrasians to reject Friedman's favorite money-credit dichotomy. They suspect that "monetary policy and monetary change" operate *both* through credit markets and through "actual and desired cash balances"'(1976, p.335). This issue was a truly sensitive one since, many years later, Tobin (1992, 776–7) devoted an entire section of his Palgrave entry 'Money' to discuss it in detail.
2.   Friedman's graphic dictum encapsulates this notion: 'The basic reason [to hold money] is to serve as a medium of circulation, or temporary abode of purchasing power … . [The] separation of the act of sale from the act of purchase is the fundamental productive function of money' (1969, 3).
3.   Galiani emphasises the huge efficiency gains brought about by the introduction of money, sustained by the motive force of self-interest. 'I saw, and all can now see, that trade and money – its prime mover – have led us from a wretched state of nature in which each thinks only of himself, to a blissful communal life in which each thinks of and labors for all. We maintain ourselves in this latter state, not simply by the principles of virtue and piety, which where entire nations are envisaged are bonds that, by themselves, do not suffice – but by the self interest and comfort of each individual. *Coins are the notes discussed here, because in the end these are the representations of credit which one has against society, either directly, by reason of the work done by him, or indirectly because of coins donated to him by others.* In reality, there are no common warehouses among us, there are only private stores which correspond to them. Notes – really coins – are not paid to and collected from general

custodians. With much greater wisdom, each person cares for his own labor and tries to fill his own store, giving up money which he receives by trading, or acquires by selling, merchandise. In other words, virtue and faith are not needed by public warehousemen, nor is the vigilance of the prince required, because notes are not squandered. Everyone is reluctant to part with them since to give up money is to dispose of one's own arduous toil. Such a disadvantage which would not be sufficiently controlled by any virtue that is presumed to prevail in that first state, is taken care of in the present state perfectly by self interest, the force of which is always found in all of us, even the most vicious' (Galiani 1751, 70, italics added).

4. In this connection, it is significant that Hicks, influenced by Dennis Robertson, recanted his view of money as a store of value (1935): 'He [Robertson] turned me back from several of the byways into which I have wandered: over-emphasis on the "speculative motive", over-use of the Temporary Equilibrium method of *Value and Capital*, to take two examples. He converted me to my present insistence on the primacy of the Means of Payment function' (1967, X). Although an examination of modern literature lies outside the scope of this chapter, recent research has given substance to allegorical descriptions of money as the lubricant of the economic mechanism without being itself a component of the mechanism. The *locus classicus* is the beginning of Hume's essay: 'Money is not, properly speaking, one of the subjects of commerce; but only the instrument which men have agreed upon to facilitate the exchange of one commodity for another. It is none of the wheels of trade: It is the oil which renders the motion of the wheels more smooth and easy' (1752, 33). To do justice to the classics, the notion of information, or lack thereof, was sometimes implicit in their analysis of lack of double coincidence of wants. Thus Galiani remarked: 'The inconvenience of ancient and primitive methods of trading, which consists of people bartering one thing for another, obviously arises from the fact that it would be too difficult for a person *to know* to whom a thing which he has in excess is lacking, or *to know* who possesses precisely what he himself is lacking' (1751, 67, italics added).

5. See Chapter 8 below. This argument has been extensively developed with regard to the evolution of the international monetary system in Cesarano (2006).

6. Thus Galiani, who went farthest identifying the informational role of money as distinct from its commodity characteristic, wanted to base the monetary system on metal because 'the prince could always print an excessive number of notes. The doubt alone which he could cause in this way would be sufficient to take away from, or reduce their price, and inhibit their circulation' (1751, 71). Episodes of governments meddling with money abound in history even under metallic standards. An often cited one (Cantillon 1755, 297; Galiani 1751, 184) is the debasement of the currency, reducing its weight by five-sixths, implemented by the Romans after the First Punic War to repay the public debt.

7. In a fiat money environment, there is much to argue about this proposition on theoretical grounds and on policy grounds as well because the ideal of monetary unification finds its ultimate limit in nations' political sovereignty, which is heightened in a fiat money regime.

8. Wicksell went so far as to call for cutting the link with gold altogether, a 'first step towards the introduction of an ideal standard of value' (1898, 193). In his *Lectures*, Wicksell stressed the policy-makers' responsibility in designing monetary institutions and the difficulty of carrying out this task: '[W]ith regard to money, everything is determined by human beings themselves, i.e. the statesmen, and (so far as they are consulted) the economists; the choice of a measure of value, of a monetary system, of currency and credit legislation – all are in the hands of society, and natural conditions (e.g. the scarcity or abundance of the metals employed in the currency, their chemical properties, etc.) are relatively unimportant. Here, then, the rulers of society have an opportunity of showing their economic wisdom – or folly. Monetary history reveals the fact that folly has frequently been paramount; for it describes many fateful mistakes' (1906, 3–4).

9. Nowadays, relating the literature on the fundamentals of money to the theory of monetary policy is a major challenge. See the contributions to the May 2002 issue of the AER *Papers and Proceedings*, pp. 51–71.

10. 'The payments mechanism in such a world would be very efficient, but money in the usual sense would not exist. Thus neither the quantity theory of money nor the liquidity preference

theory of money would be applicable' (Black 1970, 9). Fama was even more explicit Contrasting currency with an accounting system of exchange as a means of executing transactions, he remarked: 'Currency is a physical medium which can be characterized as money. An accounting system works through bookkeeping entries, debits and credits, which do not require any physical medium or *the concept of money*' (Fama 1980, 39, italics added).

11. As Hicks observed: '[I]t is with this organization [the clearing system] that we first meet a clear case of the Wicksellian phenomenon, a market in which absolute prices – money prices – are indeterminate. The money is simply a unit of account; it is not one of the traded commodities; there is therefore no supply-demand equation to determine its value. The Walras equations are sufficient to determine relative prices, prices (that is) in terms of one of the traded commodities taken as numéraire; but this numéraire is not the money in terms of which calculations are made. That money does not enter into the Walras equations; it is altogether outside them. The money prices can be at any level, yet the same Walras equilibrium will be attained' (1967, 9–10).

12. Benjamin Friedman (1999) has examined the implications of these developments for the role of the central bank, graphically depicted as 'an army with only a signal corps', stimulating a lively debate. See the contributions to *The Future of Monetary Policy*, a special issue of *International Finance*, July 2000.

13. Friedman and Schwartz (1986, 50) stress four features of the Scottish system: 1. banks only issued inside money; 2. shareholders assumed unlimited liability for the bank's obligations; 3. shareholders possessed sizeable wealth and gave great weight to their reputation; 4. some of the major banks performed central bank functions. That the lender of last resort was performed by private institutions is particularly important because it avoided a major consequence of the entering of government in the banking industry. Introducing a political dimension and the possibility of shifting future costs onto society may well heighten banks' misbehaviour, opening a Pandora's box of further regulations, whose actual effectiveness is doubtful.

14. In this respect, Patinkin's penetrating observation is quite telling: '[T]he full significance of [price level] indeterminacy ..., in brief, is that in order for the absolute price level to be determined by market-equilibrating forces, changes in it must impinge on aggregate *real* behavior in *some* market – i.e., must create excess demands in some market.' Instead, if there is no impingement on the real demand and supply functions, 'the economy does not generate resistance to any arbitrary change in the price level. Accordingly, there is nothing to prevent the frictionless flow of prices from one level to another' (1961, 113–14).

15. In this connection, the Fed's conduct in the last twenty years has, not without success, entirely diverged from the prevailing canons of the theory of monetary policy (B. Friedman 2006), maintaining a stance which, resorting to an oxymoron, may be termed 'designed ambiguity' or 'enlightened opacity.'

16. This hypothesis postulates knowledge of the 'true' model of the economy, an appropriate assumption if the model's explanatory and predictive power is substantial. Interestingly, Milton Friedman's argument for rules rested on the diametrically opposite assumption of lack of knowledge of the monetary transmission mechanism, suggesting the possibility of different positions within the classical approach (Cesarano 1983).

References

Aristotle, *Politics*, I; *Nicomachean Ethics*, V; reprinted in Arthur E. Monroe (ed.) *Early Economic Thought: Selections from Economic Literature Prior to Adam Smith*, (1924), Cambridge, Mass.: Harvard University Press.

Black, Fischer (1970) 'Banking and Interest Rates in a World Without Money: The Effects of Uncontrolled Banking', *Journal of Bank Research* 1: 9–20.

Cantillon, Richard (1755) *Essai sur la Nature du Commerce en Général*, edited by Henry Higgs, (1959), London: Frank Cass.

Cesarano, Filippo (1983) 'The Rational Expectations Hypothesis in Retrospect', *American Economic Review* 73: 198–203; reprinted in Filippo Cesarano, *Monetary Theory in Retrospect*,

(2007), London: Routledge, 125–30.

—— (2006) *Monetary Theory and Bretton Woods: The Construction of an International Monetary Order*, Cambridge: Cambridge University Press.

—— (2007) 'The History of Economic Analysis in Perspective', in Filippo Cesarano, *Monetary Theory in Retrospect*, London: Routledge, 209–33.

Clower, Robert W. (1967) 'A Reconsideration of the Microfoundations of Monetary Theory', *Western Economic Journal* 6: 1–9.

Eichengreen, Barry (1992) *Golden Fetters: The Gold Standard and the Great Depression, 1919–1939*, Oxford: Oxford University Press.

Fama, Eugene F. (1980) 'Banking in the Theory of Finance', *Journal of Monetary Economics* 6: 39–57.

Fisher, Irving (1911) *The Purchasing Power of Money: Its Determination and Relation to Credit, Interest and Crises*, (1963), New York: Augustus M. Kelley.

—— (1934) *Are Booms and Depressions Transmitted Internationally Through Monetary Standards?*, New Haven, Conn.; reprinted in Robert W. Dimand (2003) 'Irving Fisher on the International Transmission of Booms and Depressions Through Monetary Standards', *Journal of Money, Credit and Banking* 35: 49–90.

Friedman, Benjamin M. (1990) 'Targets and Instruments of Monetary Policy', in Benjamin M. Friedman and Frank H. Hahn (eds) *Handbook of Monetary Economics*, vol. 2, Amsterdam: North-Holland, 1185–230.

—— (1999) 'The Future of Monetary Policy: The Central Bank as an Army with Only a Signal Corps?', *International Finance* 2: 321–38.

—— (2006) 'The Greenspan Era: Discretion, Rather than Rules', *American Economic Review: Papers and Proceedings* 96: 174–77.

Friedman, Milton (1969) 'The Optimum Quantity of Money', in Milton Friedman, *The Optimum Quantity of Money and Other Essays*, Chicago: Aldine, 1–50.

—— (1976) Comment on 'Long-run Effects of Fiscal and Monetary Policy on Aggregate Demand' by James Tobin and Willem Buiter, in Jerome L. Stein (ed.) *Monetarism*, Amsterdam: North-Holland, 310–17.

Friedman, Milton, and Schwartz, Anna J. (1963) *A Monetary History of the United States, 1867–1960*, Princeton: Princeton University Press.

—— (1986) 'Has Government Any Role in Money?', *Journal of Monetary Economics* 17: 37–62.

Galiani, Ferdinando (1751) *On Money*, translated by Peter R. Toscano, (1977), Ann Arbor, Mich.: University Microfilms International.

Goodhart, Charles A.E. (1999) 'Myths about the Lender of Last Resort', *International Finance* 2: 339–60.

Grierson, Philip (1977) *The Origins of Money*, London: The Athlone Press, University of London.

Hahn, Frank H. (1965) 'On Some Problems of Proving the Existence of an Equilibrium in a Monetary Economy', in Frank H. Hahn and Frank P.R. Brechling (eds) *The Theory of Interest Rates*, London: Macmillan, 126–35.

Hawtrey, Ralph G. (1932) *The Art of Central Banking*, (1970), London: Frank Cass.

Hicks, John R. (1935) 'A Suggestion for Simplifying the Theory of Money', *Economica* 2: 1–19.

—— (1967) *Critical Essays in Monetary Theory*, Oxford: Oxford University Press.

Hume, David (1752) 'Of Money'; reprinted in David Hume, *Writings on Economics*, edited by Eugene Rotwein, (1970), Madison: The University of Wisconsin Press, 33–46.

—— (1769) Letter to André Morellet, 10 July 1769; reprinted in David Hume, *Writings on Economics*, edited by Eugene Rotwein, (1970), Madison: The University of Wisconsin Press, 214–16.

Jones, Robert A. (1976) 'The Origin and Development of Media of Exchange', *Journal of Political Economy* 84: 757–75.

Keynes, John M. (1923) *A Tract on Monetary Reform*, London: Macmillan.

Klein, Benjamin (1974) 'The Competitive Supply of Money', *Journal of Money, Credit and Banking* 6: 423–53.

Laidler, David (1988) 'Taking Money Seriously', *Canadian Journal of Economics* 21: 687–713.

—— (1991) *The Golden Age of the Quantity Theory: The Development of Neoclassical Monetary*

Economics, 1870–1914, Hemel Hempstead: Philip Allan.
—— (2002) 'Rules, Discretion and Financial Crises in Classical and Neoclassical Monetary Economics', *Economic Issues* 7: 11–33.
McKinnon, Ronald I. (1993) 'The Rules of the Game: International Money in Historical Perspective', *Journal of Economic Literature* 31: 1–44.
Menger, Carl (1892) 'On the Origin of Money', *Economic Journal* 2: 239–55.
Mill, John S. (1848) *Principles of Political Economy*, edited by William Ashley, (1987), New York: Augustus M. Kelley.
Mundell, Robert A. (2000) 'A Reconsideration of the Twentieth Century', *American Economic Review* 90: 327–40.
Niehans, Jürg (1978) *The Theory of Money*, Baltimore: The Johns Hopkins University Press.
Ostroy, Joseph M. (1973) 'The Informational Efficiency of Monetary Exchange' *American Economic Review* 63: 597–610.
Ostroy, Joseph M. and Starr, Ross M. (1990) 'The Transactions Role of Money', in Benjamin M. Friedman and Frank H. Hahn (eds) *Handbook of Monetary Economics*, vol. 1, Amsterdam: North-Holland, 3–62.
Patinkin, Don (1961) 'Financial Intermediaries and the Logical Structure of Monetary Theory', *American Economic Review* 51: 95–116.
Redish, Angela (1990) 'The Evolution of the Gold Standard in England', *Journal of Economic History* 50: 789–805.
—— (2000) *Bimetallism: An Economic and Historical Analysis*, Cambridge: Cambridge University Press.
Schumpeter, Joseph A. (1954) *History of Economic Analysis*, Oxford: Oxford University Press.
Tobin, James (1976) 'Reply: Is Friedman a Monetarist?', in Jerome L. Stein (ed.) *Monetarism*, Amsterdam: North-Holland, 332–6.
—— (1992) 'Money', in Peter Newman, Murray Milgate, and John Eatwell (eds) *The New Palgrave Dictionary of Money and Finance*, vol. 2, London: Macmillan, 770–79.
White, Lawrence H. (1984) *Free Banking in Britain: Theory, Experience, and Debate, 1800–1845*, Cambridge: Cambridge University Press.
Wicksell, Knut (1898) *Interest and Prices: A Study of the Causes Regulating the Value of Money*, (1965), New York: Augustus M. Kelley.
—— (1906) *Lectures on Political Economy*, vol. 2: *Money*, (1935), London: Routledge.
Woodford, Michael (2000) 'Monetary Policy in a World Without Money', *International Finance* 3: 229–60.
—— (2003) *Interest and Prices: Foundations of a Theory of Monetary Policy*, Princeton: Princeton University Press.

PART I

THE DEMAND FOR MONEY

[2]

Money and quasi-money*

Analysis of the definition of monetary aggregate was a prominent feature of the debate on money in the 1960s and early 1970s. In his 1962 survey Harry Johnson, discussing the subject in the context of money demand, underscores its significance: '[T]he chief substantive issues outstanding are three: first, what specific collection of assets corresponds most closely to the theoretical concept of money – an issue that arises as soon as the distinguishing characteristic of money ceases to be its function as a medium of exchange' (1962, p. 26). The issue of the relationship between money and quasi-money has an important bearing on other fundamental aspects of monetary theory and policy, and progress in understanding these therefore hinges on an advance in analysis of the definition of money. Numerous studies treated the issue in the fifteen years following Johnson's article. Once relatively concordant results had been reached at least on the empirical plane (Feige and Pearce 1977, p. 463), research moved on to other subjects.

The problem has not received equal attention in Italy, in part for reasons specific to the institutional framework.[1] Only recently, following the spread of money-market instruments, has the question of including these instruments in the definition of money stock been raised in various quarters. After examining the nature of the problem (section I), this paper presents an empirical analysis (section II).

I

In the initial phase of the revival of interest in monetary economics in the second half of the 1950s, analysis was conducted at a level of abstraction where it was not deemed relevant to specify the empirical aggregates corresponding to the significant variables (Johnson 1962, pp. 25–33). Still, the link between the definition of money and some key questions emerged early on. It is sufficient to cite the work of Gurley and Shaw regarding the impact of financial intermediaries on monetary policy: if the assets issued by financial intermediaries have a high degree of substitutability with money, the effectiveness of monetary policy may diminish.

The natural point from which to begin an inquiry into the definition of monetary aggregate is a theoretical analysis of the essential properties of money. As is known, assigning money a role in the general equilibrium model is quite arduous. While the abundant literature that appeared towards the end of the 1960s helped to clarify some aspects of the problem, it certainly did not solve it.[2] The difficulty of penetrating the notion of money is essentially due to the multiplicity of functions it performs and the interrelations between these functions; the phenomenon, considered as a whole, is correspondingly complex.[3] As Robert Clower observed (1977, p. 211), the crux lies in identifying the sufficient conditions for defining a monetary economy. Except for some works focusing on the mechanism of exchange, the different strands of the more recent literature concentrate on one of the fundamental functions other than that of unit of account: medium of exchange and store of value.

These conceptions of money's essential characteristics have given rise in the past to different approaches to the transmission mechanism of monetary policy.[4] Blaug (1968, pp. 154–59) succinctly labels the two hypotheses of transmission the 'direct mechanism' and the 'indirect mechanism.' In the former, given an equilibrium level of money balances, an increase in the quantity of money causes an increase in expenditure and thus in the general price level. In the latter, an injection of money produces an increase in loanable funds and a decrease in the market interest rate, which therefore is lower than the rate of return on capital; the subsequent change in the demand for funds brings the two rates back into equilibrium. The widespread interpretation positing a close connection between the direct mechanism with the means-of-payment function and the indirect mechanism with the store-of-value function should be accepted with considerable caution, for this parallelism is not always observable. Wicksell, for example (1935, Chapter 1), though stressing the pre-eminence of the medium-of-exchange function, is one of the leading proponents of the indirect mechanism of transmission (Cesarano 1983, section IV).

The two strands of thought have often overlapped, with now one, now the other prevailing, depending in part on the 'demand for theory' exerted by significant events (Pantaleoni 1898). Moreover, different interpretations of the essential properties of money can also be found in the work of the same economist. Hicks, for example, in the *Essays*, critiques fundamental aspects of the monetary theory that was current in the 1950s and 1960s, suggesting that some of its widely held tenets be dropped.[5]

The limited progress beyond these two approaches is reflected also in the attempts to define the stock of money through empirical measurement. In the wide-ranging review that introduces their study of the United States, Friedman and Schwartz (1970, pp. 89–146) stress that the different efforts to identify a criterion sufficient to provide a univocal definition of money can be divided into two major groups, each closely connected with one of the two approaches described above. On the basis of their critique of these attempts, Friedman and Schwartz come to the general conclusion, found by Keynes and many others,[6] that the quest for the definition must be based not on a principle determined a priori but on an empirical analysis.

In its present state, monetary theory is unable to indicate a specific criterion for arriving at a definition of money stock, and so work has concentrated on attempts of an empirical nature. These have followed three main approaches (Feige and Pearce 1977, p. 442). The first estimates a money demand function in order to determine the cross elasticity with respect to the interest rate on alternative assets; the cross elasticity provides a measure of the degree of substitutability between money and those assets. The second, developed by Friedman and Schwartz (1970), consists in seeking the monetary aggregate with the most stable demand function in terms of a limited number of arguments. The third, which can be traced back to the article by Chetty (1969), aims at estimating the elasticity of substitution between money and quasi-money directly from the parameters of a utility function. An immediate problem, common to all three approaches, is the difficulty of drawing the line between the assets to be included in the definition of money and those to be excluded, substitutability being a question of degree, not of kind. The convention, adopted in works of applied microeconomics, of fixing the line at the point where elasticity is equal to minus one does not contribute to a solution, given the nature of the problem. Taking the approaches individually, numerous criticisms of that adopted by Friedman have been raised in connection with the overall contours of Friedman's thinking; one specific shortcoming, underscored by Feige and Pearce (1977, p. 442), regards the non-measurability of the substitutability between money and quasi-money. Responses to Chetty's work have called into question his conclusion in favour of a high degree of substitutability between money and quasi-money.[7] Recently, Husted and Rush (1984) pointed up some analytical weaknesses of Chetty's article and obtained extremely low estimates of the elasticity of substitution. Chetty in fact is one of the few who have reached a result in line with Gurley and Shaw's hypothesis.

The survey by Feige and Pearce (1977) concludes that the empirical evidence in favour of a low degree of substitutability between money and quasi-money is, in the American case, quite decisive. This finding has not been modified in the years since then; indeed, it has been corroborated by the few works that have been published on the subject (Ewis and Fisher 1984). This lack of developments on the empirical plane, together with difficulty theory has encountered in making progress, explain the diminished attention the issue now attracts.

II

The upsurge of interest in Italy in the problems of the empirical definition of money was triggered by several developments in the financial markets during the 1970s. In particular, the high variability of inflation led to accentuated uncertainty regarding real yields. When variations in nominal interest rates are due mainly to fluctuations in the inflation rate, economic agents react by shortening the maturity of their financial assets. In fact, it can be shown that when inflation is highly variable, the mean and variance of the cost of issuing long-term securities exceed those of issuing short-term securities. Issuers consequently would demand long-term funds only if they received a premium. However, a premium of opposite sign would have to be paid to the purchaser. Obviously, this is impossible, and so the market for long-term securities tends to dry up and be replaced by short-term paper or instruments indexed to short-term rates.

The development of the market for Treasury bills and Treasury credit certificates is a clear case in point. Following the growth in the stock of these assets (the former short term, the latter indexed to money-market rates), many raised the question of whether Treasury bills or both Treasury bills and Treasury credit certificates ought to be included in the definition of the money stock, to obtain M3 and M4 respectively.

On the basis of the arguments set out in section I, the hypothesis of extending the definition of monetary aggregate is perfectly acceptable. The hard thing is to identify an a priori criterion for drawing a dividing line between the different assets. The answer to this can only be sought on the empirical plane.

The approach adopted in this study is that most frequently found in the literature and consists in estimating the cross elasticity of money demand with respect to the interest rate of the asset whose degree of substitutability with money is to be measured. The specification of the function is the 'conventional' or 'standard' specification (Goldfeld 1973) based on a simple short-term stock adjustment mechanism. At first Goldfeld's specification was widely accepted and did not generate controversy. Subsequently various criticisms were raised. Among other things, David Laidler (1982) and Robert Gordon (1984) remarked that where the supply of money is controlled by the central bank, the conventional specification could in part represent a Phillips curve 'in disguise.' In this case, there are serious reasons to doubt the possibility of identifying a short-term money demand function (Cooley and LeRoy 1981). However, this problem is of little relevance to the experience of Italy, where over the last two decades monetary policy has been conducted relying prevalently on interest rates, whether explicitly or implicitly. Laidler and Gordon's criticism does not apply in this case, since once the interest rate is set the supply of money becomes endogenous and the money demand curve is identified (Gordon 1984, p. 404). Although the necessity of estimating the equation in the context of a structural model is unanimously acknowledged, this is more a statement of principle than a practicable path, given the lack of agreement on the contents of the generally accepted 'true' structural model. This also complicates the choice of exogenous variables to be used in a two-stage estimation (Cooley and LeRoy 1981). The estimation using the ordinary least squares method can be seen as a first test of the theoretical hypothesis tying the quantity of money demanded to some variables (Hetzel 1984, p. 189).

The following equation is estimated,[8] using quarterly data for the period 1976.Q1 to 1983.Q4:

$$\ln(M/P)_t = -1.352 + 0.763\ln y_t - 0.142\ln i_t^S - 0.189\ln i_t^L + 0.272\ln(M/P)_{t-1} + \varepsilon_t$$
$$\quad\quad (1.74)\quad (9.30)\quad\quad (4.22)\quad\quad (4.86)\quad\quad (3.64) \tag{1}$$

$$\bar{R}^2 = 0.897 \quad\quad \sigma = 0.0223 \quad\quad h = -0.17$$

(the absolute value of Student's t is shown in brackets; h is the Durbin h-statistic), where M is the M2 money stock (currency in circulation plus current account and savings deposits), P is the consumer price index, y is real income, i^S and i^L are respectively the rate on short-term assets (weighted average of the rate on Treasury bills and Treasury credit certificates) and long-term assets (rate on Treasury bonds).

The short-term elasticity with respect to the short-term rate is considerably less than one (-0.142) and is also lower than the elasticity to the long-term rate (-0.189). The long-term elasticities are -0.195 and -0.260 respectively. The hypothesis of a low degree of substitutability between money and quasi-money thus appears to be confirmed also for Italy. By comparison with the case of the United States, the stock adjustment coefficient is relatively high (0.728), so that almost three fourths of the adjustment is completed within the calendar quarter. It should also be noted that the long-term elasticity with respect to income is equal to 1.048, higher than that hypothesized by a pure transaction model.

In equation (1) the own rate of return on money is not included, as the related coefficient is not significantly different from zero. The specification including the differential between the rate of return on alternative assets and the own rate, suggested by transaction models (Barro and Santomero 1972), constrains the individual rates to equality. In addition, that specification encounters a serious limit in some basic assumptions of the underlying theoretical model. Taking these observations into account, the results obtained considering the yield differentials for the same estimation period are presented:

$$\ln(M/P)_t = -3.324 + 0.775\ln y_t - 0.063\ln(i^S - i^M)_t - 0.128\ln(i^L - i^M)_t$$
$$\quad\quad (3.30)\quad (7.51)\quad\quad (3.71)\quad\quad\quad (5.06)$$
$$\quad\quad + 0.450\ln(M/P)_{t-1} + \varepsilon_t \tag{2}$$
$$\quad\quad\quad (5.71)$$

$$\bar{R}^2 = 0.852 \quad\quad \sigma = 0.0268 \quad\quad h = -0.24$$

where i^M is the weighted average rate, net of tax, on the assets composing M2. Compared with equation (1), the short-term elasticity to the short-term rate is more than halved (–0.063), while that with respect to the long-term rate falls substantially (–0.128). The respective long-term elasticities also are considerably lower (–0.115 and –0.223), although the stock adjustment coefficient is smaller. This also implies an increase in the long-term elasticity with respect to income (1.409).

These results must be interpreted with due caution. The relatively low cross elasticity of money demand with respect to the short-term rate only indicates that changes in the yield of liquid assets do not generate appreciable changes of opposite sign in the quantity of money demanded. This distinguishes M2, for its scant substitutability with money-market securities. This result is worth underscoring, since in the past there has sometimes been confusion, in Italy as elsewhere, about the criteria governing the definition of a monetary aggregate. In certain cases, specific institutional features have been taken as guideposts. Pesek and Saving (1967, pp. 122–23), for example, exclude savings deposits from the definition of money on the grounds that they are not used as a medium of exchange in transactions. Don Patinkin has rightly ridiculed this approach to the problem, pointing out the singularity of Pesek and Saving's criterion.[9]

An essential requisite for a monetary aggregate to be used as an intermediate objective is the stability of its demand function. Testing the stability hypothesis is beyond the scope of this work.[10] However, it should be remarked that the monetary aggregates do not necessarily become unreliable for the implementation of monetary policy at a time of financial innovation.[11] Following the introduction of assets serving as an alternative to money, the learning process could develop steadily over time. Control of the aggregates would become problematic only if innovation had frequent and unpredictable effects on the relevant parameters.

As noted at the beginning of this section, the high variability of real rates of return in the 1960s led to a shortening of the maturity of securities. However, the results described above show quite a pronounced distinction between money and short-term assets. The sharp increase in the stock of these assets held by the public can be attributed to a change in preferences regarding the liquidity of the form in which wealth is held. A similar phenomenon has been observed in the United States, though in a considerably different institutional context (Cagan and Schwartz 1975). The shortening of the average maturity of debt is closely connected with the impact of policies, especially as regards the manner of financing the government budget deficit,[12] on agents' behaviour. Perhaps owing to the innovative nature of the instrument the massive issuance of securities indexed to short-term rates has given the impression that it is a handy solution to far more complex problems. Some important implications of the issue of these securities for monetary control have been identified only recently.

Notes

* Translated by Daniel Dichter. Angelo Porta, Nicola Rossi, Giacomo Vaciago and Fausto Vicarelli offered useful comments on an earlier version of this article. Complete responsibility for the text remains with the author.
1. It will be sufficient here to cite the absence in Italy of a developed money market until 1975. For analogous observations regarding the British and American experience, see Sprenkle (1984).
2. See the review by Ulph and Ulph (1975) and Barro and Fischer (1976, section 7).
3. Notice the broad similarity between the following two passages of the prefaces by Hicks (1967) and Friedman (1969): 'The essays that are collected in this book ... are the record of a process, extending over many years, by which I have at last formed my present conception of monetary theory. All the while I have been learning; as time has gone on, first one thing has become clear, then another. I have realised that truth is many-sided. Any uniform presentation could only be a photograph from one angle' (Hicks 1967, p. V). 'Monetary theory is like a Japanese garden. It has esthetic unity born of variety; an apparent simplicity that conceals a sophisticated reality; a surface view that dissolves in ever deeper perspectives. Both can be fully appreciated only if examined from many different angles, only if studied leisurely but in depth. Both have elements that can be enjoyed independently of the whole, yet attain their full realization only as part of the whole' (Friedman 1969, p. V).
4. The antinomy between two distinct 'visions' of monetary theory, which dates back at least to the beginning of the nineteenth century, is found in the contemporary schools of thought (Hicks 1967, pp. VII–VIII; Vicarelli 1983).
5. 'What is it that distinguishes money, regarded as a store of value, from these other assets, which are not money? A pre-Keynesian economist, confronted with this question, would surely have given the obvious answer. Since the mere capacity of acting as a store of value does not confer monetary quality, it must be the other functions which do so. An asset becomes a money asset if it is not only a store of value, but also a unit of account; or not only a store of value, but also a means of payment. If it has these other functions, or even only one of these other functions, and is also storable, it must be reckoned as being money. This is the obvious answer; and I think I shall be able to show that it is the correct answer. But (since Keynes) it has had a rival. It is commonly said that the essential characteristic of money (regarded as an item in a balance-sheet) is that it does not bear interest, whereas other assets, in some sense or other, do. Thus, we are told by Patinkin that what has to be explained is the "peaceable co-existence" between non-interest-bearing money and interest-bearing bonds. I have myself taken this view in earlier writings, but I have come to hold that it should not be accepted. I think I shall be able to show, as we go on, that the whole theory makes better sense if we abandon it' (Hicks 1967, p. 18).
6. '[W]e can draw the line between "money" and "debts" at whatever point is most convenient for handling a particular problem' (Keynes 1936, p. 167, note 1). See, also, the discussion in Pasquale Jannaccone's *Manuale* (1959, pp. 465 ff.).
7. A new approach, but fairly well in line with Chetty's, has been taken by William Barnett and some collaborators. Starting out from the theory of aggregation and index numbers, Barnett has constructed estimates of the money stock using the Divisia index; the method should provide a measure of the quantity of money consistent with the different degree of substitutability between its different components. For an analysis of this approach, see Barnett, Offenbacker and Spindt (1981).
8. For a review of empirical works on money demand in Italy, see Calliari, Spinelli and Verga (1982). The most recent studies, not covered in that article, are those by Bedoni and Verga (1982), Caranza, Micossi and Villani (1982), and Vaciago and Verga (1982).
9. It is useful to quote Patinkin at length: 'The statement that savings deposits are not money because "we do not observe the product of the [savings] association serving as a medium of exchange, as money" reveals an extremely naive conception of the nature of empirical

observation in economics. True, we do not observe individuals in the market place making purchases with their saving pass-books. But the relevant question for the economist is not this, but whether (say) an increase in the rate of interest paid on savings account will decrease significantly the amount of money ... which individuals hold. In other words, here as elsewhere the relevant criterion of what group of goods constitute a single commodity for purposes of economic analysis is not the physical characteristics of these goods, but the cross-elasticities of demand among them' (Patinkin 1969, p. 1157).

10. In a recent article Bedoni and Verga find that the demand function of bank deposits is broadly stable (1982, p. 669).
11. A distinct and very important question regards the measure of the interest rate elasticity and the velocity of adjustment in relation to the greater or lesser variability of yields in a regime of money-stock control.
12. For a detailed analysis of these problems with reference to the Italian case, see Spaventa (1984). The most recent writings on monetary policy (Barro and Gordon 1983) underscore the importance of these aspects.

References

Barnett, William, Offenbacher, Edward and Spindt, Paul (1981) 'New Concepts of Aggregated Money', *Journal of Finance* 36: 497–505.

Barro, Robert J. and Fischer, Stanley (1976) 'Recent Developments in Monetary Theory', *Journal of Monetary Economics* 2: 133–67.

Barro, Robert J. and Gordon, David B. (1983) 'A Positive Theory of Monetary Policy in a Natural Rate Model', *Journal of Political Economy* 91: 589–610.

Barro, Robert J. and Santomero, Anthony M. (1972) 'Household Money Holdings and the Demand Deposit Rate', *Journal of Money, Credit and Banking* 4: 397–413.

Bedoni, Marisa and Verga, Giovanni (1982) 'La domanda dei depositi: un ulteriore approfondimento', *Giornale degli Economisti* 41: 659–70.

Blaug, Mark (1968) *Economic Theory in Retrospect*, Homewood, Ill.: Irwin.

Cagan, Phillip and Schwartz, Anna J. (1975) 'Has the Growth of Money Substitutes Hindered Monetary Policy?', *Journal of Money, Credit and Banking* 7: 137–59.

Calliari, Sergio, Spinelli, Francesco and Verga, Giovanni (1982) 'La domanda di moneta in Italia: una valutazione della letteratura e nuove stime', in Francesco Spinelli and Giuseppe Tullio (eds) *Saggi di politica monetaria e fiscale*, Milan: Franco Angeli, 40–80.

Caranza, Cesare, Micossi, Stefano and Villani, Marco (1982) 'La domanda di moneta in Italia: 1963–1981', ms., Banca d'Italia.

Cesarano, Filippo (1983) 'On the Role of the History of Economic Analysis', *History of Political Economy* 15: 63–82.

Chetty, V. Karuppan (1969) 'On Measuring the Nearness of Near-Moneys', *American Economic Review* 59: 270–81.

Clower, Robert W. (1977) 'The Anatomy of Monetary Theory', *American Economic Review* 67: 206–12.

Cooley, Thomas F. and Leroy, Stephen F. (1981) 'Identification and Estimation of Money Demand', *American Economic Review* 71: 821–44.

Ewis, Nabil A. and Fisher, Douglas (1984) 'The Translog Utility Function and the Demand for Money in the United States', *Journal of Money, Credit and Banking* 16: 34–52.

Feige, Edgar L. and Pearce, Douglas K. (1977) 'The Substitutability of Money and Near-Monies: A Survey of the Time-Series Evidence', *Journal of Economic Literature* 15: 439–69.

Friedman, Milton (1969) *The Optimum Quantity of Money and Other Essays*, Chicago: Aldine.

Friedman, Milton and Schwartz, Anna J. (1970) *Monetary Statistics of the United States*, New York: Columbia University Press.

Goldfeld, Stephen M. (1973) 'The Demand for Money Revisited', *Brookings Papers on Economic Activity* 4(3): 577–638.

Gordon, Robert J. (1984) 'The Short-Run Demand for Money: A Reconsideration', *Journal of Money, Credit and Banking* 16, Part 1: 403–34.

Hetzel, Robert L. (1984) 'Estimating Money Demand Functions', *Journal of Money, Credit and

Banking 16: 185–93.

Hicks, John R. (1967) *Critical Essays in Monetary Theory*, Oxford: Oxford University Press.

Husted, Steven and Rush Mark (1984) 'On Measuring the Nearness of Near Moneys. Revisited', *Journal of Monetary Economics* 14: 171–81.

Jannaccone, Pasquale (1959) *Manuale di economia politica*, Turin: UTET.

Johnson, Harry G. (1962) 'Monetary Theory and Policy', *American Economic Review* 52: 335–84; reprinted in Harry G. Johnson (1969) *Essays in Monetary Economics*, 2nd ed., Cambridge, Mass.: Harvard University Press, 15–72.

Keynes, John M. (1936) *The General Theory of Employment, Interest and Money*, London: MacMillan.

Laidler, David (1969) 'The Definition of Money', *Journal of Money, Credit and Banking* 1: 508–25.

Laidler, David (1982) *Monetarist Perspectives*, Oxford: Philip Allan.

Pantaleoni, Maffeo (1898) 'Dei criteri che debbono informare la storia delle dottrine economiche', *Giornale degli Economisti* 17: 407–31.

Patinkin, Don (1969) 'Money and Wealth: A Review Article', *Journal of Economic Literature* 7: 1140–60.

Pesek, Boris P. and Saving, Thomas R. (1967) *Money, Wealth, and Economic Theory*, New York: MacMillan.

Spaventa, Luigi (1984) 'La crescita del debito pubblico in Italia: evoluzione, prospettive e problemi di politica economica', *Moneta e Credito* 37: 251–84.

Sprenkle, Case M. (1984) 'On Liquidity Preference-Again: Comment', *American Economic Review* 74: 809–11.

Ulph A.M. and Ulph D.T. (1975) 'Transaction Costs in General Equilibrium Theory – A Survey', *Economica* 42: 355–72.

Vaciago, Giacomo and Verga, Giovanni (1982) 'Domanda di moneta e "disintermediazione" delle banche', *Moneta e Credito* 35: 59–71.

Vicarelli, Fausto (1983) 'Credito', in Giorgio Lunghini and Mariano D'Antonio (eds) *Dizionario di economia politica*, vol. 7: *Credito, crescita, crisi*, Turin: Boringhieri.

Wicksell, Knut (1935) *Lectures on Political Economy*, vol. 2, London: Routledge.

3

Applied Economics, 1990, **22**, 1437–1442

Financial innovation and demand for money: some empirical evidence

FILIPPO CESARANO

Banca d'Italia–Servizio Studi, Via Nazionale, 91 00184 Roma, Italy

Recent criticism of money growth targets has been based on the implications of spreading financial innovation, since the latter has been considered to undermine monetary policy effectiveness both by bringing about an increase in the interest elasticity of money demand and by producing instability of the money demand function. The empirical results presented in this paper – focusing on a single and specific case of financial innovation particularly suited to study the issue at stake – falsify both hypotheses.

I. INTRODUCTION

Assessing the state of the art of monetary policy, David Laidler (1986) has recently emphasized the instability of the money demand function in the last decade as the main element giving rise to widespread criticism of policy regimes based on money growth targets. Such instability, observed in many countries, 'is a well established result coming from a variety of studies' (1986, p. 4) and is chiefly related to institutional changes in the financial sector. Indeed, financial innovation has been traditionally considered to undermine monetary policy effectiveness by (a) bringing about an increase in the interest elasticity of the demand for money (Gurley and Shaw, 1960) and (b) producing instability of the money demand function. This paper presents some empirical evidence which runs counter to both propositions.

The theoretical foundation of these results can be found in Alvin Marty's (1961) penetrating review of Gurley and Shaw (1960). In particular, with regard to the former proposition, Marty (1961, pp. 59–60) argued that the development of assets rival to money may actually *reduce* rather than raise the interest elasticity. In fact, the introduction of a money substitute will have two distinct effects: (1) it will make the slope of the money demand schedule flatter for each individual; (2) it will shift each schedule to the left. The second effect, so the argument runs, is likely to be stronger for the more elastic schedules since the latter pertain to individuals who, being highly sensitive to variations in the interest rate, are more likely to substitute the new asset for a relatively large fraction of their money balances. Therefore, the final market schedule may well be less elastic than the initial one since the weight of agents whose demand is relatively inelastic will be greater.[1] With respect

---

[1] Early empirical works on the demand for money (Meltzer, 1963; Laidler, 1966; Tucker, 1966) and later articles as well (Cagan and Schwartz, 1975; Hafer and Hein, 1984), albeit using different estimation

to the second proposition, Marty has contended (1961, pp. 60–1) that possible shifts in the money demand function do not necessarily impair monetary policy effectiveness, since the latter is related to the stability of the rate at which individuals learn to substitute new assets for money.

This note focuses on the experience of Italy, where the main institutional change in the financial sector has not been fostered by the operation of competitive market forces but by the government. The development of the Treasury Bills market in 1975 was prompted by the need to finance an accelerating public deficit. This is quite a different instance of financial innovation in that it has no appreciable recognition lag, since it concerns the introduction at a given point in time of a single, widely publicized, default-free asset rival to money. In fact, the case of Italy seems to provide the uncommon opportunity of studying the issue at stake in a way close to an *in vitro* experiment. The empirical results shown in the next section corroborate Marty's conjectures against propositions (a) and (b) above, thereby falsifying the widely accepted hypothesis concerning the effects of the diffusion of a new money substitute on monetary control.

II. EMPIRICAL RESULTS

Interest elasticity

A conventional or standard demand for money function has been estimated using Italian quarterly data for two distinct periods, 1970.I–1975.IV and 1976.I–1985.IV, before and after the development of the Treasury Bills market respectively.[2] In this regard, the criticism raised by David Laidler (1982, chapter 2) and others on the conventional specification – arguing that the latter may in fact be a Phillips curve in disguise if money supply is exogenous – does not apply to the case examined in the present paper since, in Italy, the interest rate has always been, more or less explicitly, the foremost instrument of monetary policy.

Concerning the arguments of the money demand function, it should be stressed that interest payments on bank deposits were never subject to regulations and that demand deposits pay an interest rate which is almost equal to the one paid on time deposits. Therefore, the monetary aggregate chosen is M2, as the distinction between M1 and M2 is blurred and relates mainly to the payment habits of different classes of individuals. Furthermore, up to 1975, both government and private long-term bonds were the only asset in the monetary and financial menu. Hence, the long-term rate of return is to be considered not only on the basis of a firm theoretical ground (Friedman, 1977) but of factual evidence as

---

[1](continued)
periods and procedures, have reported a decline in the interest elasticity. These findings, however, all refer to a country, the US, where financial innovation has been triggered mostly by market forces responding to changing conditions in money and capital markets, i.e. 'rising and increasingly volatile nominal interest rates, regulations and regulatory changes, and ambiguities in domains of surveillance by monetary and fiscal authorities' (Hester, 1981, p. 148). Hence, by its very nature, financial innovation has been spreading at an uneven pace, giving rise to a lag in recognizing it. Hester (1981, pp. 168–71) describes in detail the different factors accounting for this lag.

[2]In May 1975, a thorough reform of the Treasury Bills auction was passed, giving rise to the growth of a money market. The reserve price was set well below current market prices, thus not binding, in principle, the search for an equilibrium interest rate. Nonetheless, the central bank acted as a residual buyer at a price coherent with the design of monetary policy. Treasury Bills were, like other kinds of government debt, tax exempt.

well. After 1975, Treasury Bills became the other asset entering the economic agent's portfolio choices; this state of affairs did not substantially change during the period under study.[3]

Keeping in mind these institutional features, the following standard demand for money equation has been estimated, using ordinary least squares:

$$\ln(M/P) = a_0 + a_1 \ln y_t + a_2 \ln i_t^D + a_3 \ln i_t^L + a_4 \ln(M/P)_{t-1} + \varepsilon_t \tag{1}$$

where M represents the stock of money M2 (currency plus total demand and time deposits), P is the consumer price level, y measures real GDP,[4] i^D and i^L stand for the deposits and the government long-term nominal interest rate respectively. Table 1 shows the regressions relative to the two different periods, before and after the introduction of Treasury Bills (i^S is the nominal interest rate on the latter). Comparing the two, a marked reduction in both the short- and long-run elasticity of money demand with respect to either the bond rate i^L or the Treasury Bills rate i^S can be observed;[5] yet, the statistical significance of the coefficient on the own rate of return i^D is rather weak. In order to overcome this difficulty, Equation 1 has been estimated substituting the interest differentials for their respective levels (Table 2). Although this specification does not allow own and cross rate effects to be determined separately (Klein, 1974, pp. 934–5), it has been regarded, from a theoretical viewpoint, as the correct specification when deposits yield interest.[6]

Table 1.

	Estimated coefficients[a]					Summary statistics[b]		
Constant	y_t	i_t^D	i_t^S	i_t^L	$(M/P)_{t-1}$	$\bar{R}^2$	σ	h
Estimation period: 1970.I–1975.IV								
1. −2.931	0.588	0.189			−0.275	0.670	0.953	0.028	0.340
(3.31)	(4.46)	(1.59)			(1.97)	(7.79)			
Estimation period: 1976.I–1985.IV								
2. −0.490	0.403	0.064			−0.195	0.603	0.571	0.042	1.430
(0.26)	(3.00)	(0.42)			(1.61)	(4.75)			
3. −1.492	0.277	0.033	−0.179		0.514	0.597	0.041	0.368
(1.02)	(2.86)	(0.32)	(2.26)		(4.26)			

[a] All variables enter logarithmically. Absolute values of t-statistics are shown in parentheses.
[b] h is Durbin's h-statistics.

[3] Not before the start of the 1980s, new monetary and financial instruments, i.e. certificates of deposit, security repurchase agreements, commercial paper, and other assets became available to investors, but did not make up a conspicuous share of their portfolios.
[4] Following Cagan and Schwartz (1975), current real income is used in Equation 1. 'We use current GNP rather than, as is common, some moving average to approximate the concept of permanent income. This transformation will affect the absolute size of the interest coefficient but very likely not the comparative size between periods' (p. 141). The consumer price level was used in place of the implicit price deflator because data on the latter were not available for the entire estimation period.
[5] The inclusion of all three rates of interest – i^D, i^S, and i^L – in the second period raises a multicollinearity problem, a common one in estimating money demand equations.
[6] A formal derivation can be found in the models by Barro and Santomero (1972), and Ando and Shell (1975).

Table 2.

Estimated coefficients[a]					Summary statistics[b]		
Constant	y_t	$(i^S - i^D)_t$	$(i^L - i^D)_t$	$(M/P)_{t-1}$	$\bar{R}^2$	σ	h
Estimation period: 1970.I–1975.IV							
1. −3.109	0.588		−0.094	0.672	0.957	0.027	0.217
(3.77)	(4.74)		(2.57)	(9.38)			
Estimation period: 1976.I–1985.IV							
2. −1.768	0.451		−0.084	0.673	0.575	0.042	1.019
(1.16)	(3.66)		(3.07)	(6.23)			
3. 0.676	0.283	−0.078		0.574	0.605	0.041	−0.475
(0.49)	(2.94)	(3.60)		(5.18)			

[a] All variables enter logarithmically. Absolute values of t-statistics are shown in parentheses.
[b] h is Durbin's h-statistics.

The equations reported in Table 2 show a decrease in both the short- and long-run elasticity of the demand for money with respect to the i^S (from −0.094 to −0.078, and from −0.288 to −0.183) and the i^L differential (from −0.094 to −0.084, and from −0.288 to −0.256). This evidence notwithstanding, a standard F-test does not allow the hypothesis of inequality of the long-term interest rate coefficient in the two periods to be accepted. These results, however, falsify the hypothesis of an increase in the interest elasticity of money demand after the introduction of an asset rival to money. Furthermore, the stronger reduction of the elasticities with respect to the Treasury Bills rate should be emphasized because during the second period – following the greater uncertainty of inflationary expectations and the prevalence of negative *ex-post* real rates of return – there was a flight by investors from bonds into short-term financial assets, with a consequent sharp fall in the average maturity of public debt. Hence, the Treasury Bills rate is beyond doubt the most representative yield on assets alternative to money and is the rate whose elasticity has decreased more.

Stability

With regard to the effectiveness of monetary policy the main issue in the context of financial innovation concerns the stability of the demand for money function. A standard Chow test based on Equations 1 and 2 of each table does allow the null hypothesis of structural stability at both the 5% and the 1% confidence level to be accepted (computed F: $F_{5,54}$ = 0.375, Table 1; and $F_{4,56}$ = 0.214, Table 2).

Dwelling upon this subject (Marty, 1961, pp. 60–1), it is important to examine the diffusion process of the new asset in order to see whether it followed a smooth, regularly shaped path or not. In this respect, the most commonly adopted assumption (Hester, 1981, pp. 169–70; see also the point made by Charles Holt in the 'General Discussion', p. 199) is that the time path of the coefficient under investigation is defined by a logistic function. This hypothesis has been tested with reference to variable $(i^S - i^D)$ of Equation 3 in Table 2 but the relevant parameters are not statistically significant. Assuming, instead, that the $(i^S - i^D)$

coefficient varies linearly with time, the following regression is estimated:

$$\ln (M/P)_t = -4.501 + 0.876 \ln y_t - 0.046 \ln (i^S - i^D)_t - 0.0026t \ln (i^S - i^D)_t$$
$$(3.58) \quad (7.60) \qquad (2.89) \qquad\qquad (6.32)$$
$$+ 0.488 \ln (M/P)_{t-1} + \varepsilon_t$$
$$(6.26)$$
$$\bar{R}^2 = 0.810 \qquad \sigma = 0.028 \qquad h = -0.039$$

In Equation 2 the time gradient is significant but very small, suggesting a rather slow increase in the parameter.[7] Furthermore, the time profile of the four $(i^S - i^D)$ coefficients – obtained by using dummy variables in order to divide the 1976.I–1985.IV period into four sub-periods, each spanning ten quarters – shows negligible increases during the first five years and a more noticeable change only in the last sub-period.[8] Thus, all three different testing procedures give no indication that the diffusion process of the new asset proceeded in a jumping and unpredictable way.

III. CONCLUDING REMARKS

The empirical evidence presented in this paper contrasts with two currently held propositions concerning the influence of financial innovation on the interest elasticity and on the stability of the demand for money respectively. First, the results run counter to the conjecture regarding the increase in the interest elasticity of money demand subsequent to the introduction of a money substitute. Second, the stability hypothesis cannot be rejected and the analysis of the agents' learning process with regard to the new single financial asset, displays a regularly shaped path which should not impair the monetary authority's power of control. All in all, these findings falsify the hypotheses which provide the basis of critiques directed at policies fixing money growth targets.

ACKNOWLEDGEMENTS

Thanks are due to David Laidler and Franco Spinelli for their useful comments on a first draft of this paper. The usual caveat applies. The views expressed herein are those of the author and not necessarily those of the Banca d'Italia.

REFERENCES

Ando, A. and Shell, K. (1975) Demand for money in a general portfolio model in the presence of an asset market that dominates money, in *The Brookings Model: Perspective and Recent Developments*, Gary Fromm and Lawrence R. Klein (Eds), Amsterdam, North-Holland.
Barro, R. J. and Santomero, A. M. (1972) Household money holdings and the demand deposit rate, *Journal of Money, Credit, and Banking*, 4 (May), 397–413.

[7]A very similar result is obtained if the same hypothesis is applied to Equation 3 in Table 1.
[8]The null hypothesis of equality of the four coefficients is rejected by a standard F-test (calculated $F_{3,33} = 9.17$).

Cagan, P. D. and Schwartz, A. J. (1975) Has the growth of money substitutes hindered monetary policy?, *Journal of Money, Credit, and Banking,* **7** (May), 137–59.

Friedman, M. (1977) Time perspective in demand for money, *Scandinavian Journal of Economics,* **79** (No. 4), 397–416.

Gurley, J. G. and Shaw, E. S. (1960) *Money in a theory of finance,* Washington, DC, Brookings Institution.

Hafer, R. W. and Hein, S. E. (1984) Financial innovations and the interest elasticity of money demand: some historical evidence, *Journal of Money, Credit, and Banking,* **16** (May), 247–52.

Hester, D. D. (1981) Innovations and monetary control, *Brookings Papers on Economic Activity,* (No. 1), 141–89.

Klein, B. (1974) Competitive interest payments on bank deposits and the long-run demand for money, *American Economic Review,* **64** (December), 931–49.

Laidler, D. (1966) The rate of interest and the demand for money – some empirical evidence, *Journal of Political Economy,* **74** (December), 543–55.

Laidler, D. (1982) *Monetarist Perspectives,* Oxford, Philip Allan.

Laidler, D. (1986) What do we really know about monetary policy?, *Australian Economic Papers,* **25** (June), 1–16.

Marty, A. L. (1961) Gurley and Shaw on money in a theory of finance, *Journal of Political Economy,* **69** (February), 56–62.

Meltzer, A. H. (1963) The demand for money: the evidence from the time series, *Journal of Political Economy,* **71** (June), 219–46.

Tucker, D. P. (1966) Dynamic income adjustment to money-supply changes, *American Economic Review,* **56** (June), 433–49.

4

Applied Economics, 1991, 23, 1649–1653

Demand for money and expected inflation

FILIPPO CESARANO

Banca d'Italia, Servizio Studi, via Nazionale, 91, 00184 Roma, Italy

The role of the expected rate of inflation in the demand for money has been highly controversial both at the theoretical and the empirical level. This note critically discusses these issues and puts forward a hypothesis accounting for the significance of expected inflation in money demand equations which is corroborated by an empirical investigation of the Italian experience, particularly suited for this specific experiment.

I. INTRODUCTION

The demand for money has represented, up to the early 1970s, one of the least controversial topics in the field of monetary economics. This is not to say that different approaches to the subject were lacking. At the empirical level, however, the majority of studies eventually came up adopting a single specification of the function which has been appropriately described as 'standard' or 'conventional'. In the mid 1970s, this quiet state of affairs was upset by the emergence of several issues. The so-called 'case of the missing money' (Goldfeld, 1976) provided a first motive of concern. Subsequently, David Laidler (1982) and Robert Gordon (1984)[1] raised an important objection arguing convincingly that, in the presence of sluggish adjustment of real balances, the short-run demand for money may partly represent a Phillips curve in disguise. Besides, the phenomenon of inertia in price changes, if money supply is exogenous, also casts a shadow on the possibility of correctly identifying a short-run structural demand for money function (Cooley and LeRoy, 1981).

Parallel to these points, other questions have been posed amid the discussion on money demand. The one examined in the following pages concerns the role of expected inflation in the specification. The latter has been strongly debated both at the theoretical and the empirical level. On the one hand, formal models have derived money demand equations which, in contrast with commonly accepted theory, do not include expected inflation among the arguments. On the other hand, empirical evidence supporting the significance of expected inflation has also been mixed in that, up to the early

1970s, it was mainly limited to instances of hyperinflations (Laidler, 1977, pp. 135–7), while afterwards such evidence has been reported for different countries, even in the presence of nominal interest rates. This finding, however, has not been satisfactorily accounted for and has rather been considered as a clue to misspecification of money demand equations based on the real adjustment mechanism.[2] As pointed out by Goldfeld and Sichel (1987), 'theory does not readily provide an explanation other than the adjustment mechanism for an inflation effect independent of the Fisher effect.' (p. 513).

The present paper critically addresses the above questions, albeit in an informal way. Following a discussion of the different foundations underlying the influence of expected inflation on the demand for money, a hypothesis accounting for such influence is put forward (Section II) and is then tested on Italian data, particularly suited for this purpose (Section III).

II. THEORETICAL ISSUES

It is a commonplace of monetary theory that 'the quantity of money demanded clearly depends on the costs and returns from holding money' (Friedman, 1977, p. 397). Thus, the standard specification of the short-run demand for money contains the relevant rates of return along with a scale variable and the lagged dependent variable. The approach followed by Friedman in his *Restatement* (1956) regards money as a way of holding wealth and the demand for money as a demand for the services yielded by this asset.

---

[1]See also Judd and Scadding (1982, pp. 1012–4).
[2]Goldfeld (1973, p. 611) first argued that the real adjustment mechanism may well yield a significant expected inflation coefficient, but this can in fact be redundant and not significant if the nominal adjustment mechanism is upheld. This proposition has been central in the research strategy followed by several scholars, e.g. Milbourne (1983), Spencer (1985), Huang (1985), Hafer and Thornton (1986).

0003–6846/91 $03.00+.12 © *1991 Chapman & Hall*

Since physical goods are an alternative form in which wealth can be held, the expected rate of change of the price level must be included among the arguments of the money demand function. This proposition – providing the basis of most of the works on this topic – has, however, remained controversial not only for the lack of conclusive empirical evidence but also for the appearance of opposite theoretical results.

A notable example is given by Ando and Shell (1975) who develop a model of portfolio choice which includes money, savings deposits, and equity. The rate of return on equities and the rate of inflation are random variables whereas the nominal interest rate on money and on savings deposits is known with certainty. Following an expected utility approach, money holdings then depend on the rate differential between savings deposits and money but not on expected inflation, wealth or the expected return on equities (1975, p. 562).[3] Yet, these results are derived from a crucial assumption, i.e. consumption in period one is determined independently of portfolio choice (1975, p. 561), which sharply contrasts with some well-grounded interpretations of a monetary economy. Dwelling upon the fact that, by holding one more dollar of cash balances, the individual is forsaking not only the yield on bonds, equities, and other assets, but also one more dollar of consumption, Friedman (1969) has clearly illustrated the existence of a negative relationship between the expected rate of inflation and the amount of desired real money balances. This relationship, it should be stressed, rests on principles quite distinct from that described in the previous paragraph focusing on the return on physical goods.[4] Thus, Friedman's 1956 and 1969 essays provide two different foundations accounting for expected inflation in the demand for money which, on interpretative grounds relate to two functions of money – store of value and

medium of exchange – and are in turn emphasized in each approach.[5]

Although the foregoing discussion contains nothing original, it nevertheless helps to make two important points. (1) Almost all works on money demand exclusively refer to the first rationale of the expected rate of inflation as an argument of the function, namely the rate of return on physical goods, neglecting the other. (2). The second rationale, stemming from 'the elementary but central principles of monetary theory' (Friedman, 1969, p. 2), unveils the limitations of those models, e.g. Ando and Shell (1975), which wave aside expected inflation from the demand for money. While stemming from two separate conceptions, the two rationales do not conflict in any way and rather reinforce one another leading, in fact, to the same result. The Keynesian perspective, approaching money as a component of wealth, stresses the first foundation; the classical view, instead, giving prominence to the role of money in facilitating transactions, emphasizes the second one underlying the notion of 'a *general* medium of exchange' (Wicksell, 1906, p. 17, italics in the original).[6] All in all, the expected rate of inflation can be viewed as the yield on physical goods and, thus, enters the money demand function as the return on an asset alternative to money (Friedman, 1956); conversely, it can be considered as (the negative of) the own return on cash balances, since it measures the depreciation cost which the individual can avoid by increasing consumption at the same rate (Friedman, 1969).[7]

Given the substantial arguments in support of expected inflation in the demand for money, Harry Johnson (1972, p. 127) has rightly considered the lack of empirical evidence in the US as a puzzle. In order to explain it, he has called attention to the mildness of the inflation phenomenon in US giving rise to threshold effects, and to Maurice Allais

---

[3]An immediate difficulty with this conclusion is that it seems to contradict one of the basic assumptions of the model which focuses on expected real rates, thus stressing the role of expected inflation: 'returns on money and savings deposits are subject to . . . uncertainty due to changes in the general price level'. (Ando and Shell, 1975, p. 561).

[4]Indeed, in Friedman's (1969) model (pp. 2–3), capital goods are in abeyance since they cannot be bought and sold and only services are exchanged for money.

[5]It is immediate to bring back the sharp dissimilarity between the intellectual climate surrounding Friedman's works. As regards the first one, the Keynesian influence on it has been pointed out by Patinkin (1969, p. 47) and Johnson (1971, p. 61) who, however, calls attention to the role of expected inflation: '. . . the restatement of the quantity theory of money did include one important and genuinely novel element, drawn not from Keynes but from his predecessors in monetary theory, which was highly relevant to the problem of inflation and which continues to distinguish quantity theorists from Keynesians; this consisted in its emphasis on the Fisherian distinction between the real and the money rate of interest and on the expected rate of price inflation or deflation as determining the difference between the two.' (Johnson, 1971, pp. 61–2).

[6]The primacy of the medium of exchange function has been consistently held by classic authors including Wicksell (1906, chapter 1), who, despite his 'Keynesian' view of monetary policy, does not consider the store of value function as a distinctive character. 'The conception of money is involved in its functions and it is usual to distinguish three such functions: as a *measure of value*, as a *store of value*, and as a *medium of exchange*. . . . Of the three main functions, only the last is in a true sense characteristic of money; as a measure of value any commodity whatever might serve. . . . Similarly, the function of acting as a *store of value* is not essentially characteristic of money. . . . It is never this utility [of precious metals] which is contemplated by those who hoard money (and seldom by those who hoard ornaments) but the object in view is nearly always that of procuring *something else* for it at a future time. In other words, it is the exchange value which it is desired to preserve; it is money as a future medium of exchange which is hoarded.' (Wicksell 1906, pp. 6- 8, italics in the original).

[7]Dutkowsky and Foote (1988), dwelling on Friedman's (1969) ideas, build a dynamic expected utility model of consumption and money demand behaviour. Although expected inflation is not explicitly considered, their empirical results support the complementarity of money and consumption through an analysis of imputed utility values. McCallum and Goodfriend (1987) thoroughly discuss the subject from a theoretical standpoint.

hypothesis according to which 'people pay more attention to current events relative to past events, the more rapidly the situation is changing' (Johnson, 1972, p. 127). Studies covering subsequent periods show instead a significant expected inflation coefficient, but they have equally prompted puzzling reactions because of the presence of nominal interest rates which should already reflect expected inflation. Apart from suggestions concerning the nature of the adjustment mechanism (see footnote 2), this finding has not yet been clarified.

An analysis of the models illustrated above, however, can throw light on the issue at stake in that it can help to find out the conditions under which expected inflation has no influence on money demand. In particular, Ando and Shell (1975) results hinge on a key assumption, i.e. the independence of consumption decisions from portfolio choice, which does away with Friedman's (1969) second foundation. This may be squared with a state of affairs in which financial markets are efficient and a competitive rate of interest is paid on all assets, particularly on demand deposits. In such a world, if the use of currency is trifling, money yields a nominal return which, like the rates of return on other assets, fully reflects expected inflation. Therefore, an individual holding money balances would not pay the annual cost imposed by the rate of inflation, as defined by Friedman (1969, pp. 14–15). In as much as, in this scenario, a critical factor is the efficiency of financial markets, a hypothesis can be advanced by conjecturing an inverse relationship between financial market efficiency and the role of expected inflation in money demand. If there are impediments to the operation of asset markets, e.g. following the enforcement of regulations meddling with equilibrium interest rates, holders of money do incur a cost and the expected rate of change in prices becomes a key explanatory variable of the demand for money. This very argument equally applies to Friedman's (1956) first foundation, because individuals would more promptly shift into physical goods the less effectively expected inflation is reckoned with nominal interest rates. Hence, the hypothesis bears on both rationales of the influence of expected inflation on the demand for money.

III. EMPIRICAL RESULTS

An empirical investigation concerning the propositions put forward in Section II is carried out by focusing on a country, Italy, where far-reaching administrative controls affecting interest rates have been in force since the early 1970s, thus providing the ideal conditions to test the hypothesis under examination. In 1973, in order to squeeze interest rates, compulsory bond purchases were imposed on commercial banks, the latter being required to invest in bonds a given percentage of the increase in total deposits. This measure was followed, in the same year, by another regulation fixing a ceiling on bank loans. As a result, nominal bond returns fell sharply below observed inflation, at some time by more than 12 percentage points as in 1974:4. Albeit these controls were in force almost uninterruptedly (only the second one was suspended for about a year and a half in 1975–6), the design of interest rate policy changed considerably at the beginning of the 1980s, allowing nominal returns to get closer to and eventually catch up expected inflation. In 1981, bond rates jumped by more than five percentage points and, after several years, became greater than current inflation.

A further, quite important, feature characterizing the Italian economy concerns the conduct of monetary policy which has been, explicitly or implicitly, centered on the interest rate instrument. Therefore, the criticism raised by David Laidler and other scholars (see p. 1 above) against the conventional specification of the short-run demand for money function does not apply to the case under examination.

Substituting the standard specification for the 'desired' stock of real money balances m^* given by

$$\ln m_t^* = \theta_0 + \theta_1 \ln y_t + \theta_2 \ln i_t + \theta_3 \ln \pi_t, \qquad (1)$$

where y is real income, i is the relevant nominal interest rate, and π is the expected rate of inflation, into the real partial adjustment mechanism

$$\ln m_t - \ln m_{t-1} = \lambda(\ln m_t^* - \ln m_{t-1}) \qquad (2)$$

where m is the actual stock of money balances – yields the following conventional equation

$$\ln m_t = \theta_0 \lambda + \theta_1 \lambda \ln y_t + \theta_2 \lambda \ln i_t + \theta_3 \lambda \ln \pi_t + (1-\lambda) \ln m_{t-1} \qquad (3)$$

The first part of Table 1 contains estimates[8] of Equation 3, using ordinary least squares, over the sample period 1973:1–1980:4 characterized by thorough government regulation of financial markets. Regressions 1 and 2 show very poor t-ratios on both i^S and i^L coefficients, with or without the presence of π. Regression 3, instead, obtained by dropping the interest rates variables, gives rather robust results corroborating the hypothesis, put forward in Section II, on the significance of expected inflation with regard to a state of affairs dominated by administrative controls.

Bearing in mind the criticism raised by Goldfeld and other authors (see footnote 2) – according to which, in case the nominal partial adjustment mechanism yields a non-significant π coefficient, Equation 3 is misspecified and the effect of

---

[8]The consumer price level is used in place of the implicit price deflator because data on the latter were not available for the entire estimation period. Furthermore, following Cagan and Schwartz (1975, p. 141), current real income is used rather than an approximation of permanent income. Finally, π has been constructed by Visco (1984) on the basis of a survey regularly conducted among business men since 1956.

Table 1. *Conventional money demand models*[a]

Real partial adjustment

	Intercept	y_t	i_t^S	i_t^L	π_t	m_{t-1}	$\bar{R}^2$	σ	h
1.	−3.035	0.638	−0.004	−0.024	−0.094	0.618	0.915	0.026	1.452
	(3.56)	(6.29)	(0.45)	(0.61)	(4.53)	(8.20)			
2.	−1.601	0.439	−0.010	0.006		0.655	0.854	0.034	2.172
	(1.54)	(3.66)	(0.87)	(0.12)		(6.66)			
3.	−2.354	0.591			−0.093	0.581	0.914	0.026	1.503
	(3.75)	(6.77)			(4.52)	(8.11)			

Nominal partial adjustment

	Intercept	y_t	i_t^S	i_t^L	π_t	M_{t-1}/P_t	$\bar{R}^2$	σ	h
1.'	−2.687	0.515	0.001	−0.035	−0.058	0.724	0.933	0.023	0.663
	(3.58)	(5.40)	(0.16)	(1.00)	(3.02)	(9.60)			
2'.	−1.915	0.370	−0.002	−0.023		0.791	0.913	0.026	0.873
	(2.38)	(3.93)	(0.21)	(0.57)		(9.63)			
3'.	−2.021	0.462			−0.057	0.694	0.934	0.023	0.635
	(3.65)	(5.45)			(3.00)	(9.62)			

[a]All variables enter logarithmically. Absolute values of t-statistics are shown in parentheses. h is Durbin's h-statistics. Variables are defined as follows:
m = nominal stock of $M2$ (currency plus total demand and time deposits) dated by the consumer price level P; y = real GNP; i^S = nominal rate of interest on Treasury Bills; i^L = nominal rate of interest on long-term government bonds; π = expected rate of change of the consumer price level (Visco, 1984).

π is only spurious[9] – part 2 of Table 1 illustrates the same regressions when the nominal adjustment is adopted.[10] As it appears, the significance of the expected rate of inflation is unambiguously maintained, the estimates of θ_3 in Equations 3 and 3' being respectively equal to −0.19 and −0.22. This conclusion is important because it shows that the hypothesis is corroborated independently of the type of adjustment mechanism, real or nominal, and, more specifically, because the result obtains in the latter adjustment model. These findings, albeit not solving the identification problem since the two kinds of adjustment represent only two points on a spectrum of possible partial adjustment mechanisms, provide a first attempt to fill the theoretical vacuum pointed up in Goldfeld and Sichel's (1987) quote (see p. 1). Equations 3 and 3' have also been estimated over the subsequent period 1981:1–1988:4 – characterized by the abandonment of regulations and high real interest rates – and both yield a non-significant π coefficient, thus further substantiating the conjecture linking expected inflation to inefficient capital

markets. Standard Chow tests do not allow acceptance of the null hypothesis of no structural change.[11]
Finally, given the restrictive nature of the partial adjustment mechanism, a more general model including four lagged values for each variable in Equation 3 has been estimated. However, the null hypothesis that the coefficients of the lagged variables are all equal to zero could not be rejected,[12] leading then to consider the results of Table 1 exclusively.

IV. CONCLUDING REMARKS

As noted by Goldfeld and Sichel (1987) in the closing sentence of their article, 'the precise source of the inflation effect [on the desired stock of real balances] remains an open question' (p. 515). This paper has attempted to offer a suggestion explaining such an elusive issue. Dwelling upon a critical analysis of theoretical models on the subject, a

[9]Goldfeld and Sichel (1987) have put this issue in a more general perspective arguing that, due to an identification problem, it is impossible to perform hypothesis tests on both the π coefficient and the real vs. nominal adjustment models.
[10]Substituting Equation 1 into the nominal partial adjustment mechanism given by
$$\ln M_t - \ln M_{t-1} = \lambda(\ln M_t^* - \ln M_{t-1}) \qquad (4)$$
yields the following equation
$$\ln m_t = \theta_0\lambda + \theta_1\lambda\ln y_t + \theta_2\lambda\ln i_t + \theta_3\lambda\ln\pi_t + (1-\lambda)\ln(M_{t-1}/P_t) \qquad (5)$$
[11]The computed F values are 32.60 and 10.45 for Equations 3 and 3' respectively, whereas the common critical value is equal to 2.54 (0.05 significance level).
[12]The computed F value is 1.99 and the critical value is 2.41 (0.05 significance level).

Demand for money and expected inflation 1653

hypothesis has been advanced focusing on the efficiency of financial markets. Examining the recent Italian experience, particularly suited for this specific experiment, the hypothesis has been corroborated independently of the type of adjustment mechanism, real or nominal. These empirical results notwithstanding, it is still necessary to develop rigorous models leading to a deeper treatment of the topic.

ACKNOWLEDGEMENTS

Thanks are due to Benjamin Friedman, Milton Friedman, Stephen Goldfeld, and David Laidler for their useful comments on a first draft of this paper. The usual caveat applies. The views expressed herein are those of the author and not necessarily those of the Banca d'Italia.

REFERENCES

Ando, A. and Shell, K. (1975) Demand for money in a general portfolio model in the presence of an asset market that dominates money, in *The Brookings Model: Perspective and Recent Developments*, Fromm, G. and Klein, L. R. (eds), North-Holland, Amsterdam.

Barro, R. J. and Santomero, A. M. (1972) Household money holdings and the demand deposit rate, *Journal of Money, Credit, and Banking*, 4, 379–413.

Cagan, P. and Schwartz, A. J. (1975) Has the growth of money substitutes hindered monetary policy?, *Journal of Money, Credit, and Banking*, 7, 137–59.

Cooley, T. F. and Le Roy, S. F. (1981) Identification and estimation of money demand, *American Economic Review*, 71, 825–44.

Dutkowsky, D. H. and Foote, W. G. (1988) The demand for money: a rational expectations approach, *Review of Economics and Statistics*, 70, 83–92.

Fama, E. F. (1970) Efficient capital markets: a review of theory and empirical work, *Journal of Finance*, 25, 383–417.

Feige, E. L. and Pearce, D. K. (1977) The substitutability of money and near monies: a survey of the time-series evidence, *Journal of Economic Literature*, 15, 439–69.

Friedman, M. (1956) The quantity theory of money: a restatement, in *Studies in the Quantity Theory of Money*, Friedman, M. (ed.), University of Chicago Press, Chicago.

Friedman, M. (1969) The optimum quantity of money, in *The Optimum Quantity of Money and Other Essays*, Friedman, M. (ed.), Aldine, Chicago.

Friedman, M. (1977) Time perspective in the demand for money, *Scandinavian Journal of Economics*, 79, 397–416.

Goldfeld, S. M. (1973) The demand for money revisited, *Brookings Papers on Economic Activity*, 4, 577–638.

Goldfeld, S. M. (1976) The case of the missing money, *Brookings Papers on Economic Activity*, 7, 683–730.

Goldfeld, S. M. and Sichel, D. E. (1987) Money demand: the effects of inflation and alternative adjustment mechanism, *Review of Economics and Statistics*, 69, 511–15.

Gordon, R. J. (1984) The short-run demand for money: a reconsideration, *Journal of Money, Credit, and Banking*, 16, 403–34.

Hafer, R. W. and Thornton, D. L. (1986) Price expectations and the demand for money: a comment, *Review of Economics and Statistics*, 68, 539–542.

Hicks, J. R., *Critical Essays in Monetary Theory*, Oxford University Press, Oxford.

Huang, Hae-shin (1985) Test of the adjustment process and linear homogeneity in a stock adjustment model of money demand, *Review of Economics and Statistics*, 67, 689–92.

Johnson, H. G. (1971) The Keynesian revolution and the monetarist counter-revolution, *American Economic Review*, 61, 1–14, repr. 1973 in *Further Essays in Monetary Economics*, Harvard University Press, Cambridge, MA.

Johnson, H. G. (1972) *Macroeconomics and Monetary Theory*, Aldine, Chicago.

Judd, J. P. and Scadding, J. L. (1982) The search for a stable money demand function. *Journal of Economic Literature*, 20, 993–1023.

Laidler, D. E. W. (1977) *The Demand for Money: Theories and Evidence*, 2nd edn, Dun-Donnelley, New York.

Laidler, D. E. (1982) *Monetarist Perspectives*. Allan, Oxford.

Laidler, D. E. and Parkin, M. J. (1975) Inflation – a survey, *Economic Journal*, 85, 741–809.

McCallum, B. T. and Goodfriend, M. S. (1987) Demand for money: theoretical studies, in *The New Palgrave. A Dictionary of Economics*, Eatwell, J., Milgate, M. and Newman, P. (eds), Macmillan, London.

Milbourne, R. (1983) Price expectations and the demand for money: resolution of a paradox, *Review of Economics and Statistics*, 65, 633–8.

Patinkin, D. (1969) The Chicago tradition, the quantity theory, and Friedman, *Journal of Money, Credit, and Banking*, 1, 46–70.

Spencer, D. E. (1985) Money demand and the price level, *Review of Economics and Statistics*, 67, 490–6.

Tobin, J. (1969) A general equilibrium approach to monetary theory. *Journal of Money, Credit, and Banking*, 1, 15–29.

Visco, I. (1984) *Price Expectations in Rising Inflation*, North-Holland, Amsterdam.

Wicksell, K. (1935) *Lectures on Political Economy*, Vol. 2, Routledge, London; first Swedish edition, 1906.

PART II

THE NEW MONETARY ECONOMICS

5

Journal of Economic Behavior and Organization
Vol. 26 (1995) 445–455

ELSEVIER

JOURNAL OF
Economic Behavior
& Organization

The New Monetary Economics and the Theory of Money [1]

Filippo Cesarano

Banca d'Italia – Servizio Studi, Via Nazionale, 91, 00184 Roma, Italy

Received June 1992, final version received September 1992

Abstract

A critical analysis of the main tenets of the New Monetary Economics (NME) is carried out from the viewpoint of received monetary theory. It is shown that the essential properties of a monetary economy are independent of the tangible character of the means of payment and, in particular, that these properties establish a relationship between the medium of exchange and the unit of account (section 2). Dwelling upon these results, the NME proposition, according to which money is a product of regulation, is found to be untenable (section 3).

JEL classification: E42

1. Introduction

The recent outgrowth of literature on competitive payments systems may seem concerned with rather esoteric matters of but little interest to the profession. When closely examined, however, the discussion appears to touch upon questions which are momentous for both the theory of money and the development of monetary arrangements. Indeed, the scope of the contributions is thought to have originated

---

[1] Thanks are due to Robert W. Clower, Milton Friedman, and Lawrence H. White for helpful comments on a first draft. The usual caveat applies. The views expressed herein are those of the author and not necessarily those of the Banca d'Italia.

446   *F. Cesarano / J. of Economic Behavior & Org. 26 (1995) 445–455*

a "new school of monetary economics" (Hall, 1982b, p. 1555) [2]. The ground-work of the new school's propositions is the institution-laden character of monetary economics. The eventual emergence of alternative institutional frameworks, forsaking a tangible means of payment, would have such far-reaching implications as to "make current monetary theory almost completely invalid...in such a world...neither the quantity theory of money nor the liquidity preference theory of money would be applicable" (Black, 1970, p. 9). A further and basic element of the new school's teachings concerns the role of the government in today's monetary arrangements. The presence of a public authority is not merely opposed following an extreme *laissez-faire* approach, but is deemed conspicuous to the point of determining the very phenomenon of money: "the money stock itself is a creature of inefficient regulation" (Hall, 1982b, p. 1555).

In the present paper, the main tenets of the New Monetary Economics (henceforth NME) are critically appraised. In particular, the separation of the unit of account from own-unit of payment media and the consequences of this separation for the different payments systems are both questioned. The relationship between the unit of account and the medium of exchange is analyzed to show that it is well grounded on the foundations of both classical and contemporary monetary theory and, above all, is independent of the tangible character of the means of payment (section 2). Dwelling upon these theoretical findings, the fundamental NME proposition, according to which money is a product of regulation, is found to be untenable (section 3).

2. The New Monetary Economics and the foundations of money

The basic feature of the NME consists in the absence of a tangible means of payment and the consequent separation of the medium of exchange from the unit of account. As Fama puts it:

"... one of our main points is that currency and an accounting system are entirely different methods for exchanging wealth. Currency is a physical medium which can be characterized as money. An accounting system works through bookkeeping entries, debits and credits, which do not require any physical medium or the concept of money" (1980, p. 39).

---

[2] The main references include Black (1970), Fama (1980), Bilson (1981), Hall (1982a,1982b), Greenfield and Yeager (1983), Yeager (1985). Critical reviews are due to White (1984,1987), McCallum (1985) and Hoover (1988); see also the short but pregnant remarks by Brunner and Meltzer (1985, pp. 1–6) and Barro (1985). Cowen and Kroszner (1987) deal with the subject from a history of economics viewpoint while, in a 1989 symposium, Mott, Yeager and White discuss these issues from a Post Keynesian perspective.

F. Cesarano / J. of Economic Behavior & Org. 26 (1995) 445–455   447

Both classical and contemporary economists, however, have pointed out the implausibility of divorcing the unit of account from the medium of exchange. Such an intimate connection is not related in any essential way to the physical character of money but to the distinguishing properties of a monetary economy as contrasted with a Walrasian economy, these properties being in fact independent of eventual progress in transactions technology. These principles characterize the development of monetary theory throughout and have been held even after a major institutional change, i.e. the evolution from a commodity to a fiat money system (Friedman, 1986), much more substantial than the transition from fiat to non-tangible money.

Before the end of the eighteenth century, the theory of money had already reached a fairly advanced status relative to other fields of economics. Although the literature on the subject is extensive, it has been dominated by a single approach – attributed to Aristotle and suitably called by Schumpeter the Metallist Theory of Money – founded on two basic principles: 1. the primacy of the medium of exchange function, and 2. the necessary assignment of the latter to a commodity. A natural implication of this theory is the use of the medium of exchange as the measure of value (Schumpeter, 1954, pp. 62–63). The overwhelming influence of this view [3] is apparent in Adam Smith's classic analysis of the inconveniences of barter (1776, chapter IV) which develops the notion of money as a 'common' or 'universal instrument of commerce'. In the fifth chapter of the *Wealth of Nations*, a penetrating passage explains the assignment of the unit of account function to the same commodity that emerges as the means of payment.

"But when barter ceases, and money has become the common instrument of commerce, every particular commodity is more frequently exchanged for money than for any other commodity. The butcher seldom carries his beef or his mutton to the baker, or the brewer, in order to exchange them for bread or for beer; but he carries them to the market, where he exchanges them for money, and afterwards exchanges that money for bread and for beer. The quantity of money which he gets for them regulates too the quantity of bread and beer which he can afterwards purchase. It is more natural and obvious to him, therefore, to estimate their value by the quantity of money, the commodity for which he immediately exchanges them, than by that of bread and beer, the commodities for which he can exchange them only by the intervention of another commodity; and rather to say that his butcher's meat is worth three or four pounds of bread, or three or four quarts of small beer. Hence it comes to pass, that the exchangeable value of every commodity is more frequently estimated by the quantity of money, than by the quantity

---

[3] "Whatever its shortcomings, this theory, though never unchallenged, prevailed substantially to the end of the nineteenth century and even beyond. It is the basis of the bulk of all analytic work in the field of money" (Schumpeter, 1954, p. 63).

448   *F. Cesarano / J. of Economic Behavior & Org. 26 (1995) 445–455*

either of labour or of any other commodity which can be had in exchange for it'' (1776, p. 36) [4].

An analysis as perspicuous as Smith's is not easy to find in previous and subsequent periods, albeit for opposite reasons. Earlier writers – like Law, Cantillon, and Hume – though they discussed the functions of money separately, did not examine the relationships between them. In the nineteenth century, the principles linking the medium of exchange and the unit of account are taken for granted and often are just mentioned in passing. Representative examples are McCulloch (1825, pp. 77–78), J.S. Mill (1848, pp. 483–488, 564), Menger (1871, ch. VIII), Jevons (1875, pp. 13–14), and Wicksell (1906, pp. 6–8).

The momentous changes affecting monetary arrangements after 1914 led to "the emergence of a world monetary system that ... is unprecedented: a system in which essentially every currency in the world is, directly or indirectly, on a pure fiat standard'' (Friedman and Schwartz, 1986, p. 38). These events brought about an equally unprecedented evolution in the theory of money as theoretical metallism began to fade away [5]. However, the basic proposition concerning the primacy of the medium of exchange function – and its corollary establishing the necessary identity of the means of payments and the unit of account – did not collapse with the abandonment of the Metallist Theory of Money. Indeed, this proposition was reinforced by recognizing that, from an analytical standpoint, it is not a requisite for money to consist in a commodity. This appears from contemporary contributions prompted by the challenging problem of money in a Walrasian economy. An explicit analysis of the unit of account is absent in this literature because the latter envisages a general equilibrium setting where an arbitrary numeraire is assumed. Nevertheless, some authors do grapple with the issue. In

---

[4] It should be stressed that, in the *Wealth of Nations*, Smith reversed his previous opinion on the primacy of the medium of exchange function. As Cannan recalls in his introduction, in the *Lectures on Justice, Police, Revenue and Arms* – reported by a student in 1763 – Smith considers money "first as the measure of value and then as the medium of permutation or exchange'' (1776, p. 32, footnote 3), this view being borrowed by Hutcheson's *System of Moral Philosophy* (1776, pp. XVII–XVIII; XLII–XLIII).

[5] The latter development, it should be noticed, followed rather than anticipated the institutional reforms, as the majority of economists firmly abided by metallism. The article "Money", written by Hawtrey for the Encyclopaedia Britannica, conveys the intellectual climate of that period. "A metallic standard is the universally accepted monetary policy. Departures from it occur only at times of emergency and transition. Nevertheless such departures do occur, and some times years, and even generations pass before the theoretically normal standard is restored. ... Apart from schemes of the type favoured by Mr. Keynes, paper money dissociated from gold is a monetary disease. The abuse of paper money became so prevalent during and after the World War, that it has been given an almost disproportionately important place in latter-day monetary theory'' (Hawtrey, 1929, pp. 692–698).

F. Cesarano / J. of Economic Behavior & Org. 26 (1995) 445–455   449

particular, Niehans (1978, chapter 7) formally demonstrates the ancillary character of the unit of account with respect to the medium of exchange by dwelling upon the notion of 'accounting costs' [6]. Likewise, Ostroy (1973) views money as an abstract 'record-keeping device' which saves time in the attainment of equilibrium since it preserves the enforcement of budget constraints without imposing *quid pro quo* at each exchange. The introduction of a monetary authority – that receives 'checks' by all individuals providing information about their trading history – leads to a competitive equilibrium allocation. In order to measure quantities traded at the competitive price vector, a convention must require the use of a common unit of account but the latter does not define the specific role of money. "While this convention is essential to the operation of the record-keeping system, it is not identical to it. Money is not simply a unit of account" (Ostroy, 1973, p. 608).

Modern literature has not provided a settled treatment of money, the main difficulty, in this respect, being the identification of *sufficient* conditions for monetary exchange to emerge in an Arrow–Debreu economy (Clower, 1977, p. 211). However, it has arrived at a much deeper understanding of the distinctive character of money. The different ways of tackling the subject all point to the informational role of money in solving the problem of enforcing budget constraints (Ostroy and Starr, 1990). Despite the variety of approaches, these contributions regard the physical or tangible configuration as incidental and link the essential property of money to other specific factors: the role of transactions costs (Hahn, 1971; Niehans, 1971; Clower and Howitt, 1978), the transmission of information about market prices and the qualities of goods and services (Brunner and Meltzer, 1971; Alchian, 1977; King and Plosser, 1986), the provision of a record-keeping device to avoid inconsistent claims on resources (Ostroy, 1973). In particular, Ostroy and Starr (1974) investigate the logistics of exchange and identify the function of a common medium of exchange with allowing decentralization of the trading process. In order to perform such a function, tangibility is

---

[6] "It should be noted that the advantages of a common medium of account can only be realized if the medium of account is also elevated to the role of the common medium of exchange. Clearly, as long as all $\frac{1}{2} q(q-1)$ potential trading posts are active, it does not help to provide each individual with a price list giving all prices just in terms of apples; he would still have to take the time and trouble to compute the prices at all other trading posts from this basic set. The saving of accounting costs only materializes if the other markets are closed down" (1978, p. 121). James Tobin makes the same point and adds the following remark: "... the use of a common numeraire or unit of account does not logically compel the use of a common money in transactions. Commodity-for-commodity barters could be and are made with values equated by reference to numeraire or unit-of-account prices. But it is hard to imagine, and I suspect even harder to illustrate historically, a unit of account disembodied from a generally accepted means of payment" (1980, p. 87).

450   *F. Cesarano / J. of Economic Behavior & Org. 26 (1995) 445–455*

not required [7]. Other works by Hahn, Starrett, Kurz, Ulph and Ulph, in which alternative organizational structures are postulated, similarly approach money as "a kind of transfer credit system" (Ulph and Ulph, 1975, p. 370), the physical character of the money 'object' being irrelevant.

Therefore, the transition from a theory which requires money to be a commodity to another one which does not, leaves the main proposition linking the unit of account to the means of payment unaffected. From a theoretical point of view, such a transition has far more momentum than the one considered by NME theorists – i.e. passing from physical fiat money to an accounting system of exchange – as the latter development involves nothing but the mere shape of an irredeemable payment instrument. Thus, the innovation doing away with tangible exchange media could hardly falsify the proposition in question. All in all, money can well be immaterial but this does not mean that its 'services' disappear. As far as monetary theory is concerned, the important point is not so much the tangibility of the means of payments as the medium of exchange *function* which, in a real world monetary system without central coordination of trade, allows us to depart from barter exchange.

3. The New Monetary Economics and regulation

Although the teachings of the NME differ among its exponents, a common starting-point can be identified with the critique of the role of government in a monetary system based on a tangible asset, so that in "the new school's view ... money is exactly a creation of regulation" (Hall, 1982b, p. 1554) [8]. Following the

---

[7] "The sole purpose of trade in commodity *m* (the money commodity) is to establish a counting device to insure that the sum of additions to and subtractions from the value of one's holdings during the course of trade is zero. That the device is embodied in a tangible commodity is clearly inessential" (Ostroy and Starr, 1974, p. 1111). In their recent survey, Ostroy and Starr state: "The problem is how to enforce the overall budget constraint underlying market-clearing excess demands while also permitting individuals temporarily to violate those constraints in the course of fulfilling those excess demands. Again, what is called for is a record-keeping device. ... Of course a commodity record-keeping device is a relatively crude instrument. The same function could be abstracted by a system of electronic funds transfers provided that accounts were monitored by an agency with sufficient police powers to punish 'overissuers'." (1990, p. 11).

[8] "The new monetary economics views the quantity theory as nothing more than an artifact of government regulation. An economy organized along free-market principles could function without money at all. ... the government's monetary liability – call it a reserve – has some economic value, either because it is intrinsically useful or because the government creates an artificial demand for it through regulation. Through manipulation of the quantity of reserves or changes in regulations, the government controls the relative price of reserves and goods and services in general. Because prices are quoted in terms of reserves, the government thereby controls the price level" (Hall, 1982b, pp. 1552–1553).

arguments put forward in section 2, this proposition does not seem valid since the basic features of a monetary economy have little to do with either the physical character of the means of payment or the nature of the issuer. In fact, both rationales of the usefulness of money set forth by Hall – i.e. the intrinsic value of a money commodity and the artificial demand for money created by the government – are analytically irrelevant inasmuch as the foundations of monetary theory respectively prescind from the outward form of money and the presence of government. The relevant contrast is between Walrasian and decentralized exchange economies, not between tangible money and intangible accounting systems.

The immediate implication of the correct taxonomy is that monetary institutions, needed to ensure operationality, do not belong to the realm of general equilibrium theory. Specifically, the latter does not set out to analyze the implementation of trades and the related problems raised by informational decentralization. Indeed, these issues are not even contemplated by equilibrium theory. From a historical viewpoint, government involvement in monetary affairs (White, 1984, section II; Friedman and Schwartz, 1986, p. 43) has been prompted by the need to standardize the coinage and certify its quality, i.e. information producing activities germane to a commodity standard. Monetary arrangements, then, do not primarily impinge upon relative prices or resource allocation. These arrangements, which may aptly be called *rules of the game*, vary with the kind of monetary system but their nature is quite distinct from that of *regulations*. While the former concern the specific requirements stipulated for granting viability of a monetary standard, the latter concern intervention on the part of the government in resource allocation. Price ceilings, licensing, and price support programs are typical examples of regulations; fixing the gold content of the monetary unit in the gold standard and setting a limit to the quantity of fiat money in order to maintain its value are examples of rules. Thus, the mere fact that the paper money circulating today in all countries is issued by the government bears no relation whatsoever to regulation. Hall's statement (see footnote 8) about the 'artificial demand' for money created by the government through regulation is not easy to follow. Menger's (1892) classic hypothesis about the origin of money is based on an 'invisible hand', involving no collective decision, driven by self-interested individuals striving to overcome the inconveniences of barter. There too, it is difficult to see any artificiality or any instance of regulation, in the phenomenon of money; money is an artifact of efficient decentralized market behavior.

Of course, the question concerning the role to be assigned to the government and to private agents respectively arises with regard to rules as well (King, 1983). In this connection, the relevant issue is to explain both the emergence and the necessity of rules. The unfettered working of market forces is sufficient to account for the origin of money and for the successive stages of monetary development, fostered by the thrust of resource saving. Indeed, the whole history of monetary arrangements can be seen as a search for less costly ways to settle transactions [9]. On the other hand, such a resource saving can be attained only if suitable institutions are set up (Hicks, 1967, chapter 1). From the reading of the historical record, there seems to be an inverse relationship between the amount of resources saved and the complexity of the institutional structure of exchange.

Once the establishment of rules is deemed a necessary element of the standard, the next question regards their scope. Investigating the minimum requirements of a monetary system, Patinkin has indicated the principle that solves the problem of price level determinacy. A solution exists only if there is a mechanism – involving the control of some nominal quantity – which acts as a pivot or peg in the monetary system, thus linking the monetary to the real sector of the economy. The same conclusion is reached by Hicks whose analysis (1967, pp. 8–10) of the 'clearing system' – in which there is no delivery of intermediate commodities – shows the limits of the Walrasian apparatus to tackle the problem at stake [10]. To make the general price level determinate, there must be a demand for and supply of a medium of exchange acting as an 'anchor' of the system. Thus, viable monetary standards must rest on a peg. More than often, proposals about new monetary arrangements have simply changed the type of peg [11].

---

[9] "There is the same incentive to find ways of reducing transaction costs as of reducing other costs; one way of looking at monetary evolution is to regard it as the development of ever more sophisticated ways of reducing transaction costs" (Hicks, 1967, p. 7). Lawrence White (1984, section II) admirably illustrates this evolutionary process.

[10] "... in order for the absolute price level to be determined by market-equilibrating forces, changes in it must impinge on aggregate *real* behavior in *some* market – i.e., must create excess demands in some market" (Patinkin, 1961, p. 113, italics in the original). See also Patinkin (1965, p. 309).

In his Lecture I, Hicks observes: "... it is with this organization (the clearing system) that we first meet a clear case of the Wicksellian phenomenon, a market in which absolute prices – money prices – are indeterminate. The money is simply a unit of account; it is not one of the traded commodities; there is therefore no supply–demand equation to determine its value. The Walras equations are sufficient to determine relative prices, prices (that is) in terms of one of the traded commodities taken as numéraire; but this numéraire is not the money in terms of which calculations are made. That money does not enter into the Walras equations; it is altogether outside them. The money prices can be at any level, yet the same Walras equilibrium will be attained. ... It is inevitable, even in a market of the kind we are discussing, that the seller, when he is deciding whether or not to sell (or how much to sell) at a particular price, should implicitly consider what that price may be worth in terms of other goods; he must have some idea about other prices before he can say whether or not a particular price–offer is acceptable" (Hicks, 1967, pp. 9–10).

[11] The following comment by Wicksell about Fisher's plan for a compensated dollar is quite telling. "The real advantage of Fisher's method is that, externally, everything would continue as at present, so that the general public would not even notice the change. Such an *argumentum ad ignoratum* seems, however, of doubtful value. The very substance of the proposed reform is to raise something *else* to the position of a *measure of value*, and not gold, as is now the case. Why not, therefore, go the whole way, and choose something different by which the goal in view, a stable price level, may be secured with reasonable certainty?" (1906, p. 228, italics in the original).

F. Cesarano / J. of Economic Behavior & Org. 26 (1995) 445–455 453

Monetary institutions mostly find their rationale in the necessity of rules to preserve viability of the monetary system. The analysis of the latter pertains to the theory of a monetary economy being, in fact, the 'applied' counterpart to the theoretical foundations of money examined in section 2 above. Therefore, the proposition that money is a product of regulation appears to derive from a price-theoretical approach that is downright misleading when the subject is money.

4. Conclusion

The Metallist Theory of Money, albeit generally disparaged at present, reigned almost unchallenged for over two millennia. Without enquiring about the reasons for such a puzzling development (a tentative explanation may hinge on the difficulty of accounting for the value of fiat money and the fatal outcome of some early experiments, e.g. John Law's System), it is astonishing that almost all leading economists up to the nineteenth century rejected, on *theoretical* grounds, a fiduciary standard [12]. This is suggestive of the complexity of monetary theory which has often lagged behind innovation stimulated by market forces. It may well be that monetary economics currently is not sufficiently advanced to deal satisfactorily with the issues raised by an accounting system of exchange. In fact, an undeniable merit of the NME is to have raised several provocative and intellectually stimulating questions, thus originating a debate on the relationships between analytical and institutional aspects of money that are, as yet, largely unexplored.

References

Alchian, Armen, 1977, Why Money?, Journal of Money, Credit, and Banking 9, 133–140.
Barro, Robert J., 1985, Bank Deregulation, Accounting Systems of Exchange, and the Unit of Account: A Critical Review – A Comment on the McCallum Paper, Carnegie-Rochester Conference Series on Public Policy 23, 47–54.
Barro, Robert J. and David B. Gordon, 1983, A Positive Theory of Monetary Policy in a Natural Rate Model, Journal of Political Economy 91, 589–610.
Bilson, John F.O., 1981, A Proposal for Monetary Reform (University of Chicago).
Black, Fischer, 1970, Banking and Interest Rates in a World Without Money: The Effects of Uncontrolled Banking, Journal of Bank Research 1, 9–20.
Brunner, Karl and Allan H. Meltzer, 1971, The Uses of Money: Money in the Theory of an Exchange Economy, American Economic Review 61, 784–805.

---

[12] Referring to Jevons' *Money and the Mechanism of Exchange*, Laidler notes: "Even though, according to Jevons (1875), "There is plenty of evidence to prove that an inconvertible paper money, if carefully limited in quantity, can retain its full value" (p. 235), inconvertible paper money was regarded as an 'abnormal phenomenon', to use his own (p. 191) phrase, associated in particular, though not exclusively with wartime finance" (1988, p. 77).

454   *F. Cesarano / J. of Economic Behavior & Org. 26 (1995) 445–455*

Brunner, Karl and Allan H. Meltzer, 1985, The 'New Monetary Economics', Fiscal Issues, and Unemployment, Carnegie-Rochester Conference Series on Public Policy 23, 1–12.

Clower, Robert W., 1967, A Reconsideration of the Microfoundations of Monetary Theory, Western Economic Journal 6, 1–9; reprinted in Clower (1969).

Clower, Robert W. (ed.), 1969. Monetary Theory (Harmondsworth, Penguin Books).

Clower, Robert W., 1977, The Anatomy of Monetary Theory, American Economic Review 67, 206–212.

Clower, Robert W. and Peter W. Howitt, 1978, The Transactions Theory of the Demand for Money: A Reconsideration, Journal of Political Economy 86, 449–466.

Cowen, Tyler and Randall Kroszner, 1987, The Development of the New Monetary Economics, Journal of Political Economy 95, 567–590.

Fama, Eugene F., 1980, Banking in the Theory of Finance, Journal of Monetary Economics 6, 39–57.

Friedman, Milton, 1960, A Program for Monetary Stability (Fordham University Press, New York).

Friedman, Milton, 1986, The Resource Cost of Irredeemable Paper Money, Journal of Political Economy 94, 642–647.

Friedman, Milton and Anna J. Schwartz, 1986, Has Government Any Role in Money?, Journal of Monetary Economics 17, 37–62.

Greenfield, Robert L. and Leland B. Yeager, 1983, A Laissez–Faire Approach to Monetary Stability, Journal of Money, Credit and Banking 15, 302–315.

Greenfield, Robert L., 1986, Competitive Payments Systems: Comment, American Economic Review 76, 848–849.

Hahn, Frank H., 1971, Equilibrium with Transaction Costs, Econometrica 39, 417–439.

Hahn, Frank H., 1973, On Transaction Costs, Inessential Sequence Economies and Money, Review of Economic Studies 40, 449–461.

Hall, Robert E., 1982a, Explorations in the Gold Standard and Related Policies for Stabilizing the Dollar, in: Inflation: Causes and Effects (University of Chicago Press, Chicago).

Hall, Robert E., 1982b, Monetary Trends in the United States and the United Kingdom: A Review from the Perspective of New Developments in Monetary Economics, Journal of Economic Literature 20, 1552–1556.

Hawtrey, Ralph G., 1929, Money, in: The Encyclopaedia Britannica, 14th edition (Encyclopaedia Britannica Company, London).

Hicks, John R., 1967, Critical Essays in Monetary Theory (Oxford University Press, Oxford).

Hoover, Kevin D., 1988, Money, Prices and Finance in the New Monetary Economics, Oxford Economic Papers 40, 150–167.

Jevons, Stanley W., 1875, Money and the Mechanism of Exchange (C. Kegan Paul & Co., London).

Jones, Robert A., 1976, The Origin and Development of Media of Exchange, Journal of Political Economy 84, 757–775.

Kareken, John H. and Neil, Wallace (eds.), 1980, Models of Monetary Economies (Federal Reserve Bank of Minneapolis, Minneapolis).

King, Robert G., 1983, On the Economics of Private Money, Journal of Monetary Economics 12, 127–158.

King, Robert G. and Charles I. Plosser, 1986, Money as the Mechanism of Exchange, Journal of Monetary Economics 17, 93–115.

Laidler, David, 1988, British Monetary Orthodoxy in the 1870s, Oxford Economic Papers 40, 74–109.

McCallum, Bennett T., 1985, Bank Deregulation, Accounting Systems of Exchange, and the Unit of Account: A Critical Review, Carnegie–Rochester Conference Series on Public Policy 23, 13–46.

McCulloch, John R., 1864, The Principles of Political Economy (Black, Edinburgh) (first edition 1825).

Menger, Carl, 1981, Principles of Economics, translated by James Dingwall and Bert F. Hoselitz, Introduction by F.A. Hayek (New York University Press, New York) (first edition 1871).

Menger, Carl, 1892, On the Origin of Money, Economic Journal 2, 239–255.

F. Cesarano / J. of Economic Behavior & Org. 26 (1995) 445–455   455

Mill, John Stuart, 1909, Principles of Political Economy, William Ashley (ed.) (Longmans, Green & Co., London) (first edition 1848).

Mott, Tracy, 1989, A Post Keynesian Perspective on a 'Cashless Competitive Payments System', Journal of Post Keynesian Economics 11, 360–369.

Niehans, Jürg, 1971, Money and Barter in General Equilibrium with Transactions Costs, American Economic Review 61, 773–783.

Niehans, Jürg, 1978, The Theory of Money (Johns Hopkins University Press, Baltimore)

Ostroy, Joseph M., 1973, The Informational Efficiency of Monetary Exchange, American Economic Review 63, 597–610.

Ostroy, Joseph M. and Ross M. Starr, 1974, Money and the Decentralization of Exchange, Econometrica 42, 1093–1113.

Ostroy, Joseph M. and Ross M. Starr, 1990, The Transactions Role of Money, in: Benjamin M. Friedman and Frank H. Hahn (eds.), Handbook of Monetary Economics (North-Holland, Amsterdam).

Patinkin, Don, 1961, Financial Intermediaries and the Logical Structure of Monetary Theory, American Economic Review 51, 95–116.

Patinkin, Don, 1965, Money, Interest, and Prices (Harper & Row, New York).

Schumpeter, Joseph A., 1954, History of Economic Analysis (Oxford University Press, Oxford).

Selgin, George A. and Lawrence H. White, 1987, The Evolution of a Free Banking System, Economic Inquiry 25, 439–457.

Smith, Adam, 1976, An Inquiry into the Nature and Causes of the Wealth of Nations, Edwin Cannan (ed.) The University of Chicago Press, Chicago) (first edition 1776).

Tobin, James, 1980, The Overlapping Generations Model of Fiat Money: Discussion, in: Kareken and Wallace.

Ulph, A.M. and D.T. Ulph, 1975, Transaction Costs in General Equilibrium Theory – A Survey, Economica 42, 355–372.

Wärneryd, Karl, 1989, Legal Restrictions and the Evolution of Media of Exchange, Journal of Institutional and Theoretical Economics 145, 613–626.

Wärneryd, Karl, 1990, Legal Restrictions and Monetary Evolution, Journal of Economic Behavior and Organization 13, 117–124.

White, Lawrence H., 1984, Competitive Payments Systems and the Unit of Account, American Economic Review 74, 699–712.

White, Lawrence H., 1986, Competitive Payments Systems: Reply, American Economic Review 76, 850–853.

White, Lawrence H., 1987, Accounting for Non-interest-bearing Currency: A Critique of the Legal Restrictions Theory of Money, Journal of Money, Credit and Banking 19, 448–456.

White, Lawrence H., 1989, Alternative Perspectives on the Cashless Competitive Payments System, Journal of Post Keynesian Economics 11, 378–384.

Wicksell, Knut, 1935, Lectures on Political Economy, Vol. 2 (Routledge, London) (first edition 1906).

Yeager, Leland B., 1985, Deregulation and Monetary Reform, American Economic Review 75, 103–107.

Yeager, Leland B., 1989, A Competitive Payments System: Some Objections Considered, Journal of Post Keynesian Economics 11, 370–377.

6

The Manchester School Vol LXII No. 2   June 1994
0025-2034   199-208

LEGAL RESTRICTIONS THEORY AND THE RATE-OF-RETURN DOMINANCE OF MONEY*

by

FILIPPO CESARANO†

Banca d'Italia

I   INTRODUCTION

Monetary theory has often lagged behind market innovations in monetary arrangements. Notable examples relate to the conception of money considered either from an analytical or an empirical viewpoint. Notwithstanding the evolution of the payments system through the early introduction of fiduciary media, for over two millennia economists stood by Theoretical Metallism, i.e., the theory that it is logically essential for money to consist of some commodity (Schumpeter, 1954, p. 288). In addition, new payment instruments were not always included in the money stock and, in fact, whether deposits should be so included was for long a controversial question (Mints, 1945, Chapters VI and X). The complex and elusive nature of the subject has at times hindered the development of monetary institutions. At present, the major advances in payments technology have not yet been matched by an equally substantial progress in monetary theory grappling with an economy devoid of tangible media of exchange. These topics have been tackled by the New Monetary Economics[1] but its teachings remain controversial. Stressing the distinction between currency and an accounting system of exchange (Fama, 1980, p. 39), the new school argues for the separation between the unit of account and the medium of exchange and emphasizes the actual role of the government as the sole issuer of currency. Money is, then, considered as a product of regulation (Hall, 1982b). A related though distinct development, due to Bryant and Wallace, is the Legal Restrictions Theory which aims to answer the problem viewed by Hicks as "the central issue in the pure theory of money" (1935, p. 5), namely the coexistence of non-interest-bearing money and bonds. Wallace (1983) ascribes the interest rate dominance of money to certain legal restrictions on private intermediation, e.g., the prohibition of

---

* Manuscript received 23.9.91; final version received 11.3.93.
† Thanks are due to Robert Clower, Milton Friedman, Larry White and two anonymous referees for their useful comments on a first draft of this paper. The usual caveat applies.
[1]This term is due to Hall (1982b). The main contributions include Black (1970); Fama (1980); Hall (1982a); and Greenfield and Yeager (1983). For a critical appraisal, see White (1984b) and McCallum (1985). Cowen and Kroszner (1987) and Sumner (1990) examine the topic from a history of economics standpoint.

private note issue. This theory deserves careful attention because its policy implications purportedly call into question the traditional treatment of monetary policy, holding that the effectiveness of the latter is due only to the presence of legal restrictions. In contrast, under *laissez-faire*, open market operations or discount window lending do not affect anything, not even the price level (Wallace, 1983, p. 1).

White (1987) has recently criticized this approach on two grounds. He provides historical evidence against it and also sets forth the argument of costly payment of interest on currency as an explanation of the coexistence of non-interest-bearing currency with interest-bearing bonds. Both White's contentions, however, have been countered. Cowen and Kroszner (1989) dispute his historical evidence (see, however, White's 1990 reply) and, moreover, Bryant (1989) takes him to task for failing to consider Friedman's (1969) suggestion to resort to deflation as a costless way to ensure a positive yield on money. Then, Bryant maintains that costs of paying interest on currency are not sufficient to account for the rate-of-return dominance of currency which, as Friedman (1969) would argue, arises instead from legal restrictions on private note issue.

The purpose of this note is to clarify the debate by bringing out the distinctive elements of the legal restrictions theory as compared with received monetary economics. In particular, it is shown that, contrary to Bryant's interpretation, Friedman's view of the subject is based on principles quite opposite to the legal restrictions theory (Section II). Furthermore, it is contended that a government monopoly of currency issue is just one of the possible ways of setting a limit on the quantity of fiat money, but that it has little if any bearing on interest rate dominance. The latter is instead strictly related to the theoretical foundations of money and thus is consistent with the essential properties of a monetary economy (Section III).

II FRIEDMAN AND THE LEGAL RESTRICTIONS THEORY

Bryant's defence of the legal restrictions theory is centred on Friedman's optimum quantity of money chapter (1969) which allegedly upholds the legal restrictions theory. According to Bryant, the prohibition of private note issue "may, then, be the crucial legal restriction for explaining the rate of return dominance of currency, as Friedman suggests" (1989, p. 241). When closely examined, however, Friedman's essay clashes with the legal restrictions approach, as does the rest of his work spanning more than four decades. Bryant's assertion notwithstanding, Friedman has always been critical of competitive money supply schemes, e.g., the proposals of Klein and Hayek (Friedman and Schwartz, 1986, pp. 45–6). Indeed, his analysis of "why should government intervene in monetary and banking questions?" (1960, pp. 4–9) is often referred to as the classic statement in support of an active role by government. He maintains that, in a fiat money standard, the incentive for any individual issuer to supply the currency whose market value is greater than its cost of production would make the system collapse into a "paper standard". Thus, the government must place an external limit on the quantity of fiat money.[2]

A quarter of a century later, Friedman, in the article co-authored by Anna Schwartz (1986, p. 58), defends and restates the same views after pointedly analysing various problems raised in the recent literature. It is not surprising, then, that this position is coherently upheld in the 1969 essay. Discussing the payment of interest on currency as an alternative way to implement the optimum quantity of money, Friedman envisages allowing free entry into banking and permitting banks to issue interest-bearing currency and deposits. Nevertheless, he calls for a limit on the stock of money (1969, pp. 38–9) and thus, far from maintaining the legal restrictions theory as Bryant suggests, goes in quite the opposite direction. This is not merely a matter of textual interpretation, fondly pursued by historians of economics but deemed trifling by fellow economists. Underlying this interpretative query, in fact, there is a disagreement on the fundamentals of money. On the one hand, the legal restrictions theory emphasizes a *laissez-faire* approach and considers government activity in monetary arrangements as an interference, as in commodity markets. Hence, a distinctive feature of fiat money is that it is government-issued and thus that it "is exactly a creation of regulation" (Hall, 1982b, p. 1554). On the other hand, Friedman's analysis follows the traditional transactions and asset motives for holding money, noting that both "depend critically on ... the existence of individual uncertainty" (1969, p. 3). In his theoretical framework, a public authority is regarded as a vital element, rather than a disturbing one, since it preserves the viability of a fiat money system. The source of Bryant's misinterpretation seems due to the failure to recognize that while on microeconomic grounds Friedman advocates competition in the banking industry in order to pay interest on money, he does maintain the principle of setting an external limit to the quantity of fiat money as a rule governing the standard. This appears in the key passage cited by Bryant when quoted in full.[3] In a recent contribution, in fact,

[2]Renewed interest in the subject of monetary reform has prompted a variety of studies (e.g., White, 1984a; Selgin, 1988; Dowd, 1989; and Glasner, 1989) which have thrown doubt on the technical monopoly argument and, especially, on the role of government. Early contributions to this debate are Klein (1974); Hayek (1976); and Taub (1985). A discussion of these matters, however, goes beyond the range of the present paper, which focuses on government monopoly of fiat currency issue and, in Section II, specifically aims at clarifying Friedman's standpoint in relation to the legal restrictions theory.

[3]"Competition among banks would force them to pay interest on deposits at a rate falling short of r_B [the bond rate] by the costs of running the banks, *including loss of interest on assets required to be held as non-interest bearing fiat money*. Competition would force banks also to pay interest on currency at a rate below the rate paid on deposits by the extra costs of administering the payment of interest on currency. They would, of course, have an incentive to devise an economical way to pay such interest." (Friedman, 1969, p. 39, italics added; quoted by Bryant, 1989, p. 240). The italicized sentence, drawing attention to the limit on the money stock, is skipped by Bryant.

Friedman has openly dissociated himself from the legal restrictions theory (1984, p. 49), thus validating the foregoing analysis.

Finally, Bryant's (1989) treatment of interest rate dominance requires a brief comment. In his article, banks back their notes by holding bonds which must be purchased by "spending" the entire supply of the government currency. The latter is exclusively used to buy bonds and is ultimately held by the government only. Yet, the government currency has no role but to set a surreptitious limit on the quantity of money since it does not perform any of the standard monetary functions. It is not a medium of exchange, or a store of value and, Bryant's assertion notwithstanding (1989, p. 242), not even a unit of account because this notion still entails its use in exchange.[4] In this model, it is difficult to account for both the "price level of government currency, $P_{c,t}$," and the proposition according to which "bank notes dominate government currency" (Bryant, 1989, pp. 243–4) if such currency does not have any monetary properties.

III   THE RATE-OF-RETURN DOMINANCE OF MONEY

The contrast between the legal restrictions view and received monetary economics on the role of government in monetary affairs has its roots in the different approaches to the theory of money. This point, hinted at in Section II (see p. 201 above), will be developed below in connection with the question of interest rate dominance.

Recently, Friedman has buttressed his analysis of the technical monopoly character of a pure fiduciary currency by putting forward an argument which, although based on historical experience, bears heavily on the theoretical aspects of the subject. He draws attention to the conspicuous revenue levied by governments through inflating fiat money and, considering this as a measure of the price that individuals are willing to pay to preserve the money they are used to, emphasizes the "value that communities attach to having a single unit of account and medium of exchange" (Friedman and Schwartz, 1986, p. 44). Friedman notes that except for major inflationary episodes such as the ones observed in Israel and Latin America, resort has not usually been made to alternative monetary media or units despite their availability. This empirical observation, advanced earlier by Keynes (1923, pp. 48–50) and Robertson (1959, pp. 12, 20), has its theoretical counterpart in both classical monetary economics and the modern literature on the foundations of money.

---

[4]The ECU (European Currency Unit) is a unit of account because it enters a number of financial and, to a lesser extent, non-financial transactions. It could hardly be considered a unit of account if its parity were just announced and served no other purpose. To make an analogy, the yard is not thought of as a unit of measure in continental Europe, although it is known that it equals 0·9144 metre, since no one would ever measure anything in yards. An analysis of the relationship between the unit of account and the medium of exchange can be found in Niehans (1978, Ch. 7).

Classical economists identified the medium of exchange with the primary function of money, the other ones — unit of account and store of value — playing a subordinate role. An important corollary of this proposition is the strict connection between the medium of exchange and the unit of account functions in that the latter naturally attaches itself to the same commodity performing the former. The opening chapter of Wicksell's *Lectures* contains a lucid statement of both principles:

> "Of the three main functions [measure of value, store of value, and medium of exchange], only the last is in a true sense characteristic of money; as a measure of value any commodity whatever might serve. ... Similarly, the function of acting as a *store of value* is not essentially characteristic of money. ... the object in view [contemplated by those who hoard money] is nearly always that of procuring *something else* for it at a future time. In other words, it is the exchange value which it is desired to preserve; it is money as a future medium of exchange which is hoarded" (1906, pp. 6–8, italics in the original).

Commenting on the then fashionable proposal of monetary reform based on indexation, Wicksell notes: "... a commodity which serves as a medium of exchange naturally comes to be used also as a measure of value for transactions in goods and service which are near or simultaneous in time" (1906, p. 7). These tenets are not peculiar to Wicksell but represent the mainstream classical position since they have been treated, in even greater detail, by Smith, McCulloch, Stuart Mill, Menger, Jevons and many others. According to the classical approach, the essential properties of money, centred on the medium of exchange function, entail a resource-enhancing role which distinguishes a monetary economy from a barter economy. The *locus classicus* of this analysis is Adam Smith's discussion of the difficulties of commodity trading as related to the division of labour (1776, Book I, Ch. IV) and of money considered as "the great wheel of circulation" (1776, Book II, Ch. II).

In the 1960s, the acknowledged failure of the general equilibrium model to arrive at a meaningful treatment of money stimulated an extensive literature attempting to probe the properties of an exchange economy in which, in contrast with the Walrasian economy, agents exchange goods between themselves. This research programme has deepened our understanding of a monetary economy and has corroborated the hypotheses advanced by the classics. Clower's (1967) analysis of the microfoundations of monetary theory dwells on the distinction between money and non-money commodities, the former's key characteristic stemming from the medium-of-exchange function. The primacy of this function is shown by Ostroy (1973, pp. 607–8) while the ancillary character of the unit of account with respect to the medium of exchange is formally demonstrated by Niehans (1978, Ch. 7) and analysed by White (1984b). In general, most works point at the problem of enforcing budget constraints and thus stress incomplete information as a key aspect of the "inconveniences of barter". Therefore, an essential property of money is to provide a record-keeping device which makes up for the informational decentralization of an exchange economy (Ostroy and Starr, 1990, pp. 8–14). This principle has been analysed in different contexts: the dynamic one-good, two-agent sequence economy model or the static n-good, m-agent pure exchange economy $(n, m \geqslant 3)$. Both, however, build on the same foundations, i.e., the conflict between the need for net trades to be zero and the potential for exploiting all the gains from trade. The role of money is to help to resolve this conflict (Ostroy and Starr, 1990, p. 26).

The informational element also provides the groundwork of the theory of the origin of money (Menger, 1871, 1892; Jones, 1976). The independent behaviour of individuals, driven only by market forces, triggers a process in which one commodity emerges as the unique medium of exchange. The crucial issue, then, is the distinction between a barter economy and a monetary economy and the welfare gains generated by the presence of money. These gains are so large that people are willing to hold currency with a conspicuously negative real rate of return. This explains not only the non-resurgence of barter during hyperinflations but also the failure to resort to a different money. In fact, recent developments in the literature on the foundations of money emphasize strategic elements in the phenomenon, and origin, of money so that the latter may be regarded as "a self-fulfilling prophecy" (Iwai, 1988; Kiyotaki and Wright, 1989a, 1989b; Oh, 1989; Wärneryd, 1989, 1990). This approach, partly anticipated by Menger, corroborates previous work on the subject and provides a further rationale for the high opportunity cost of doing away with actual money. Thus, the Keynes-Robertson-Friedman and Schwartz historical observation finds its way into monetary theory, and particularly into the analysis of the essential properties of money, which explains the high value that societies attribute to a single unit of account and medium of exchange.

These arguments cast serious doubts on the legal restrictions view as an explanation of the interest rate dominance of money and, more generally, as a hypothesis of the demand for money. Legal restrictions on private intermediation are not a sufficient condition for dominance since, as Bryant himself acknowledges (1989, p. 244), the government can well provide currency yielding a positive return through deflation. Furthermore, the failure to resort to alternative payment media makes unnecessary the presence of legal restrictions to account for dominance because such alternatives have generally been available. Indeed, what is striking during major inflationary episodes is the persistence in the use of the depreciating currency even though this entails the appropriation of a considerable amount of resources by the government. Underlying this phenomenon, there should be some rationale for money holdings other than the existence of legal restrictions. The latter could hardly explain the unwillingness on the part of individuals to substitute for a dominant money whose real rate of return is hugely negative, i.e., over

50 per cent *per month* in absolute terms, as in hyerinflations (Cagan, 1956).[5] These considerations turn the question of dominance upside-down. In fact, it may be argued that people do not adopt alternative exchange media *despite* government monopoly in currency issue, rather than because of it.

A closer examination of the contributions to the legal restrictions theory does not clarify the problem. In particular, Wallace's (1983) main argument — that non-negotiability of U.S. savings bonds and the large denomination of Treasury bills account for the coexistence of assets having highly different rates of return — rather than corroborating the legal restrictions theory, shows the essential properties of money. His conclusion, according to which Treasury bills would sell at par when issued in small denominations, is eminently correct but provides a further illustration of a basic character of money, namely divisibility. When Treasury bills are assigned such a typical monetary property, their interest rate falls to zero because they become indistinguishable from money, not because of the removal of any legal restrictions on private intermediation which seemingly eliminates dominance. In Wallace's example, both "green" Federal Reserve notes and "red" Treasury bills finally circulate together like an enlarged money stock since the two assets share the same "monetary" properties. These properties, listed in nineteenth-century textbooks as portability, homogeneity, cognizability, etc. (Jevons, 1875, Ch. V), relate to *market* not to physical characteristics of goods (Jones, 1976, p. 775) and have little to do with government regulation.

An alternative explanation of dominance can then be advanced by dwelling on the previous analysis of the distinction between a barter economy and a monetary economy, emphasized by both classical and modern monetary theory. Transition from one to the other involves a substantial welfare gain to society that, given the informational foundation of money, is strictly related to the uniqueness of the medium of exchange and thus accounts for the lack of incentive to do away with dominant money during hyperinflations. Therefore, the main point is not the substitutability between outside and inside money (Wallace, 1988, p. 26) but rather the very existence of "money", qua medium of a decentralized indirect exchange economy.

IV   Conclusion

The present paper has attempted to clarify some interpretative and analytical issues concerning the interest rate dominance of money and the legal restrictions theory. In the light of the criticisms raised here, the policy implications of the legal restrictions theory, e.g., the ineffectiveness of monetary policy under *laissez-faire* and the defence of the real bills doctrine, should be treated with considerable caution. Nevertheless, the legal restrictions

[5]A 15 per cent Treasury bill rate, although considered as a substantial piece of evidence in support of the legal restrictions theory (Bryant, 1989, p. 244), is a mere trifle if compared with the highly negative returns on cash balances observed in several inflationary experiences.

literature has stimulated a lively debate on major questions relating to both the theoretical and the institutional aspects of the economics of money, thereby contributing to a deeper understanding of the subject.

REFERENCES

Black, F. (1970). "Banking and Interest Rates in a World Without Money: The Effects of Uncontrolled Banking", *Journal of Bank Research*, Vol. 1, No. 3, pp. 9–20.
Bryant, J. (1989). "Interest-Bearing Currency, Legal Restrictions, and the Rate of Return Dominance of Money", *Journal of Money, Credit, and Banking*, Vol. 21, No. 2, pp. 240–246.
Bryant, J. and Wallace, N. (1979). "The Inefficiency of Interest-Bearing National Debt", *Journal of Political Economy*, Vol. 87, No. 2, pp. 365–381.
Bryant, J. and Wallace, N. (1980). "Open Market Operations in a Model of Regulated, Insured Intermediaries", *Journal of Political Economy*, Vol. 88, No. 1, pp. 146–173.
Cagan, P. (1956). "The Monetary Dynamics of Hyperinflation" in Milton Friedman (ed.), *Studies in the Quantity Theory of Money*, Chicago, The University of Chicago Press.
Clower, R. W. (1967). "A Reconsideration of the Microfoundations of Monetary Theory", *Western Economic Journal*, Vol. 6, No. 1, pp. 1–9.
Cowen, T. and Kroszner, R. (1987). "The Development of the New Monetary Economics", *Journal of Political Economy*, Vol. 95, No. 3, pp. 567–590.
Cowen, T. and Kroszner, R. (1989). "Scottish Banking before 1845: A Model for Laissez-Faire?", *Journal of Money, Credit, and Banking*, Vol. 21, No. 2, pp. 221–231.
Dowd, K. (1989). *The State and the Monetary System*, New York, Philip Allan.
Fama, E. F. (1980). "Banking in the Theory of Finance", *Journal of Monetary Economics*, Vol. 6, No. 1, pp. 39–57.
Friedman, M. (1942). "Discussion of the Inflationary Gap", *American Economic Review*, Vol. 32, No. 2, pp. 314–320; reprinted in Friedman (1953).
Friedman, M. (1953). *Essays in Positive Economics*, Chicago, The University of Chicago Press.
Friedman, M. (1960). *A Program for Monetary Stability*, New York, Fordham University Press.
Friedman, M. (1969). "The Optimum Quantity of Money" in *The Optimum Quantity of Money and Other Essays*, Chicago, Aldine.
Friedman, M. (1984). "Monetary Policy for the 1980s" in J. H. Moore (ed.), *To Promote Prosperity: U.S. Domestic Policy in the Mid-1980s*, Stanford, Hoover Institution Press.
Friedman, M. and Schwartz, A. J. (1986). "Has Government Any Role in Money?", *Journal of Monetary Economics*, Vol. 17, No. 1, pp. 37–62.
Glasner, D. (1989). *Free Banking and Monetary Reform*, Cambridge, Cambridge University Press.
Greenfield, R. L. and Yeager, L. B. (1983). "A Laissez-Faire Approach to Monetary Stability", *Journal of Money, Credit, and Banking*, Vol. 15, No. 3, pp. 302–315.
Hall, R. E. (1982a). "Explorations in the Gold Standard and Related Policies for Stabilizing the Dollar" in *Inflation: Causes and Effects*, Chicago, University of Chicago Press.
Hall, R. E. (1982b). "*Monetary Trends in the United States and the United Kingdom*: A Review from the Perspective of New Developments in Monetary Economics", *Journal of Economic Literature*, Vol. 20, No. 4, pp. 1552–1556.

Legal Restrictions Theory and the Rate-of-Return Dominance of Money 207

Hayek, F. A. (1976). *The Denationalization of Money*, London, Institute of Economic Affairs.

Iwai, K. (1988). "The Evolution of Money: A Search Theoretic Foundation of Monetary Economics", *University of Pennsylvania CARESS Working Paper 88-03*.

Jevons, S. W. (1875). *Money and the Mechanism of Exchange*, London, C. Kegan Paul & Co.

Jones, R. A. (1976). "The Origin and Development of Media of Exchange", *Journal of Political Economy*, Vol. 84, No. 4, pp. 757–775.

Keynes, J. M. (1923). *A Tract on Monetary Reform*, London, Macmillan.

Kiyotaki, N. and Wright, R. (1989a). "On Money as a Medium of Exchange", *Journal of Political Economy*, Vol. 97, No. 4, pp. 927–954.

Kiyotaki, N. and Wright, R. (1989b). "A Contribution to the Pure Theory of Money", *Federal Reserve Bank of Minneapolis Research Department Staff Report 123.*

Klein, B. (1974). "The Competitive Supply of Money", *Journal of Money, Credit, and Banking*, Vol. 6, No. 4, pp. 423–453.

McCallum, B. T. (1985). "Bank Deregulation, Accounting Systems of Exchange, and the Unit of Account: A Critical Review", *Carnegie-Rochester Conference Series on Public Policy*, Vol. 23, Amsterdam, North-Holland, pp. 13–46.

Menger, C. (1981 [1871]). *Principles of Economics*, translated by J. Dingwall and B. F. Hoselitz with an Introduction by F. A. Hayek, New York, New York University Press.

Menger, C. (1892). "On the Origin of Money", *Economic Journal*, Vol. 2, No. 6, pp. 239–255.

Mints, L. W. (1945). *A History of Banking Theory in Great Britain and the United States*, Chicago, The University of Chicago Press.

Niehans, J. (1978). *The Theory of Money*, Baltimore, The Johns Hopkins University Press.

O'Driscoll, G. P. (1985). "Money in a Deregulated Financial System", *Federal Reserve Bank of Dallas, Economic Review*, pp. 1–12.

Oh, S. (1989). "A Theory of a Generally Acceptable Medium of Exchange and Barter", *Journal of Monetary Economics*, Vol. 23, No. 1, pp. 101–119.

Ostroy, J. M. (1973). "The Informational Efficiency of Monetary Exchange", *American Economic Review*, Vol. 63, No. 4, pp. 597–610.

Ostroy, J. M. and Starr, R. M. (1990). "The Transactions Role of Money" in B. M. Friedman and F. H. Hahn (eds.), *Handbook of Monetary Economics*, Amsterdam, North-Holland.

Robertson, D. H. (1959). *Lectures on Economic Principles, Vol. III*, London, Staples Press.

Schumpeter, J. A. (1954). *History of Economic Analysis*, Oxford, Oxford University Press.

Selgin, G. A. (1988). *The Theory of Free Banking*, Totowa, N.J., Rowman & Littlefield.

Smith, A. (1976 [1776]). *An Inquiry into the Nature and Causes of the Wealth of Nations*, edited by Edwin Cannan, Chicago, The University of Chicago Press.

Sumner, S. (1990). "The Forerunners of 'New Monetary Economics' Proposals to Stabilize the Unit of Account", *Journal of Money, Credit, and Banking*, Vol. 22, No. 1, pp. 109–118.

Taub, B. (1985). "Private Fiat Money with Many Suppliers", *Journal of Monetary Economics*, Vol. 16, No. 2, pp. 195–208.

Wallace, N. (1983). "A Legal Restrictions Theory of the Demand for 'Money' and the Role of Monetary Policy", *Federal Reserve Bank of Minneapolis Quarterly Review*, Vol. 7, No. 1, pp. 1–7.

Wallace, N. (1988). "A Suggestion for Oversimplifying the Theory of Money", *Economic Journal*, Conference Papers, Vol. 98, No. 390, pp. 25–36.

Wärneryd, K. (1989). "Legal Restrictions and the Evolution of Media of Exchange", *Journal of Institutional and Theoretical Economics*, Vol. 145, No. 4, pp. 613–626.

Wärneryd, K. (1990). "Legal Restrictions and Monetary Evolution", *Journal of Economic Behavior and Organization*, Vol. 13, No. 1, pp. 117–124.

White, L. H. (1984a). *Free Banking in Britain*, Cambridge, Cambridge University Press.

White, L. H. (1984b). "Competitive Payments Systems and the Unit of Account", *American Economic Review*, Vol. 74, No. 4, pp. 699–712.

White, L. H. (1987). "Accounting for Non-Interest-Bearing Currency: A Critique of the Legal Restrictions Theory of Money", *Journal of Money, Credit, and Banking*, Vol. 19, No. 4, pp. 448–456.

White, L. H. (1990). "Scottish Banking and the Legal Restrictions Theory: A Closer Look", *Journal of Money, Credit, and Banking*, Vol. 22, No. 4, pp. 526–536.

Wicksell, K. (1935 [1906]). *Lectures on Political Economy*, Vol. 2, London, Routledge.

7

The New Monetary Economics and Keynes' Theory of Money

Filippo Cesarano
Banca d'Italia, Rome, Italy

In the last three decades, the momentous progress in payments technology has fostered the notion of a monetary system entirely devoid of a tangible medium of exchange. The implications of these developments for the theory of money have been considered so far-reaching as to affect the foundations of the subject and to originate a "new monetary economics" (Hall, 1982b, p. 1552). In his pioneering article, Fischer Black argues that the introduction of a cashless competitive payments system would explode current monetary theories altogether:

> In such a world, it would not be possible to give any reasonable definition of the quantity of money. The payments mechanism in such a world would be very efficient, but money in the usual sense would not exist. Thus neither the quantity theory of money nor the liquidity preference theory of money would be applicable (Black, 1970, p. 9).

Given the original and provocative character of this literature, careful examination of the main contributions to the new monetary economics (NME henceforth) – including Fama (1980), Greenfield and Yeager (1983) and Hall (1982a) – cannot be avoided. Critical assessments (Burkett, 1990; Hoover, 1988; McCallum, 1985; Richter, 1989; White, 1984) and historical treatments (Cowen and Kroszner, 1987, 1992; Sumner, 1990) of the NME have already appeared. However, these studies focus on individual works and do not attempt to draw an overall picture – which is admittedly no easy task, because the NME does not exhibit a homogeneous body of knowledge. The following pages attempt to fill this void, gathering up the threads of the subject in order to set forth the basic principles of the new school. But the chief aim is to appraise the NME on the basis of Keynes' monetary economics, which bear heavily on the issues raised by this modern approach. Therefore the NME's rejection of both the quantity theory and liquidity preference in a cashless world is critically analysed with specific reference to Keynes' theory of money.

The New Monetary Economics
The NME aims at a variety of analytical objectives: the payments system, the role of banks, the stabilization of output and of the price level, monetary reform and the like. However, the central proposition is the distinction between a tangible and a non-tangible means of payment, since the latter does not involve the notion of money. As Fama puts it:

Journal of Economic Studies
Vol. 21 No. 3, 1994, pp. 39-53.
© MCB University Press, 0144-3585

Journal of
Economic
Studies
21,3

40

One of our main points is that currency and an accounting system are entirely different methods for exchanging wealth. Currency is a physical medium which can be characterized as money. An accounting system works through bookkeeping entries, debits and credits, which do not require any physical medium or the concept of money (1980, p. 39).

The technological feature of tangibility is essential for the definition of money so that monetary theory becomes institution-laden[1]. Since the basic character of today's monetary arrangements is the governmental monopoly of currency issue, "the new monetary economics views the quantity theory as nothing more than an artifact of government regulation" and, thus, "the Government's monetary liability ... has some economic value, either because it is intrinsically useful or because the Government creates an artificial demand for it through regulation" (Hall, 1982b, pp. 1552-3). Instead, in an accounting system of exchange managed by an unregulated banking system, money does not exist and transactions are settled in prices stated in terms of a *numéraire*, i.e. a real commodity. Stressing the tangibility, or lack thereof, of the means of payment, the NME assigns a central role to the unit of account function of money *vis-a-vis* the medium of exchange and the store of value functions. In this environment, banks are indistinguishable from other portfolio managers, e.g. mutual funds, because they will compete to provide portfolios with different degrees of risk against deposits. Individuals benefit from the transaction services offered by banks and choose the type of account with the risk characteristic that best suits them. Furthermore, the portfolio management activities of banks are pure financing decisions covered by the Modigliani-Miller theorem (Fama, 1980, p. 40).

The banking system plays a key role in administering payments in a world lacking a tangible medium of exchange, but is nevertheless regarded just as any other industry. Following Tobin (1963), the NME attributes to banks, and to their products, no peculiar characteristics. Therefore banks affect neither real variables nor the price level, but simply bring together the demand for and supply of securities. It is rather the Government's regulatory activity which assigns banks a special place in monetary arrangements.

As Fama recognizes (1980, pp. 44, 49), this theoretical framework concerns a non-monetary economy, i.e. the Walrasian economy in which exchange is carried out, not between agents but through the auctioneer. In the absence of a physical means of payment, the NME soon meets the Wicksellian problem of price level indeterminacy[2], the solution of which requires the control of a nominal quantity which acts as a peg or an anchor for the price level (Patinkin, 1961)[3]. In this connection, NME theorists (Black, 1970, pp. 13-14; Fama, 1980, pp. 49-55) also call for a tangible currency, but on an entirely different basis. Besides the micro-economic consideration that, for small payments, a hand-to-hand medium of exchange may be more efficient than an accounting system, they focus on the unit of account function and aim to bring forth the *numéraire* of the Walrasian model as that very unit. As Fama notes: "The precise problem is not rendering a monetary system determinate, but rather giving content to a pure nominal unit of account (a dollar) as a separate, well-defined economic good" (1980, p. 55). Beside these interpretative queries, however, the introduction of currency is considered a solution to price level indeterminacy[4] that eliminates the need to control deposits, securities or any other banking activity.

The emphasis on the micro-economics of the banking industry notwithstanding, the NME ultimately points at macro-economic targets. In the present monetary arrangements, characterized by the governmental monopoly of money issue, the adjustment mechanism of eventual shocks in the money market necessarily entails output and price level changes:

> Money matters in today's economy because we have chosen to quote prices in terms of money, or, to be completely specific, in terms of the high-powered money issued by the Government. The price of money cannot change. Every shift of supply or demand in the money market must ultimately be accommodated by a change in the prices of all other goods and services. In the frictionless Walrasian economy, money controls the price level. In the real world, prices seem to have an element of fixity in the short run, and the money stock influences interest rates and real activity (Hall, 1982b, p. 1553).

A main objective of the NME is, therefore, to do away with income and price fluctuations by building an alternative monetary system. The new school is not unanimous in suggesting such an institutional framework and several proposals have been put forward. A notable one, originated by Greenfield and Yeager (1983), is the so-called "BFH system" – after the initials of Black (1970), Fama (1980), and Hall (1982a) – which is based on a unit of account physically defined in terms of a large number of non-storable commodities, separated from the medium of exchange, and not convertible. While the prices of the goods composing the unit change, the price of the bundle would be fixed at one analogous to units of length and weight, thus making the BFH system immune from both the price level and income variability which, in actual monetary arrangements, arise from adjustments in the demand for and supply of money.

There is a close relationship between the NME proposals for monetary reform and the underlying theoretical framework. A non-tangible medium of exchange calls forth the Walrasian model of general equilibrium as the relevant "box of tools", so that money is viewed as the unit of account in that model with no further distinctive characteristic. In this price-theoretical approach, Government activity in monetary arrangements is considered as analogous to Government intervention in the goods market, i.e. as an interference which makes money a product of regulation and ultimately reduces social welfare. In today's monetary system, the equilibrating mechanism in the money market generates price level and income variability. The NME aims to avoid these effects through divorcing the unit of account from the medium of exchange.

To complete this examination of the NME, a short account of the closely-related Legal Restriction Theory of money (LRT henceforth), developed by Bryant and Wallace (1980), is in order. The LRT analyses the coexistence of interest-bearing bonds and non-interest-bearing money which, according to

Journal of
Economic
Studies
21,3

42

Hicks, "is really the central issue in the pure theory of money. Either we have to give an explanation of the fact that people do hold money when rates of interest are positive, or we have to evade the difficulty somehow" (1935, p. 5). According to the LRT, the rate of return dominance of money arises from legal restrictions on private intermediation, i.e. the prohibition against private bank note issue. Wallace (1983) points in particular to large denominations of Treasury bills and non-negotiability of savings bonds to explain the coexistence of these assets with currency. If those legal restrictions were waived, Wallace argues, bills and savings bonds would sell at par.

Although it focuses on the specific issue of interest rate dominance of money, the LRT shares most of the NME theoretical framework and may be viewed as an application of the latter to a specific problem. In fact, the LRT identifies no distinctive property of money *vis-à-vis* other assets, so that both are valued in terms of their pecuniary returns. Furthermore, the LRT does not assign a role to the Government but to meddle with the market. This bears not only on the explanation of the interest rate dominance of money, but also on the effectiveness of monetary policy, since both would vanish under *laissez-faire*. An open market purchase of Treasury bills would merely substitute Government currency for privately issued bank notes, with no further effects on interest rates, the price level and real income.

The New Monetary Economics and the Quantity Theory
The theory of money often lags behind major changes in monetary institutions spurred on by market forces. Nowadays, the substantial progress in payments technology has paved the ground for the NME. Likewise, the demise of the gold standard after World War I stimulated much reflection on monetary theory. In this regard, Keynes' *A Tract on Monetary Reform* (1923) stands out in that it gave an original analysis of the role of money in the economy and of monetary arrangements which fostered the modern conception of monetary policy.

The opening sentence of the *Tract* – "Money is only important for what it will procure" – concisely describes the starting-point of classical monetary theory, i.e. the medium of exchange function of money. The classical theorists identified the other functions as well – unit of account and store of value – but considered them as subsidiary to, or as a necessary implication of, the medium of exchange function[5], thus having no major place in the analysis. Therefore money, as distinct from commodities, has the particular property of yielding indirect utility in the form of purchasing power. This provides the basis of the quantity theory:

> The [Quantity] Theory flows from the fact that money as such has no utility except what is derived from its exchange-value, that is to say from the utility of the things which it can buy ... A Currency Note has no utility in itself and is completely worthless except for the purchasing power which it has as money (Keynes, 1923, p. 75).

The notion of money as a medium of exchange, then, involves the irrelevance of the substance of which it is made. The role of money is to avoid the "inconveniences of barter" or, in modern terminology, to provide an information-producing mechanism which allows the decentralization of exchange (Ostroy and Starr, 1990). To perform such a function, the physical shape of the means of payment is clearly accidental.

The NME turns upside-down the foundations of the classical theory. Contrasting currency with an accounting system of exchange, the NME emphasizes the unit of account function and calls for the Walrasian model as the appropriate analytical tool. In fact, the NME research strategy is to deny any peculiar characteristic which distinguishes money from commodities in order to bring money under the realm of general equilibrium theory. However, this openly clashes with the emphasis laid, in the last quarter-century, on the absence of any meaningful role of money in the general equilibrium framework[6]. Indeed, a major task of monetary economics has been to analyse the properties of an economy in which money enters in an essential way. This is the central problem of monetary theory. Though a complete answer has not yet been given, this research programme has clarified the role of money in allowing the decentralization of exchange and the exploitation of the gains from trade without violating the budget constraint. The eventual obsolescence of tangible money will merely reflect the technological progress in the payments system, but will have little if anything to do with the characteristics of a monetary economy. The disappearance of any physical means of payment will not of course mean that the medium of exchange function of money will have vanished, since this function is connected with the essential properties of a monetary economy, contrasted with a barter economy, which do not relate to the outer form of the means of payment[7].

The NME disregards these tenets because it emphasizes the unit of account as the key function of money. Yet, an important corollary of the classical viewpoint is that, if a commodity is used as a medium of exchange, it naturally becomes the unit of account (Smith, 1776, p. 36; Wicksell, 1906, p. 7). In fact, in order to enhance the gain in information stemming from a monetary economy, individuals will post prices in that unit which coincides with the medium of exchange. This emerges from both Menger's theory of the origin of money (White, 1984) and from the hypothesis of minimizing "accounting costs" (Niehans, 1978, ch. 7). Hinging on the reduction of trading costs, these theories account for the ancillary character of the unit of account in respect of the medium of exchange function[8].

Although the NME does not consider these principles, the latter come out in connection with the problem of price level determinacy, which is another way of looking at the primacy of the medium of exchange *vis-à-vis* the unit of account function. As clearly stated by Hicks (see note 2), in a "clearing system" in which money is only a unit of account, the equations of the Walrasian model determine relative prices but not the absolute price level, since there is no demand-supply equation that determines the value of money. Yet, the purchasing power of money crucially enters into the agent's maximizing behaviour[9] and, hence, a nominal anchor is required. NME theorists do not evade the Wicksellian indeterminacy problem and, in the main, accept the standard solution, i.e. the

Journal of
Economic
Studies
21,3

44

introduction of a fiat nominal aggregate. But their interpretation of this solution is quite misleading in some cases. In particular, Fama looks at the use of currency as a way of "transforming the unit of account into a real economic good" (1980, p. 51). This is a peculiar way of tackling the determinacy issue, which specifically relates to the need for anchoring the price level. Fiat currency, even metallic money, can hardly be thought of as a real economic good, since its essential property, namely to yield indirect utility in the form of general purchasing power, sharply distinguishes it from commodities. Therefore Fama's interpretation is confusing because it brings us back to the metallist conception[10]. In addition to treating the metallist argument, Hall (1982b) explains the demand for, and thus the value of, money by the existence of governmental monopoly. But this seems to turn the arguments around, because it is the lack of convertibility that necessitates a limit on money issue in order to prevent a fiat money system from collapsing (Friedman, 1960). Furthermore, the emergence of a monetary economy and the demand for fiat money arise not from monopoly, whether public or private, but from the unconcerted behaviour of individuals driven only by market forces[11].

These criticisms of the NME address substantial and not merely interpretative issues. In fact, once a monetary aggregate is introduced to solve the Wicksellian indeterminacy problem, it is hard to claim the invalidity of the quantity theory, since the price level is tightly related to that aggregate. It is worth noting that major developments in the monetary system, e.g. the demise of the gold standard, did not entail abrupt changes in the theoretical framework. Again, Keynes' *Tract* is a prime example because the proposals for reform, as the title of his book indicates, are based on the quantity theory and on the foundations of classical monetary economics. Therefore Keynes revolutionized the whole conception of central bank behaviour by placing the targets of output and employment stabilization, in addition to price level stabilization, at the centre of the stage:

> In truth, the gold standard is already a barbarous relic. All of us, from the Governor of the Bank of England downwards, are now primarily interested in preserving the stability of business, prices and employment, and are not likely, when the choice is forced on us, deliberately to sacrifice these to the outworn dogma, which had its value once, of £ 3:17:10½ per ounce (Keynes, 1923, pp. 172-3).

This innovative conception of the role of the monetary authority is momentous since it sets out central bank behaviour within the modern instrument-target optimizing framework[12], as opposed to the rigid rules of a metallic standard. Yet, the reform advanced by Keynes, essentially involving the separation of the gold reserve from the note issue (1923, p. 196), far from disposing of the classical theory of money, is founded on that very theory. In fact, the characteristics of the monetary system are tightly related to the nature of money. The recognition of the distinctive properties of money, contrasted with commodities, brings us to the necessary introduction of specific arrangements which ensure the viability of the system. A case in point is the limit on the quantity of fiat money

(Friedman, 1960, ch. 1). But such arrangements do not pertain to resource allocation as studied by general equilibrium theory and, thus, Government activity in this field can hardly be thought of as regulation. It is rather connected with the "rules of the game", i.e. the stipulations which are needed for the smooth operation of the system. Regulation, instead, relates to Government interference with the market mechanism, which drives the system away from optimality.

Government regulation is also the basis of the LRT explanation of the interest rate differential between money and bonds. However, the large denomination of Treasury bills, which is assumed to be the cause of the rate of return differential between currency and US Treasury bills (Wallace, 1983, pp. 1-4), accounts for a key property of money, i.e. divisibility. In fact, the disappearance of the interest differential between currency and Treasury bills, when the latter are issued in small denominations, simply shows the importance of divisibility. If Treasury bills share this crucial monetary property, the interest rate dominance of money vanishes – not because a regulation has been cancelled, but because an asset has acquired a key monetary property.

The explanation suggested by these arguments, contrary to that of the LRT, are based on the distinctive properties of money *vis-à-vis* non-monetary assets. The rate of return dominance of money stems from the momentous role of money as an information-producing mechanism, as stressed by the modern literature on the foundations of monetary theory (Ostroy and Starr, 1990). An empirical observation that corroborates this hypothesis is the persistence in the use of money during hyperinflations. The interest rate differential between money and bonds becomes extremely high, yet money does not disappear or is not substituted for other means of payments, e.g. foreign currency, unless the inflation rate exceeds some critical threshold. This argument has been advanced by Keynes (1923, pp. 48-50) with regard to the German hyper-inflation. It has also been offered by Robertson (1957, pp. 12, 20) and, more recently, by Friedman and Schwartz (1986, p. 44), in order to emphasize the conspicuous benefits of the use of money. The latter have to do with the essential characteristics of a monetary economy contrasted with a barter economy. These characteristics do not relate to the unit of account function and to the tangibility of the means of payment only, as the NME contends, but also to the information-producing role of money which allows the decentralization of exchange.

The New Monetary Economics and Liquidity Preference
The NME makes the theory of money depend on monetary institutions. Therefore the introduction of a cashless payments system would completely invalidate current monetary theory, whether classical or Keynesian. The NME's contentions are open to serious criticism with regard to Keynesian theory, too, since, though building on principles quite different from the classical, Keynes

Journal of
Economic
Studies
21,3

46

does characterize a monetary economy with distinctive properties which are quite independent of the tangibility of the means of payments.

The classical theorists identified the store of value function of money – John Law (1705, pp. 7-8) is an early example – but did not draw any momentous analytical implications. Wicksell is a case in point. While his contribution to monetary policy foreshadows the so-called indirect transmission mechanism centred on the rate of interest, he firmly maintains a conception of money based on the medium of exchange function[5]. In Keynes' theory of liquidity preference, the speculative motive for holding money is, instead, strictly related to the store of value function. Uncertainty as to the future course of the interest rate is, then, a key element in the explanation of the demand for money. Uncertainty is central to the definition of a monetary economy, in that changes in the state of expectations vary money holdings and affect the economy via interest rate changes. The high liquidity premium that money commands *vis-à-vis* other assets assigns money peculiar properties that characterize a monetary economy contrasted with a stationary economy: "*For the importance of money essentially flows from its being a link between the present and the future*" (Keynes, 1936, p. 293; italics in the original).

The basic principles characteristic of a monetary economy in *The General Theory* are not in any way related to the outer shape of the money object and of monetary arrangements. Uncertainty about the future rates of return, and the related notion of liquidity, do not disappear with the disposal of tangible money. Indeed, if such an institutional innovation has any bearing on Keynesian liquidity preference, it is in the direction of reinforcing rather than weakening it. In fact, in an accounting system of exchange (Fama, 1980), agents choose not between currency and bonds, but between bank deposits with different degrees of risk characterizing the portfolio of financial assets against which the account has claim. As each deposit increases or decreases, the bank respectively buys or sells assets. However, agents select the riskiness of the deposit they hold and banks supply asset portfolios matching these deposits. In this payments system, the demand for "money" is dominated by the speculative motive in so far as both the transactions and the precautionary motives can be satisfied by the agent's whole portfolio. It is the allocation of the latter, then, and thus the state of expectations on the future course of interest rates, that become the crucial issue[13]. Indeed, on interpretative grounds, the NME lays further stress on the key hypothesis of Keynesian monetary theory: the role of uncertainty.

But the foregoing discussion hardly exhausts the issue, since there is much more in the *General Theory* that bears critically on the NME. The disappearance of tangible money does not affect liquidity preference theory[14], except to emphasize its essential aspects. In an accounting system of exchange, in fact, even the most short-term assets in the agent's portfolio[15] yield a positive rate of return, with the effect of increasing the interest rate threshold at which agents will shift into "money", i.e. into a greater share of highly liquid assets. Hence the central principles of Keynes' analysis do not fade away in a cashless world, but become more relevant. In particular, a main property of money, i.e. the reluctance of its own rate of return to decline, remains undiminished. Further, and more important, the existence of uncertainty can hardly be suppressed and is embedded in the definition of a monetary economy. Yet, the latter necessitates the presence not of a money object, but of any other asset with the same characteristics:

The New
Monetary
Economics

47

> Money in its significant attributes is, above all, a subtle device for linking the present to the future; and we cannot even begin to discuss the effect of changing expectations on current activities except in monetary terms. We cannot get rid of money even by abolishing gold and silver and legal tender instruments. So long as there exists any durable asset, it is capable of possessing monetary attributes and, therefore, of giving rise to the characteristic problems of a monetary economy (Keynes, 1936, p. 294).

In this regard, a brief comment on the hypothesis put forward by the LRT, closely related to the NME, is in order. From the viewpoint of Keynes' theory of money, the interest rate differential between non-interest-bearing money and interest-bearing bonds is to be explained by the essential property of money, "that its yield is *nil*, and its carrying cost negligible, but its liquidity-premium substantial" (Keynes, 1936, p. 226). In particular, Keynes singles out the very small elasticities of production and substitution to account for the liquidity premium:

> The first characteristic ... is the fact that money has, both in the long and in the short period, a zero, or at any rate a very small, elasticity of production ... The second *differentia* of money is that it has an elasticity of substitution equal, or nearly equal, to zero; which means that as the exchange value of money rises there is no tendency to substitute some other factor for it; – except, perhaps, to some trifling extent, where the money-commodity is also used in manufacture or the arts. This follows from the peculiarity of money that its utility is solely derived from its exchange-value, so that the two rise and fall *pari passu*, with the result that as the exchange value of money rises there is no motive or tendency, as in the case of rent-factors, to substitute some other factor for it.
>
> Thus not only is it impossible to turn more labour on to producing money when its labour-price rises, but also money is a bottomless sink for purchasing power, when the demand for it increases, since there is no value for it at which demand is diverted – as in the case of other rent-factors – so as to slop over into a demand for other things (Keynes, 1936, pp. 230-31).

The LRT, however, denies any distinctive property of money *vis-à-vis* other assets and assesses them only in terms of their pay-offs. The interest rate dominance of money is then viewed as an interference with equilibrium owing to Government regulations, since money is indistinguishable from other forms of wealth. This manifestly exhibits a general equilibrium approach which, as Hicks has cautioned, "is hopelessly misleading when our subject is money" (1967, p. 6). The peculiar properties of a monetary economy cannot be captured by the Walrasian model simply because there is no role for money in such a model. Once this role is recognized, non-interest-bearing money commands a liquidity premium that is again related to the essential properties of a monetary economy. This is Keynes' answer to the rhetorical question he raised while introducing liquidity preference: "But, given that the rate of interest is never

Journal of
Economic
Studies
21,3

48

negative, why should anyone prefer to hold his wealth in a form which yields little or no interest to holding it in a form which yields interest?" (1936, p. 168)[16].

The relevance of this issue clearly emerges when the implications of cancelling the interest rate differential between bonds and money are considered. An important instance is Friedman's (1969) solution to the optimum quantity of money problem, arising from the difference between the zero social cost of supplying fiat money and the positive private opportunity cost of holding it. In order to eliminate the externality, Friedman proposes to engineer a deflation rate such that the nominal interest rate on bonds is driven down to zero. But this result, as early critics (Hahn, 1971, p. 71; Tsiang, 1969, p. 267) pointed out, would make the bond market disappear: facing the same rate of return on money and bonds, agents would hold only money, given the liquidity premium it commands.

To conclude, Keynes emphasized that the peculiar features of a monetary economy do not derive from the existence of money: even if money were abolished, these properties would remain:

> If by *money* we mean the standard of value, it is clear that it is not necessarily the money-rate of interest which makes the trouble. We could not get out of our difficulties (as some have supposed) merely by decreeing that wheat or houses be the standard of value instead of gold or sterling. For, it now appears that the same difficulties will ensue if there continues to exist *any* asset of which the own-rate of interest is reluctant to decline as output increases. It may be, for example, that gold will continue to fill this role in a country which has gone over to an inconvertible paper standard (1936, p. 229; italics in the original).

Even in a non-monetary economy, in which there are only consumer goods and capital and "there is no asset for which the liquidity-premium is always in excess of the carrying-costs" (Keynes, 1936, p. 239), there will be a "scale of liquidity" relative to the different forms of holding wealth. In certain historic circumstances, land has been considered as a highly liquid asset, since, like money, it has low elasticities of production and substitution (Keynes, 1936, pp. 240-42). All in all, the essential characteristic of a monetary economy cannot be disposed of even if money does not exist.

Conclusions
The main message of this article is the independence of the essential properties of a monetary economy from the tangible character of money, in contrast with a basic proposition of the NME, according to which the introduction of a cashless payments system would invalidate received monetary theory. Both the classical and the Keynesian theories of money consider specific characteristics that define a monetary economy. The former points to the decentralization of exchange, while the latter emphasizes the existence of uncertainty as the foundation of liquidity. However, neither analysis relates the essential properties of a monetary economy to the institutional or technological features of the monetary system. While the classical and the Keynesian theories,

respectively, probe the medium of exchange and the store of value function, the NME calls attention to the unit of account function and contends that, in an accounting system of exchange, not just the money object, but also the concept of money itself disappears.

The merit of the NME is to have called attention to the evolution of monetary arrangements; but the implication that the NME has drawn as to the invalidity of received monetary theory is highly dubious. On a purely theoretical plane, the transition from tangible currency to non-tangible payments media seems a much less substantial change than the transition from metallic money to fiat money. And the latter change has not essentially altered the fundamentals of monetary theory[17]. Hence, though technological progress will probably drive towards more or less differentiated forms of cashless payment systems, it is hard to imagine that such progress would make the theory of a monetary economy invalid or altogether irrelevant. The evolution of institutions may well affect the superstructure of the theory of money without significantly falsifying its core. Keynes' contributions to the main paradigms of monetary economics corroborate this hypothesis.

Notes

1. "Let us suppose that all payments in this simpler world are handled by check or credit card, and that currency is not used. In this world, money does not exist" (Black, 1970, p. 12). Black gives credit to William Vickrey (1955, 1964) for stressing the key role of institutions in shaping monetary theory. "[Vickrey] emphasizes the fact that current monetary theory depends heavily on a rather restricted form of financial institution. He says that other institutional arrangements would make current monetary theory almost completely invalid" (1970, p. 9).

2. Wicksell's analysis of a "pure credit system" (1906, pp. 79-126) treats many of the issues raised by the NME. In his discussion of the "clearing system", Hicks explains the problem originally raised by Wicksell. "For it is with this organization [the clearing system] that we first meet a clear case of the Wicksellian phenomenon, a market in which absolute prices – money prices – are indeterminate. The money is simply a unit of account; it is not one of the traded commodities; there is therefore no supply-demand equation to determine its value. The Walras equations are sufficient to determine relative prices, prices (that is) in terms of one of the traded commodities taken as *numéraire*; but this *numéraire* is not the money in terms of which calculations are made. That money does not enter into the Walras equations; it is altogether outside them. The money prices can be at any level, yet the same Walras equilibrium will be attained" (1967, pp. 9-10).

3. "In order for the absolute price level to be determined by market-equilibrating forces, changes in it must impinge on aggregate *real* behavior in *some* market – i.e. must create excess demand in some market" (Patinkin, 1961, p. 113; italics in the original).

4. "If the term 'outside money' is interpreted as currency, and 'inside money' is taken to mean unregulated deposits, then the contention of Patinkin's statement is exactly our conclusion that controlling the supply of currency alone is sufficient to render the price level (the real value of the unit of account) determinate" (Fama, 1980, p. 53).

5. Wicksell illustrates this point: "Of the three main functions [measure of value, store of value, and medium of exchange], only the last is in a true sense characteristic of money; as a measure of value any commodity whatever might serve ... Similarly, the function of acting as a *store of value* is not essentially characteristic of money ... It is never this utility

[of precious metals] which is contemplated by those who hoard money but the object in view is nearly always that of procuring *something else* for it at a future time. In other words, it is the exchange value which it is desired to preserve; it is the money as a future medium of exchange which is hoarded" (1906, pp. 7-8; italics in the original).

6. The literature on this topic is conspicuous. See the recent survey by Ostroy and Starr (1990).

7. "The problem is how to enforce the overall budget constraint underlying market-clearing excess demands while also permitting individuals temporarily to violate these constraints in the course of fulfilling those excess demands. Again, what is called for is a record-keeping device ... Of course a commodity record-keeping device is a relatively crude instrument. The same function could be abstracted by a system of electronic fund transfers provided that accounts were monitored by an agency with sufficient police powers to punish 'over-issuers' " (Ostroy and Starr, 1990, p. 11).

8. James Tobin makes the same point. "The use of a common *numéraire* or unit of account does not logically compel the use of a common money in transactions. Commodity-for-commodity barters could be and are made with values equated by reference to *numéraire* or unit-of-account prices. But it is hard to imagine, and I suspect even harder to illustrate historically, a unit of account disembodied from a generally accepted means of payment. The dollar is our unit of account because physical dollars are generally acceptable in transactions" (1980, p. 87).

9. "It is inevitable, even in a market of the kind we are discussing, that the seller, when he is deciding whether or not to sell (or how much to sell) at a particular price, should implicitly consider what that price may be worth in terms of other goods; he must have some idea about prices before he can say whether or not a particular price-offer is acceptable" (Hicks, 1967, p. 10). On the issues raised by the notion of money considered solely as a unit of account, see Davidson (1978, pp. 148-9).

10. Schumpeter defines Theoretical Metallism as "the *theory* that it is logically essential for money to consist of, or to be 'covered' by, some commodity so that the logical source of the exchange value or purchasing power of money is the exchange value or purchasing power of that commodity, considered independently of its monetary role" (Schumpeter, 1954, p. 288; italics in the original). According to Schumpeter, the Metallist Theory of Money, "though never unchallenged prevailed substantially to the end of the nineteenth century and even beyond. It is the basis of the bulk of all analytic work in the field of money" (1954, p. 63).

11. Robert Jones, dwelling on Menger's (1892) theory of the origin of money, argues: "The approach suggests that a very common good would emerge as a first commodity money in a barter economy. The important point is that this commonness is a market characteristic of goods rather than an intrinsic physical characteristic such as portability, divisibility, or cognizability" (1976, p. 775).

12. The contemporary two-stage process of monetary policy, involving instruments, intermediate targets, and final goals, is clearly illustrated in the following passage. "The volume of the paper money, on the other hand, would be consequential, as it is at present, on the state of trade and employment, bank-rate policy and Treasury Bill policy. The governors of the system would be bank-rate and Treasury Bill policy, the objects of Government would be stability of trade, prices and employment, and the volume of paper money would be a consequence of the first (just – I repeat – as it is at present) and an instrument of the second, the precise arithmetical level of which could not and need not be predicted" (Keynes, 1923, p. 196).

13. The stronger relevance of liquidity preference theory, in the presence of interest-bearing assets which do not involve capital losses, has often been pointed out (Niehans, 1978, pp. 21, 52).

14. The only state of affairs which would do away with the speculative motive is a world with no uncertainty. "In a static society or in a society in which for any other reason no one feels any uncertainty about the future rates of interest, the Liquidity Function L_2, or the propensity to hoard (as we might term it), will always be zero in equilibrium" (Keynes, 1936, pp. 208-09).

15. According to Keynes, the maturity of the assets to be classified as "money" is a relative matter. "Without disturbance to this definition, we can draw the line between 'money' and 'debts' at whatever point is most convenient for handling a particular problem. For example, we can treat as *money* any command over general purchasing power which the owner has not parted with for a period in excess of three months, and as *debt* what cannot be recovered for a longer period than this; or we can substitute for 'three months' one month or three days or three hours or any other period; or we can exclude from *money* whatever is not legal tender on the spot. It is often convenient in practice to include in *money* time-deposits with banks and, occasionally, even such instruments as (e.g.) treasury bills. As a rule, I shall, as in my *Treatise on Money*, assume that money is co-extensive with bank deposits" (1936, p. 167 n. 1; italics in the original).

16. A similar, and better known, passage is in Keynes' *QJE* 1937 article: "Money, it is well known, serves two principal purposes ... it facilitates exchanges ... In the second place it is a store of wealth. So we are told, without a smile on the face. But in the world of the classical economy, what an insane use to which to put it! For it is a recognised characteristic of money as a store of wealth that it is barren ... Why should anyone outside a lunatic asylum wish to use money as a store of wealth?" (quoted in Davidson, 1978, p. 141).

17. In this regard, Schumpeter, in his discussion of eighteenth century contributions to monetary economics, notes: "It is but natural that most of such advance as the analysis of monetary processes made links up with metallist foundations, even where, in strict logic, the antimetallist starting-point would have been more appropriate. This should not surprise us, however: in spite of its shortcomings, theoretical metallism, properly handled, gets us almost as far as would a more correct theory – which is precisely one of the reasons why it proved so hardy a plant" (1954, p. 293).

The New
Monetary
Economics

51

References

Black, F. (1970), "Banking and Interest Rates in a World without Money: The Effects of Uncontrolled Banking", *Journal of Bank Research*, Vol. 1, Autumn, pp. 9-20.

Bryant, J. and Wallace, N. (1980), "Open Market Operations in a Model of Regulated, Insured Intermediaries", *Journal of Political Economy*, Vol. 88, February, pp. 146-73.

Burkett, P. (1990), "The Competitive Payments System: Some Stability Problems", *Journal of Post-Keynesian Economics*, Vol. 12, Summer, pp. 572-90.

Cowen, T. and Kroszner, R. (1987), "The Development of the New Monetary Economics", *Journal of Political Economy*, Vol. 95, June, pp. 567-90.

Cowen, T. and Kroszner, R. (1992), "German-language Precursors of the New Monetary Economics", *Journal of Institutional and Theoretical Economics*, Vol. 148, September, pp. 387-410.

Davidson, P. (1978), *Money and the Real World*, Macmillan, 1st edition, London, 1972.

Fama, E.F. (1980), "Banking in the Theory of Finance", *Journal of Monetary Economics*, Vol. 6, January, pp. 39-57.

Journal of
Economic
Studies
21,3

52

Friedman, M. (1960), *A Program for Monetary Stability*, Fordham University Press, New York, NY.

Friedman, M. (1969), "The Optimum Quantity of Money", in Friedman, M. (Ed.), *The Optimum Quantity of Money and Other Essays*, Aldine, Chicago, IL.

Friedman, M. and Schwartz, A.J. (1986), "Has Government Any Role in Money?", *Journal of Monetary Economics*, Vol. 17, January, pp. 37-62.

Greenfield, R.L. and Yeager, L.B. (1983), "A *Laissez-faire* Approach to Monetary Stability", *Journal of Money, Credit and Banking*, Vol. 15, August, pp. 302-15.

Hahn, F.H. (1971), "Professor Friedman's Views on Money", *Economica*, Vol. 38, February, pp. 61-80.

Hall, R.E. (1982a), "Explorations in the Gold Standard and Related Policies for Stabilizing the Dollar", in Hall, R.E. (Ed.), *Inflation: Causes and Effects*, University of Chicago Press, Chicago, IL.

Hall, R.E. (1982b), "Monetary Trends in the United States and the United Kingdom: A Review from the Perspective of New Developments in Monetary Economics", *Journal of Economic Literature*, Vol. 20, December, pp. 1552-6.

Hicks, J.R. (1935), "A Suggestion for Simplifying the Theory of Money", *Economica*, Vol. 2, February, pp. 1-19.

Hicks, J.R. (1967), *Critical Essays in Monetary Theory*, Oxford University Press, Oxford, UK.

Hoover, K.D. (1988), "Money, Prices and Finance in the New Monetary Economics", *Oxford Economic Papers*, Vol. 40, March, pp. 150-67.

Jones, R.A. (1976), "The Origin and Development of Media of Exchange", *Journal of Political Economy*, Vol. 84, August, pp. 757-75.

Keynes, J.M. (1923), *A Tract on Monetary Reform*, Macmillan, London.

Keynes, J.M. (1936), *The General Theory of Employment, Interest and Money*, Macmillan, London.

Law, J. (1705), *Money and Trade Considered*, Anderson, Edinburgh; new edition, Kelley, New York, NY, 1966.

McCallum, B.T. (1985), "Bank Deregulation, Accounting Systems of Exchange, and the Unit of Account: A Critical Review", *Carnegie-Rochester Conference Series on Public Policy*, Vol. 23, pp. 13-46.

Menger, C. (1892), "On the Origin of Money", *Economic Journal*, Vol. 2, June, pp. 239-55.

Niehans, J. (1978), *The Theory of Money*, The Johns Hopkins University Press, Baltimore, MD.

Ostroy, J.M. and Starr, R.M. (1990), "The Transactions Role of Money", in Friedman, B.M. and Hahn, F.H. (Eds), *Handbook of Monetary Economics*, North-Holland Publishing Company, Amsterdam.

Patinkin, D. (1961), "Financial Intermediaries and the Logical Structure of Monetary Theory", *American Economic Review*, Vol. 51, March, pp. 95-116.

Richter, R. (1989), *Money: Lectures on the Basis of General Equilibrium Theory and the Economics of Institutions*, Springer-Verlag, New York, NY.

Robertson, D.H. (1957), *Lectures on Economic Principles*, Vol. III, Staples Press, London.

Schumpeter, J.A. (1954), *History of Economic Analysis*, Oxford University Press, Oxford.

Smith, A. (1776), *An Inquiry into the Nature and Causes of the Wealth of Nations*, 1st edition; new edition, Cannan, E. (Ed.), The University of Chicago Press, Chicago, IL, 1976.

Sumner, S. (1990), "The Forerunners of 'New Monetary Economics' Proposals to Stabilize the Unit of Account", *Journal of Money, Credit and Banking*, Vol. 22, February, pp. 109-18.

Tobin, J. (1963), "Commercial Banks as Creators of 'Money' ", in Carson, D. (Ed.), *Banking and Monetary Studies*, Irwin, Homewood, IL.

Tobin, J. (1980), "The Overlapping Generations Model of Fiat Money: Discussion", in Karken, J.H. and Wallace, N. (Eds), *Models of Monetary Economies*, Federal Reserve Bank of Minneapolis, Minneapolis, MN.

Tsiang, S.C. (1969), "A Critical Note on the Optimum Supply of Money", *Journal of Money, Credit and Banking*, Vol. 1, May, pp. 266-80.

Vickrey, W.S. (1955), "Stability through Inflation", in Kurihara, K.K. (Ed.), *Post-Keynesian Economics*, Allen & Unwin, London.

Vickrey, W.S. (1964), *Metastatics and Macroeconomics*, Harcourt, Brace & World, New York, NY.

Wallace, N. (1983), "A Legal Restrictions Theory of the Demand for 'Money' and the Role of Monetary Policy", Federal Reserve Bank of Minneapolis *Quarterly Review*, Vol. 7, Winter, pp. 1-7.

White, L.H. (1984), "Competitive Payments Systems and the Unit of Account", *American Economic Review*, Vol. 74, September, pp. 699-712.

Wicksell, K. (1906), *Lectures on Political Economy*, Vol. 2, 1st edition; new edition, Routledge, London, 1935.

Further Reading

Greenfield, R.L. and Yeager, L.B. (1986), "Competitive Payments Systems: Comment", *American Economic Review*, Vol. 76, September, pp. 848-9.

Jevons, S.W. (1875), *Money and the Mechanism of Exchange*, C. Kegan Paul & Co., London.

The New
Monetary
Economics

53

PART III

MONETARY SYSTEMS

[8]

Kredit und Kapital, Heft 2/1999
Seiten 192 - 208

Monetary Systems and Monetary Theory

By Filippo Cesarano*, Rome

The focus of research on the international monetary system has shifted towards the study of exchange rate regimes as the evolution of monetary arrangements culminated in the abandonment of any form of convertibility. The chain of events begun in the interwar period eventually led to the overall emergence of fiat money. Milton Friedman has thus remarked: "(T)he world's current monetary system is, I believe, unprecedented. No major currency has any link to a commodity" (1986, p. 643). This epoch-making change was accompanied by the development of modern monetary policy, which, in contrast with the rules of a metallic standard, assigns the central bank an active role in the pursuit of price stability and other welfare targets. On the international plane, the choice of the exchange rate regime becomes a key issue,[1] but this is simply a necessary implication, or a mirror image, of the transformation of commodity money into a fiat instrument. The present paper, therefore, is concerned with the characteristics of the money object and, laying emphasis on the close connection between theory and institutions, investigates the changes in arrangements from a money-theoretical perspective. In a sense, it inverts the traditional approach to the subject since, instead of taking the monetary set-up as given, it looks at its evolution through the lens of theory.

The first part of this article discusses the relationships between monetary institutions and monetary theory, showing that besides contributing to the understanding of institutions, theory is an essential factor in their development. Together with the level of technology, the state of the art of monetary economics shapes monetary arrangements, which thus adapt to

---

* Thanks are due to David Laidler, Milton Friedman, Jürg Niehans, Larry White, and an anonymous referee for their perceptive comments. The usual caveat applies. The views expressed herein are those of the author and not necessarily those of the Banca d'Italia.

[1] *Krugman* regards the choice of an exchange regime "as the central intellectual question of international monetary economics" (1993, p. 4). The literature on these topics is extensive. Recent references include *Bordo* (1993), *McKinnon* (1993), and *Eichengreen* (1995).

the prevailing theory. The second part considers the development of non-tangible payment media thanks to advances in information technology. The importance of this innovation lies in its potential impact on institutional design, rather than, as the new monetary economics holds (Fama 1980; Hall 1982), on the theory of money. In fact, the complete abandonment of tangible exchange media could have far-reaching implications for the monetary system by reintroducing some of the positive features that characterized commodity standards.

I. Monetary Systems and the Theory of Money

The influence of monetary theory on the evolution of the monetary system is manifest inasmuch as the latter, throughout its history up to the early twentieth century, has been the outcome of a mistaken hypothesis, i.e. metallism.[2] Paradoxically, this very mistake, when translated into a policy norm, gave the system its strength through the credibility of the rules of the game epitomized by the so-called "gold standard mythology". However uninteresting nowadays, metallism dominated monetary economics from Aristotle onwards.[3] In classical writings the distinction between theoretical and practical metallism is often blurred since it is hard to separate the abstract argument for commodity money from the policy goal of monetary discipline. In any case, the predominance of this doctrine for such a prolonged period is puzzling.

Menger (1892) explains the emergence of exchange media as a spontaneous process, driven by market forces, through which commodities with

---

[2] *Schumpeter's* definition runs as follows: "By Theoretical Metallism we denote the *theory* that it is logically essential for money to consist of, or to be 'covered' by, some commodity so that the logical source of the exchange value or purchasing power of money is the exchange value or purchasing power of that commodity, considered independently of its monetary role. ... By Practical Metallism we shall denote sponsorship of a principle of monetary policy, namely, the principle that the monetary unit 'should' be kept firmly linked to, and freely interchangeable with, a given quantity of some commodity. Theoretical and Practical Cartalism may best be defined by the corresponding negatives" (1954, p. 288, italics in the original).

[3] "Whatever may be its shortcomings, this theory (the Metallist Theory of Money), though never unchallenged, prevailed substantially to the end of the nineteenth century and even beyond. It is the basis of the bulk of all analytic work in the field of money" (*Schumpeter* 1954, p. 63). Indeed, as recently as 1929, Hawtrey remarked: "Apart from schemes of the type favored by Mr. Keynes, paper money dissociated from gold is a monetary disease. The abuse of paper money became so prevalent during and after the World War, that it has been given an almost disproportionately important place in latter-day monetary theory" (1929, p. 698).

the highest "saleability" are selected. Modern theory dwells upon Menger's hypothesis and maintains that a very common good happens to be chosen as a first commodity money because of its market rather than physical characteristics (Jones 1976, p. 775). All the goods that performed monetary functions – cattle, salt bars, cowry shells, and the like – possessed, to varying degrees, those market properties. The selection process was guided by the search for informationally more efficient ways of settling transactions and, as a result, converged towards metals. This advance was conditioned by the state of technology. In the sixth century B.C., progress in metallurgy was in fact essential to start minting coins of uniform quality in Lydia and, hence, to fix the standard more precisely, further enhancing the informational efficiency of commodity money. The innovation soon spread to neighboring Ionian cities and throughout the Greek world (Hicks 1969, pp. 65 - 66). The singular experience of the introduction of paper money in China in the ninth century A. D. was favored by the invention of paper, ink, and printing (Tullock 1957, p. 395). But technology alone cannot account for the prevalence of metallic money for almost three thousand years; the reason must be sought elsewhere.

Primitive money may not have performed all of the traditional three functions. Evidence of an embryonic monetary mechanism can be traced back to ancient societies, such as the Sumerian, which resorted to standardized silver bars as a means of payment. Yet to the economist, a fully-fledged monetary economy emerges with the medium of exchange function which allows the decentralization of exchange. In a commodity money system, information about the quality of the means of payment is a main issue. With regard to the earliest forms of money, this guarantee was provided by merchants (Mélitz 1974, p. 92), but was then appropriated by the political authority, which at first might have commanded a higher reputation. Eventually, the role of fixing the standard and supplying the currency became instrumental to the extraction of seignorage (Friedman 1960, p. 5). In fact, throughout the whole history of metallic money, the government imposed seignorage when it had sufficient power to enforce it (Mundell 1993, p. 2) and when the economy was relatively closed (De Cecco 1987, p. 539). The opposition to this form of disguised taxation provides an early analytical basis for a tightly disciplined commodity money on grounds of distributional justice.

However, the entrance of the government into monetary arrangements has momentous implications for the role of theory in that, as soon as the operation of the system is taken over by a monopolist, an element of volition is introduced. The exercise of this power requires knowledge of the working of a monetary economy and, thus, even at the most rudimentary stage, the theory of money becomes a central factor in the evolution of monetary institutions. On the other hand, innovation in the payments system and the development of inside money have their roots in competitive market forces so that theory has had little or no effect on the growth of banks and financial intermediaries. The present paper, therefore, disregards the latter topic and concentrates exclusively on the "core" of the monetary system, i.e. the ground rules governing the standard. In contrast with the unplanned spread of banking and finance, the early role of the government as the sole issuer of the currency entailed the design of those rules on the basis of the prevailing state of the art, however backward it was. In particular, an understanding of the nature of money and of the effects of money stock variations was needed.

The classics fully grasped the functions of money, but seldom made the further analytical step to show that the performance of those functions does not require, in principle, an intrinsically useful object.[4] The most insightful writers intuited the conventional character of money but stopped short of advocating a paper standard. In his penetrating analysis, Galiani (1751, pp. 67 - 71) puts forward the key concepts of today's literature relating to the notion of money as a record-keeping device and its role in enforcing budget constraints. Nonetheless, he staunchly supports a metallic system. Hume contrasts the nature of money with that of commodities and recognizes the greater security and transportability of paper money but rejects it because of its inflationary effects (1752, pp. 35 - 36).[5] These works pave the way for the metallist view, common

---

[4] The contrast between the first and the second paragraph of the following passage by Say is eloquent: "If ... money be employed as a mere intermedial object of exchange between an object in possession and the object of desire, the choice of its material is of no great importance. Money is not desired as an object of food, of household use, or of personal covering, but for the purpose of re-sale, as it were, and re-exchange for some object of utility, after having been originally received in exchange for one such already. Money is, therefore, not an object of consumption; it passes through the hands without sensible diminution or injury; and may perform its office equally well, whether its material be gold or silver, leather or paper.

Yet, to enable it to execute its functions, it must of necessity be possessed of inherent and positive value; for no man will be content to resign an object possessed of value, in exchange for another of less value, or of none at all" (1803, pp. 220 - 21).

[5] In a letter sent to Morellet dated 10 July 1769, *Hume*, while still arguing for a commodity standard in order to maintain purchasing power stability, points out the conventional nature of money. "It is true, money must always be made of some materials, which have intrinsic value, otherwise it would be multiplied without

in classical works, which calls for a convertible paper standard in order to restrain the money stock. This policy prescription, however, does not exclude the conventional character of money on a purely abstract plane. As Mill shows (1848, pp. 542 - 55), an inconvertible paper currency circulates on the sole basis of convention[6] and its value is regulated by the principle of fixing the quantity, which ultimately depends on the fiat of the monetary authority. This lucid analysis notwithstanding, Mill fiercely opposes the introduction of paper money because it would allow discretion in monetary management, the effects of which are pernicious.

> "Such a power (of issuing inconvertible currency), in whomsoever vested, is an intolerable evil. All variations in the value of the circulating medium are mischievous: they disturb existing contracts and expectations, and the liability to such changes renders every pecuniary engagement of long date entirely precarious. ... Not to add, that the issuers may have, and in the case of a government paper, always have, a direct interest in lowering the value of the currency, because it is the medium in which their own debts are computed." (1848, p. 544)

The originality and modernity of Mill's contribution is evident. On theoretical grounds, inflation tampers with the price system and heightens uncertainty about long-run commitments. Underlying this approach is an equilibrium or natural rate hypothesis that excludes increases in output through engineered changes in money. In the realm of policy, he stresses the need to check money creation and to design a system that attains this objective. The high information content of a commodity standard effectively constrains policymakers' behavior. This provides the rationale for preferring a metallic system to a rule governing an inconvertible paper currency, i.e. maintaining the market price of bullion at the mint price (Mill 1848, pp. 545 - 46). Such an advanced analysis is

---

end, and would sink to nothing. But, when I take a shilling, I consider it not as a useful metal, but as something which another will take from me; and the person who shall convert it into metal is, probably, several millions of removes distant. ... Our shillings and sixpences, which are almost our only silver coin, are so much worn by use, that they are twenty, thirty, or forty per cent below their original value; yet they pass currency which can arise only from a tacit convention. Our colonies in America, for want of specie, used to coin a paper currency; which were not bank notes, because there was no place appointed to give money in exchange; yet this paper currency passed in all payments, by convention; and might have gone on, had it not been abused by the several assemblies, who issued paper without end, and thereby discredited the currency" (1752, pp. 214 - 15).

[6] "In the case supposed (of an inconvertible paper currency), the functions of money are performed by a thing which derives its power for performing them solely from convention; but convention is quite sufficient to confer the power; since nothing more is needful to make a person accept anything as money, and even at any arbitrary value, than the persuasion that it will be taken from him on the same terms by others" (*Mill* 1848, p. 542).

hard to find in later works which also advocate metallism but support it with much less refined arguments. Jevons's discussion of inconvertible paper money (1875, pp. 234 - 37), for instance, compares rather poorly with Mill's.

This concise account of classical thinking points to the overall dominance of metallism and of a model of the economy based on the existence of a stable equilibrium, which both bear upon the widespread support of a commodity money system. There were, of course, exceptions to this ruling paradigm – e.g. the inflationist views of Thomas Attwood and the Birmingham School – but they had little or no following. The classics consider the economy as self-adjusting and, thus, do not even conceive of an activist use of the monetary instrument within a welfare optimizing framework. This theoretical approach goes hand in hand with the rules of a metallic standard inhibiting variations in the money stock. The latter were, in fact, resorted to only in exceptional circumstances.

A metallic system, however, can suffer from an excess of discipline in that it may not allow sufficient growth in the money stock to stabilize the price level. In the last quarter of the nineteenth century, characterized by declining prices, a wide debate developed on monetary reforms designed to attain a stable purchasing power (Laidler 1991, ch. 6). A gradual but steady process led to support for the introduction of discretional elements into the rigid rules of commodity standards. Throughout this period and even beyond the First World War, a stable price level remained the only target and the analysis was still based on the model of classical economics with the assumption of equilibrium stability. Afterwards, however, both metallism and the equilibrium hypothesis were criticized and eventually overturned, thus ending a tradition that dated back to the dawn of monetary theory. Keynes's *Tract* (1923) marks this epoch-making intellectual departure by providing a thorough critique of the gold standard. The monetary authority is assigned an active role in stabilizing the price level, output, and employment (1923, pp. 172 - 73).[7]

---

[7] Keynes's analysis was at the time a radical one and represented a minority position. Only in the thirties, after the shock of the Great Depression, did his ideas gain ground. Nonetheless, a group of continental writers continued to advocate a metallic standard emphasizing the problem arising from its demise. Ludwig von Mises gave an early warning of the danger of discretionary monetary policy, both from a political and a macroeconomic viewpoint. In particular, he anticipates the key argument, i.e. the lack of knowledge of the transmission mechanism underlying Friedman's simple rule. "The ideal of a money with an exchange value that is not subject to variations due to changes in the ratio between the supply of money and the need for it – that is, a money with an invariable *innere objektive*

To this end Keynes turns the design of monetary arrangements upside-down: instead of setting up rules to constrain central bank behavior, the system must allow freedom of action to the policymaker.

From an international economics viewpoint, the counterpart to this position is the call for flexible exchange rates. Keynes discusses at length (1923, ch. IV) the choice between price level and exchange rate stabilization and supports the former since, under fixed exchange rates, the adjustment mechanism is too slow and costly in terms of employment and real income. A flexible exchange rate regime complements an analytical framework in which the stock of fiat money is maneuvered by the central bank to control the price level and the business cycle. Hence, a key aspect underlying the choice between fixed and flexible exchange rates hinges on alternative views about the nature of money and the equilibrium properties of the economy. Once the target of stabilizing output and employment opens the Pandora's box of a fiat medium of exchange, it seems hard to go back to commodity money, or to any other system whose rules strictly constrain central bank behavior. It is eloquent that Milton Friedman, the arch-enemy of discretionary monetary policy, regards "a return to a gold standard as neither desirable nor feasible" (1986, p. 646) despite the cost of a low degree of long-run price-level predictability in the presence of fiat money. In such a system, it may be further remarked, deflation is an unlikely event since it is difficult to imagine a persistent decline in prices engineered by the monetary authority. To use a recurrent metaphor, today's monetary system is, in a sense, exposed to inflationary drift insofar as it lacks a monetary anchor and exchange rate flexibility reflects this state of affairs.

A main implication of the transition to fiat money is the possibility of implementing continuous as opposed to once-and-for-all changes in the money stock. This is important not only from the viewpoint of pure theory, but also on policy grounds. First, it raises the time inconsistency

---

Tauschwert – demands the intervention of a regulating authority in the determination of the value of money; and its continued intervention. But here immediately most serious doubts arise from the circumstance, already referred to, that we have no useful knowledge of the quantitative significance of given measures intended to influence the value of money. More serious still is the circumstance that we are by no means in a position to determine with precision whether variations have occurred in the exchange value of money from any cause whatever, and if so to what extent, quite apart from the question of whether such changes have been effected by influences working from the monetary side. Attempts to stabilize the exchange value of money in this sense must therefore be frustrated at the outset by the fact that both their goal and the road to it are obscured by a darkness that human knowledge will never be able to penetrate" (*Mises* 1912, p. 269).

problem, which, in a metallic standard, was solved by the very rules of the system. Second, it allows monetary financing of the public deficit even for sizable amounts, with virtually no time limit. Under the gold standard, this policy could only be temporary since it involved a publicly announced breaking of the rules, namely the suspension of convertibility or a variation of the unit of account, but the latter could not be implemented day to day and the former was subject to the limit of the "restoration rule" (McKinnon 1993, pp. 6 - 7), which required the re-establishment of the traditional mint parity. True, even metallic standards had elements of discretion but a crucial difference compared with fiat money was the exceptional nature of recourse to them. Indirect evidence is provided by the behavior of the price level which remained roughly constant in both Britain and the United States during the periods 1740 - 1930 and 1832 - 1932 respectively (Friedman 1986, p. 643). In a fiat money system, instead, no announcement is needed about policy shifts, which, in any case, are not constrained by pre-set rules. When all countries are on an irredeemable paper standard, a fixed exchange rate regime is a fragile construction.[8] The refusal to disinflate the American economy in 1971 in order to prolong the Bretton Woods system was, rather than a schizophrenic attitude as argued by McKinnon (1993, p. 39), simply the consequence of the epochal change in the approach to money and monetary policy. Having assigned a central place to discretionary policymaking, it was natural for the U.S. not to sacrifice domestic targets to maintain the stability of the international monetary system. Indeed, the factors singled out by Bordo to account for the short life of the Bretton Woods system – 1. two fatal flaws in its design: the gold exchange standard and the adjustable peg; 2. the failure of the United States to maintain price stability after 1965; and 3. the reluctance of the other major industrial countries to follow U.S. leadership when it conflicted with their national interests (1993, p. 83) – all boil down to the spread of managed fiat money.

All in all, the history of monetary institutions has been conditioned by the government having early arrogated to itself the role of fixing the standard and supplying the currency. This monopolistic element has pushed market forces, which were a key factor in the origin of money

---

[8] According to *Giovannini*, "a fixed-exchange-rate system under a fiat currency regime is a monetary rule ... only under two rather strong conditions: that the exchange rate is a more credible target than any other monetary target and that the international system has built-in features that discourage global inflation (penalties for deficit countries or independent and conservative central bankers)" (1993, p. 114).

and the introduction of fiduciary instruments as less costly ways of settling transactions, away from the core of the monetary system and has
given theory a prominent place. Indeed, the transition from commodity
to fiat money was accompanied by the major turn in theory away from
metallism and the model of classical economics.

II. Non-Tangible Payment Media and the Monetary System

Technical progress has often been the driving force in the development
of monetary institutions. A notable example is the introduction of the
steam-powered stamping press in the early eighteenth century, which set
the pace of the diffusion of the gold standard (Redish 1990). In recent
decades, an equally momentous breakthrough has been determined by
computing technology that substitutes electronic signals for physical
payment media. From a theoretical viewpoint, however, the shift from
commodity to fiat money is much more significant than that from fiat to
non-tangible money, since the latter merely concerns the outer shape of
the means of payment already severed from its commodity characteristic.[9] Replacing dollar bills with electronic signals is, in analytical terms,
a much less dramatic change than introducing irredeemable paper
money in place of metallic currency. Nevertheless, the substitution of an
accounting system of exchange for tangible fiat money may considerably
influence the design and operation of monetary arrangements.

The quantum jump in information and computation technology has
brought about substantial changes in the financial industry, fostering the
growth of new products, increasing social welfare, raising the industry's
overall efficiency. This development is not without consequences for the
main properties of the monetary system. Indeed, the introduction of fiduciary elements in the metallic standards of the nineteenth century set in
motion major innovations, which eventually gave rise to central banking
and modern monetary policy. Likewise, the current innovations in pay-

---

[9] "Increasing the use of cash-cards substituting for cash is comparable to
increasing the use of checks relative to cash. ... The mentioned developments
increase the efficiency of the MOE (medium of exchange) because they allow individuals to transact without incurring 'shoe-leather costs' for obtaining cash and
for gathering information about products and services. The developments do not
fundamentally change the payment system, however, because they still depend
strongly on national banking systems. In the terminology of monetary theory the
cash cards and the use of credit and payment cards for electronic payments
increase the velocity of money issued by central banks" (*Eliasson* and *Wihlborg*
1998, pp. 8 - 9).

ment technology, pointing towards non-tangible money, may well introduce entirely new features in the monetary mechanism.[10] The enhanced efficiency of payment media supplied by private issuers will erode central banks' seignorage. Moreover, in countries experiencing substantial price increases, the base of the inflation tax will shrink, thus reducing this source of government revenue. In the short run, however, a significant role remains for central banks, not because of the issuing monopoly granted by law, but rather for reasons relating to the microfoundations of money. On empirical grounds, Friedman and Schwartz (1986, p. 44) emphasize the continued use of money in countries hit by hyperinflation, even if alternatives are available, in order to call attention to the value people attach to a single unit of value and medium of exchange. The basis of this observation is the notion of money as a record-keeping device, i.e. as an information-producing mechanism allowing the decentralization of exchange. The cost, in the form of an information loss, of parting with the money already in circulation is so great that it overcomes the huge tax due to hyperinflation. Hence, private competitors are challenging the central bank not by offering a different money but by dramatically improving the efficiency of the payment system to the point of making physical exchange media totally obsolete.

This is the state of affairs envisaged by Fama (1980) in a well-known article which pioneered the so-called "new monetary economics". The main function of banks is to maintain an accounting system of exchange that, in contrast with currency, does not require a physical medium. Banks invest customers' deposits in securities and thus perform a second major function, portfolio management. Since the portfolio management activities of banks, in a competitive environment, are subject to the Modigliani-Miller theorem, there is no need to control the stock of either deposits or securities to obtain a stable general equilibrium with respect to output and the price level. As Fama (1980, p. 49) acknowledges, however, this result relates to a Walrasian, not to a monetary economy. The accounting system of exchange reflects a Walrasian world, in which money plays no essential role, and thus runs into the Wicksellian price level indeterminacy problem. There are, in fact, no well-defined demand and supply functions for money by means of which to assign the unit of account determinate prices in terms of other commodities.[11] As long as

---

[10] The effects of the advance in electronic payment systems on commercial banks are not addressed in the present paper but are examined by *Eliasson* and *Wihlborg* (1998).

[11] In his discussion of the "clearing system", *Hicks* explains the problem originally raised by Wicksell's analysis of a "pure credit system" (1906, pp. 79 - 126).

currency survives because of a higher level of efficiency, the indeterminacy problem does not arise. Yet, this state of affairs may not last. Currency velocity would then tend to infinity, which is but another angle from which to view the indeterminacy problem (Eliasson and Wihlborg 1998, p. 9).

The principle of bank clearing is of course not new. The growth of the banking industry prompted classical economists to envisage universal bank accounts together with the elimination of cash as an "ideal case" (Mill 1848, p. 524). Jevons (1875, pp. 303 - 304) even imagined a "world's clearing house". Amid this widespread debate, Wicksell's analysis of a "pure credit economy" (1906, pp. 87 - 126) was a main contribution to the understanding of a payment system devoid of currency. The present-day advance in communications and computing has given content to a pure abstract framework and represents a further stage of an evolutionary process. The cashless society may not be at hand insofar as transaction costs, accounting and anonymity features make currency hard to replace (Shubik 1990, pp. 191 - 92), although this opinion may underestimate future progress in transaction technology.[12] However, the issue here is not factual. The important point is whether the set of rules governing non-tangible money can restore monetary discipline.

Viable standards must rest on a peg and, very often, proposals for reform have simply changed the type of peg. Any monetary system is organized on the basis of "rules of the game" that assure its viability: fixing the metal content of the monetary unit in the gold standard and

---

"For it is with this organization (the clearing system) that we first meet a clear case of the Wicksellian phenomenon, a market in which absolute prices – money prices – are indeterminate. The money is simply a unit of account; it is not one of the traded commodities; there is therefore no supply-demand equation to determine its value. The Walras equations are sufficient to determine relative prices, prices (that is) in terms of one of the traded commodities taken as numeraire; but this numeraire is not the money in terms of which calculations are made. That money does not enter into the Walras equations; it is altogether outside them. The money prices can be at any level, yet the same Walras equilibrium will be attained" (1967, pp. 9 - 10). Patinkin's solution of the Wicksellian problem hinges on the following point. "(I)n order for the absolute price level to be determined by market-equilibrating forces, changes in it must impinge on aggregate *real* behavior in *some* market – i.e., must create excess demand in some market" (*Patinkin* 1961, p. 113, italics in the original).

12 According to *The Economist* (29 January 1994, vol. 330, pp. 71 - 72), the National Westminster Bank is experimenting with a smart card that can be used both to pay and to receive money in up to five different currencies. Furthermore, the recent technology of "digital cash" allows to preserve the payer's anonymity in electronic deposit transfers. I owe this information to Larry White.

setting a limit on the quantity of fiat money are examples of rules. Commodity standards have dominated throughout history because of the simplicity of their rules.[13] A pure commodity-money system, as long as there is no interference in the market of the money commodity, only requires the definition of the unit of account. The momentous implication of the simplicity of such rules is the easy detection of breaking them: this enhances enforcement and, thus, credibility. These characteristics are maintained even after the introduction of fiduciary elements through convertibility (see the discussion of Mill's views in section I.). Things become quite different, however, in a fiat money standard, which not only lacks a mechanism to control money creation but also, and more importantly, lacks a direct and timely informational device to monitor the behavior of the issuing authority. Commodity money, which rested on the myth of metallism, was immune from such failures. Nowadays, a new myth is not available and the system must be built on more solid foundations.

In a fiat money regime, the degree of discipline characteristic of commodity standards seems difficult to restore. Resort to written, constitutional rules to bind policymakers' behavior would not do insofar as any commitment technology is doomed to fail if it is difficult to monitor and is not based upon widely held tenets. Credible rules should be founded on principles that are derived from theory, not artificially constructed. In the past, the unyielding trust in commodity money gave rise to the principles of metallism. Today, the eventual evolution towards an accounting system of exchange could bring forth a different set of principles to fill the void left by the collapse of the metallist myth. With the disappearance of tangible means of payment, theory calls for the control of a nominal quantity which acts as a peg or an anchor of the price level (Patinkin 1961) and thus solves the Wicksellian indeterminacy problem. In an advanced monetary environment where physical exchange media have long vanished, a constant stock of a fiat instrument – even, say, a single dollar bill, if we disregard the inconvenience of quoting prices in trillionths – simply satisfies the technical requirement of making the price

---

[13] Commenting on the difficulty of implementing a plan designed to prevent inflation, *Peter Bernholz* notes: "The pure gold and silver standards had one clear advantage. The rule of convertibility of bank notes against the precious metal and vice versa, at a fixed parity, could always be tested by everybody and could not be easily reinterpreted by governments, central banks, or supreme courts" (1987, p. 103). He then puts forward a radical proposal, i.e. to "institute a pure gold standard, and allow free banking" (1987, p. 104), inspired by the successful Scotch free banking system.

level determinate. This requirement, it should be emphasized, is quite distinct from a guideline for monetary policy. More important, it is dictated by theory and is difficult to tamper with precisely because it admits no variation at all. Thus, violations are immediately detectable[14] and the system regains the simple, easily enforceable and credible rules of commodity money. Paradoxically, the complete demise of tangible payment media leads to an institutional framework whose properties are, in some respects, like those of the earlier commodity standards. This result rests on the solution of Wicksellian indeterminacy, which necessitates a clear-cut technical requirement to assure viability. If this were thought of as natural and ineluctable, as metallism was, then the system would lose the man-made character of fiat money and re-establish unquestionable rules of the game as in a commodity standard proper.

Besides currency and commodity money, price level determinacy can also be obtained by imposing reserve requirements (Fama 1980, pp. 51 - 53). Such requirements are a form of government regulation because the demand for non-interest bearing central bank reserves would otherwise not exist. But this may be short-lived. In fact, in a context of accelerating technological progress, the problem common to all the solutions – currency, commodity money, and reserve requirements – is their long-term survival. The exploitation of profit opportunities can hardly be stopped by government. Indeed, the search for less costly ways of executing transactions has been the driving force of monetary evolution since its dawn. The only limit to this spontaneous, natural process is the specific requirement for assuring the system's viability, as suggested by the prevailing theory. Hence, credible solutions of the determinacy problem should not have the character of regulation but must rest on firm analytical foundations.

A final word of caution is in order. In this advanced state of monetary arrangements, money supply changes aimed at pursuing welfare targets are excluded, though the government can still influence economic activ-

---

14 *Friedman* has called for such a rule, albeit in the traditional context of monetary policy in a tangible money world. "Why zero growth? Zero has a special appeal on political grounds that is not shared by any other number. If 3 percent, why not 4 percent? It is hard, as it were, to go to the political barricades to defend 3 rather than 4, or 4 rather than 5. But zero is – as a psychological matter – qualitatively different. It is what has come to be called a Schelling point – a natural point at which people tend to agree, like 'splitting the difference' in a dispute over a monetary sum. Moreover, by removing any power to create money it eliminates institutional arrangements lending themselves to discretionary changes in monetary growth" (1984, p. 50).

ity through other policies. The financial industry is completely deregulated and banks, besides managing the payments system, are portfolio managers matching the demand for and supply of assets held by the public. The disappearance of monetary policy may be either hailed as progress or viewed as a step backward, depending on whether the equilibrium hypothesis is accepted or refused. During the last quarter of a century, the pendulum has swung back towards the classical model, thus rejecting the possibility of steering the economy on a superior welfare trajectory through active monetary management. But the subject, one of the most controversial in economics, is far from being settled. A necessary condition for the emergence of the state of affairs described in the present section is the rejection of discretionary monetary policy on the basis of an equilibrium model. Then, the flexibility of the real sector of the economy, enhanced by the removal of regulation and the spread of information, could match the advance in transaction technology and draw near the kind of frictionless world underlying the classical paradigm. In this scenario, the rules of an accounting system of exchange would allow only once-and-for-all changes in the money stock in response to extraordinary events, as in commodity standards.

III. Concluding Remarks

The early appropriation by the government of the money issuing function has introduced a volitional element in the design of the monetary system whose evolution has thus been conditioned by the progress of monetary theory. Throughout history up to the early twentieth century, metallism and the equilibrium model of the economy provided the analytical foundations of commodity standards. The critique of both principles after the First World War turned the approach to monetary arrangements upside down paving the way for the development of fiat money. However, the benefit of the resource saving associated with the abandonment of commodity money must be set against the lack of long-term price level predictability. In the current system, discipline is hard to impose and, thus, the credibility problem, which the rules of a commodity standard solved from the very start, is now rather intractable. Hence, Friedman has noted "that there is need for either some anchor to provide long-term price predictability, some substitute for convertibility into a commodity, or, alternatively, some device that would make predictability unnecessary" (1986, p. 646).

Substantial advances in information and communication technology could bring forth such a device in order to assure the viability of an accounting system of exchange. The constant stock of a fiat instrument needed to make the price level determinate is indeed a technical device to anchor the system, much like convertibility in metallic standards. Underneath this institutional framework, it should be recalled, there is a conception of the equilibrium properties of the economy that leads back to the classical approach. Unless this "vision" were firmly held by both policymakers and society at large, the new monetary order could hardly emerge despite the available technology. The history of monetary arrangements is indeed conditioned by the limitations of theory.

The foregoing discussion should not be interpreted as a proposal for reform – exercises of this kind are as abundant as they are ephemeral and uninteresting – but as an analysis of the evolution of monetary arrangements. Innovation in domestic money is eventually transferred to the international arena, although reform projects, even the most brilliant and original ones, such as Wicksell's and Fisher's, are often checked by the influence of the prevailing theory. The diffusion of a new monetary system is, in fact, a complex process and difficult to initiate.[15] The progress in payment technology may eventually foster theoretical advances providing the foundation of an innovative and more stable monetary system.

References

Bernholz, Peter: "The Implementation and Maintenance of a Monetary Constitution", in James A. Dorn and Anna J. Schwartz, eds., *The Search for Stable Money. Essays on Monetary Reform*, Chicago, The University of Chicago Press, 1987. – *Bordo*, Michael D.: "The Bretton Woods International Monetary System: A Historical Overview", in Bordo and Eichengreen (1993). – *Bordo*, Michael D./*Eichengreen*, Barry, eds.: *A Retrospective on the Bretton Woods System. Lessons for International Monetary Reform*, Chicago, The University of Chicago Press, 1993. –

---

15 The following episode is reported by Gordon *Tullock:* "The necessity of a lengthy indoctrination in the use of paper money before an inflationary policy becomes possible can be illustrated by an incident which occurred during the Mongol dynasty. The Mongol IlKhans in Persia, impressed by the use of paper money by their suzerain in China, decided to use the same device themselves. Technical advisers were sent from Peking, and an elaborate organization was set up. The Persians, however, had not been accustomed to the use of paper currency by several hundred years of gradual developments. They simply refused to believe that these nicely printed pieces of paper were worth anything, and the experiment was a failure" (1957, p. 395, f. 5).

De Cecco, Marcello: "Gold Standard", in John Eatwell, Murray Milgate and Peter Newman, eds., *The New Palgrave. A Dictionary of Economics*, London, Macmillan, 1987. – *Eichengreen*, Barry: "The Endogeneity of Exchange Rates Regimes", in Peter B. Kenen, ed., *Understanding Interdependence*, Princeton, Princeton University Press, 1995. – *Eliasson*, Gunnar/*Wihlborg*, Clas: "Electronic Money. New Markets for Banks, Markets for New Banks, or Markets for Non-Banks", Paper presented at the International Joseph A. Schumpeter Conference, Vienna, June 1998. – *Fama*, Eugene F.: "Banking in the Theory of Finance", *Journal of Monetary Economics*, January 1980, *6*, 39 - 57. – *Friedman*, Milton: *A Program for Monetary Stability*, New York, Fordham University Press, 1960. – *Friedman*, Milton: "Monetary Policy for the 1980s", in John H. Moore, ed., *To Promote Prosperity: U.S. Domestic Policy in the Mid-1980s*, Stanford, Hoover Institution, 1984. – *Friedman*, Milton: "The Resource Cost of Irredeemable Paper Money", *Journal of Political Economy*, June 1986, *94*, 642 - 47. – *Friedman*, Milton/*Schwartz*, Anna J.: "Has Government Any Role in Money?", *Journal of Monetary Economics*, January 1986, *17*, 37 - 62. – *Galiani*, Ferdinando: *On Money*, (1751), translated by Peter R. Toscano, Ann Arbor, University Microfilms International, 1977. – *Giovannini*, Alberto: "Bretton Woods and Its Precursors: Rules versus Discretion in the History of International Monetary Regimes", in Bordo and Eichengreen (1993). – *Hall*, Robert, E.: "*Monetary Trends in the United States and the United Kingdom*: A Review from the Perspective of New Developments in Monetary Economics", *Journal of Economic Literature*, December 1982, *20*, 1552 - 56. – *Hawtrey*, Ralph G.: "Money", in *The Encyclopaedia Britannica*, 14th edition, London, The Encyclopaedia Britannica Company, 1929. – *Hicks*, John R.: *Critical Essays in Monetary Theory*, Oxford, Oxford University Press, 1967. – *Hicks*, John R.: *A Theory of Economic History*, Oxford, Oxford University Press, 1969. – *Hume*, David: "Of Money", (1752) in Eugene Rotwein, ed., *Writings on Economics*, Madison, The University of Wisconsin Press, 1970. – *Jevons*, Stanley W.: *Money and the Mechanism of Exchange*, London, C. Kegan Paul & Co., 1875. – *Jones*, Robert A.: "The Origin and Development of Media of Exchange", *Journal of Political Economy*, August 1976, *84*, 757 - 75. – *Keynes*, John M.: *A Tract on Monetary Reform*, London, Macmillan, 1923. – *Krugman*, Paul: "What Do We Need to Know About the International Monetary System?", Essays in International Finance No. 190, Princeton, N. J., Princeton University, International Finance Section, July 1993. – *Laidler*, David: *The Golden Age of the Quantity Theory. The Development of Neoclassical Monetary Economics 1870 - 1914*, New York, Allan, 1991. – *McKinnon*, Ronald, I.: "The Rules of the Game: International Money in Historical Perspective", *Journal of Economic Literature*, March 1993, *31*, 1 - 44. – *Mélitz*, Jacques: *Primitive and Modern Money*, Reading, Mass., Addison Wesley, 1974. – *Menger*, Carl: "On the Origin of Money", *Economic Journal*, June 1892, *2*, 239 - 55. – *Mill*, John Stuart: *Principles of Political Economy*, (1848), edited with an introduction by William Ashley, London, Longmans, Green & Co., 1909. – *Mises*, Ludwig von: *The Theory of Money and Credit*, (1912), Indianapolis, IN, Liberty Classics, 1981. – *Mundell*, Robert: "Prospects for the International Monetary System", Paper presented at the Conference on "The Future of the International Monetary System and its Institutions", Geneva, September 2 - 4, 1993. – *Patinkin*, Don: "Financial Intermediaries and the Logical Structure of Monetary Theory", *American Economic Review*, March 1961, *51*, 95 - 116. – *Redish*, Angela: "The Evolution of the Gold Standard in England", *Journal of Economic History*, December 1990, *50*, 789 - 805. – *Say*,

Jean-Baptiste: *A Treatise on Political Economy*, (1803), New York, Kelley, 1971. – *Schumpeter*, Joseph A.: *History of Economic Analysis*, Oxford, Oxford University Press, 1954. – *Shubik*, Martin: "A Game Theoretic Approach to the Theory of Money and Financial Institutions", in Benjamin M. Friedman and Frank H. Hahn, eds., *Handbook of Monetary Economics*, Amsterdam, North-Holland, 1990. – *Tullock*, Gordon: "Paper Money – A Cycle in Cathay", *Economic History Review*, April 1957, *9*, 393 - 407. – *Wicksell*, Knut: *Lectures on Political Economy*, (1906), vol. 2, London, Routledge, 1935.

Summary

Monetary Systems and Monetary Theory

The evolution of monetary arrangements is analyzed from a theoretical perspective showing that, together with technology, the theory of money is an essential factor in the development of monetary institutions. The diffusion of non-tangible payment media will impinge on the monetary system, possibly allowing for the reestablishment of some of the positive features that characterized commodity standards. (JEL E 42, F 33)

Providing for the optimum quantity of money

Filippo Cesarano
Banca d'Italia, Rome, Italy

Milton Friedman's theory of the optimum quantity of money (1969) is a most original contribution to monetary economics. The outcome of this analysis, the Friedman Rule or Chicago Rule involving a rate of deflation sufficient to bring the nominal interest rate down to zero, "is undoubtedly one of the most celebrated propositions in modern monetary theory, probably the most celebrated proposition in what one might call 'pure' monetary theory" (Woodford, 1990, p. 1068). However, as Woodford points out in his thorough survey, the subject is much more complex than Friedman's argument would suggest and, consequently, the results may not be immediately applicable to actual policy. In fact, some critical observations have been made from a purely theoretical standpoint. In particular, it was soon noted (Barro and Fischer, 1976, p. 144; Hahn, 1971, p. 71; Tsiang, 1969, p. 267) that the implementation of the Chicago Rule would make the bond market disappear. If the nominal interest rate is zero, the rates of return on money and bonds are equal and agents hold only money given its "liquidity" character. Hence, far from satiating people with cash balances, the rule would instead make the demand for money insatiable, as long as no one would be willing to borrow or lend but would hold cash exclusively. Moreover, in formal models of monetary economies, the Friedman Rule leads to the indeterminacy of stationary equilibrium, since agents would accumulate money balances beyond the minimum needed for transactions (Grandmont and Younès, 1973, p. 159; Niehans, 1978, p. 79). The present paper discusses these strictures and argues that they stem from the application of the welfare theorems of general equilibrium theory to a monetary economy. It then shows how, the consistency of those critical observations notwithstanding, the optimal solution can still be implemented.

The optimum quantity of money
The optimum quantity of money proposition is founded on the externality that affects the level of real cash balances. In order to accumulate money, the agent must bear the cost of forsaking consumption, but this pushes down the price level and, thus, confers benefits to others for which he/she receives no compensation. However, whereas it appears costly to the individual to raise real money holdings, society can increase them at no cost by engineering a fall in the

Thanks are due to Robert Clower, Frank Hahn, David Laidler, Jacques Mélitz, Jürg Niehans, and two anonymous referees for their useful comments. The usual caveat applies. The views expressed herein are those of the author and not necessarily those of the Banca d'Italia.

Journal of Economic Studies,
Vol. 25 No. 6, 1998, pp. 441-449,
© MCB University Press, 0144-3585

Journal of
Economic
Studies
25,6

442

price level[1]. The same point can be made more directly in the presence of assets alternative to money. While agents perceive the opportunity cost of increasing their money balances as equal to the foregone interest on non-monetary assets, society can costlessly carry out such an increase through a reduction of the price level. These arguments account for the non-optimality of cash balances in *laissez-faire* insofar as the agent holds that amount whose benefit, at the margin, matches the perceived private cost. The socially optimal solution, i.e. the Friedman Rule, involves a rate of deflation equal to the rate of time preference, which brings the nominal interest rate to zero and real money balances to the satiation level.

This theory is widely accepted. Distinguishing between a weak and a strong form of the Friedman proposition, Woodford (1990, pp. 1070-3) argues for the general validity of the former since the latter (which requires superneutrality) holds in special cases only. Although this represents the prevailing view of the profession, Friedman's clear-cut analysis, as mentioned in the introduction, raises problems which demand a detailed examination.

The Chicago Rule drives to zero the discrepancy between the social and the private cost of holding real cash balances. Since these are regarded as a free good, the quantity should be increased to satiety, i.e. to the point that the marginal utility becomes zero, in order to satisfy Pareto optimality. This proposition of course refers to the *stock* marginal utility of money, which is the increase in utility from holding a unit of real cash balances. In fact, the *flow* marginal utility of money, i.e. the utility of an additional dollar spent, can never be zero. It is a commonplace of monetary theory that money, as contrasted with commodities, yields indirect utility in the form of purchasing power. Consequently, no one would ever refuse an additional dollar unless the purchasing power of money were zero or resources were not scarce as in a state of perfect bliss. Satiation of real cash balances thus relates to the stock marginal utility of money (Niehans, 1978, pp. 74-5). Yet a tight relationship links marginal stock to flow values because, for any asset or durable consumer good, individuals will make the marginal stock value equal to its opportunity cost, i.e. its yield. The Chicago Rule, by driving the nominal interest rate down to zero in order to have zero stock marginal utility of money, puts a wedge between the stock and the flow marginal utility of money since the latter is strictly positive. Hence, the eventual outcomes of the optimal rule, namely the disappearance of the bond market and the insatiety of the demand for money[2], are accounted for by the discrepancy between the stock and flow marginal value of money holdings that the rule itself creates. The Chicago Rule focuses on money as an asset to be held, i.e. on its stock characteristic. But it is hard to imagine the stock of an asset severed from its flow of services. And all the harder in the case of money, since its service flow has the peculiar property of maintaining a strictly positive marginal utility. This explanation ultimately rests on the postulate of the indirect utility of money, which, in turn, derives from the essential properties of a monetary economy.

98 Money and Monetary Systems

The lack of any meaningful role for money in the general equilibrium model, underlined by Hahn and Clower in the mid-1960s, has generated a copious literature (see the excellent survey by Ostroy and Starr (1990) that attempts to spell out the distinctive characteristics of an exchange economy in which, in contrast with a Walrasian economy, trade takes place between agents. An important result of this literature is that money allows the decentralization of exchange through the enforcement of budget constraints, thus providing for an information-producing mechanism which entails the exploitation of the gains from trade. These modern contributions have buttressed the classical theory of money, which considers money's medium of exchange function as primary, the others – unit of account and store of value – playing a subordinate role[3].

The Chicago Rule seems to overlook the distinctive properties of a monetary economy, insofar as it considers money like a free good in the Walrasian model, on the same score as air in an unpolluted environment. However, while no one would ever think of paying a price for air, everybody eagerly accepts a dollar bill insofar as it can purchase scarce commodities. In fact, only the stock marginal utility of money can conceivably be driven to zero, but the flow marginal utility cannot. In the latter sense, satiety of cash balances would imply satiety of commodities. Hence, the straightforward application of general equilibrium theory to money is quite misleading, given the positive flow marginal utility of money embedded in the medium of exchange function. This property reflects the essential features of a monetary economy as contrasted with a barter economy and holds not only for the single agent but for the society as a whole because the very existence of a monetary economy presupposes a positive exchange value of money (Hahn, 1965). In the past, the problem of monetary theory has indeed been to develop a rationale for a positive exchange value of an intrinsically useless money.

In this connection, Keynes's (1936, ch. 17) penetrating analysis of wealth allocation impinges on the issue at stake. He considers three types of wealth: real assets, commodities, and money. In equilibrium, their expected yields, net of carrying costs, must be equal. Although its pecuniary return is zero, money has a substantial liquidity premium[4] with the special characteristic of being downward rigid relative to the rate of return on alternative assets. This property stems from the uniqueness of money services, i.e. "from the peculiarity of money that its utility is solely derived from its exchange-value, so that the two rise and fall *pari passu*, with the result that as the exchange value of money rises there is no motive or tendency, as in the case of rent-factors, to substitute some other factor for it". Thus, because of the stickiness of the liquidity premium, "money is a bottomless sink for purchasing power" (Keynes, 1936, p. 231).

The superiority of money in providing liquidity services is clearly acknowledged by Friedman: "Intuitively, money seems to be a more efficient carrier of non-pecuniary services ... than bonds (this is the central idea imbedded in Keynesian liquidity preference)" (1969, p. 25). However, in the formal representation of this conjecture, he admits the possibility that the

The optimum quantity of money

443

Journal of
Economic
Studies
25,6

444

marginal value of non-pecuniary consumption services yielded by money, $MNPS_M$, can be equal to $MNPS_B$ (the same variable referred to bonds) when $MNPS_M$ is zero, that is when the individual is sated with both money and bonds. This equality is, in fact, a necessary condition for the Chicago Rule (Friedman, 1969, p. 33), but is not congruous with Friedman's emphasis on the superiority of money as *the* liquid asset: "[M]oney dominates bonds in the provision of non-pecuniary services" (1969, pp. 25-6). Following the main message of this section, $MNPS_M$ cannot be equal to $MNPS_B$ and, more important, cannot go to zero or become negative. The flow marginal utility of money is, in fact, strictly positive and, given the link between the flow and the stock marginal utility of money, people can hardly be sated with cash balances. Besides, even abstracting from the flow aspect of money services and focusing on the asset characteristics exclusively, the superior liquidity of money translates into the absence of risk of capital losses. Hence, if the yield differential between money and bonds is driven to zero, agents will prefer to hold money only. This is but another angle from which to view the implications of money's liquidity premium for the Friedman Rule.

Finally, these results raise doubts concerning the standard proposition that if the cash-in-advance constraint is not binding, people are sated with money and the nominal interest rate is zero (Woodford, 1990, pp. 1074-5). In fact, such constraint is normally slack[5], but this does not imply satiation of cash balances owing to the unique property of money of yielding indirect utility in the form of purchasing power. Once again, a source of confusion is the identification of money with the commodities of the Walrasian model and the consequent application of the theorems of general equilibrium theory to money. In particular, the equilibrium conditions for a Pareto optimal allocation of cash and credit goods, from which that proposition is derived, do not pertain to a monetary economy but to a Walrasian set-up. All in all, the Chicago Rule goes too far when it corrects the externality in cash balances behavior because it does not take account of the liquidity premium that money commands over other assets.

The optimum quantity of money and the monetary system
In his seminal essay, Friedman defines the money stock as "consist[ing] of strict fiat money, i.e., pieces of paper, each labelled 'This is one dollar'" (1969, p. 3). This assumption looks innocuous, but it turns out to be critical for the validity of the Chicago Rule.

The evolution of monetary arrangements after the First World War gradually cancelled all forms of convertibility so that all countries are nowadays in a regime of inconvertible paper money. Questions concerning the monetary standard have long since ceased to be of interest for the theorist. Yet the subject has recently attracted attention following the momentous progress in the technology of payment systems. The potential development of non-tangible media of exchange has given rise to a novel stream of literature, the so-called "new monetary economics"[6]. A main tenet of this doctrine is the contrast between currency and an accounting system of exchange in that the latter does "not require any physical medium or *the concept of money*" (Fama, 1980, p. 39, italics added). Although this proposition is hard to accept, in that there is no necessary relationship between the money stuff and the essential properties of a monetary economy (Cesarano, 1995; Ostroy and Starr, 1990, p. 11), Fama's distinction is decisively relevant to the issue at stake.

The optimum quantity of money

445

An accounting system of exchange, which recalls Wicksell's "ideal banking system" (1906, pp. 87 ff.), has momentous implications for optimality. In such a system, individuals earn the nominal interest rate on "bonds", i.e. on the bank's portfolio assets aside from the cost of running the banks. Since currency does not exist, there is no perfectly liquid asset which commands a liquidity premium and, also, there is no interest rate differential between bonds and currency. The point is simply that the absence of a physical medium of exchange does away with a claim on commodities whose flow marginal utility is strictly positive. Bank deposits, which sum up to the agent's financial wealth, yield the rate of return on "bonds" equal to the rate of time preference. Agents can thus solve their intertemporal allocation problem without running into the externality problem raised by Friedman. The transition to Wicksell's pure credit system, therefore, drives to the optimal solution. In fact, the disposal of tangible money removes the discrepancy between flow and stock marginal utility that is the basis of the insatiability of cash balances. As Niehans (1978, p. 96) has remarked, the Chicago Rule puts the economy on a knife-edge between scarcity of money and a pathological addiction to ever-increasing cash balances. This peculiar state of affairs, however, applies only to a world of tangible money in which currency embodies a liquidity premium. It is the liquidity premium that, under the Friedman Rule, makes cash balances insatiable and the bond market vanish. Non-tangible money eliminates these problems at source and, since the return on "bonds" matches, dollar for dollar, the rate of time preference, agents behave as if money did not matter. One may well conclude that, in a sense, the optimum quantity of tangible money is zero.

An accounting system of exchange runs into the problem, also raised by Wicksell, of price level indeterminacy, but this is easily solvable. Discussing the minimum requirements of a monetary system, Patinkin (1961, pp. 113-16) has shown that a necessary condition for price level determinacy is the control by the central bank of a nominal quantity because there must be at least one economic unit, in this case the central bank, which reacts to changes in the price level. Hence, following Patinkin, Fama argues for the introduction of currency in order to give content to a pure nominal unit of account (1980, p. 55). Viewed from a different standpoint, the question of price level determinacy witnesses the primacy of the medium of exchange function in accounting for the essential properties of a monetary economy. The notion of money as a temporary abode of purchasing power, or generalized purchasing power (Friedman, 1969, p. 3), entails a determinate price level inasmuch as an abstract unit of account will not do to fulfill the information-producing role of money in the decentralization of exchange[7].

Journal of
Economic
Studies
25,6

446

The design of monetary arrangements, therefore, must be such that the basic functions of an exchange economy can actually be performed. In the current state of the art, the control of a nominal quantity is required in order to anchor the price level. Even if technological progress eventually disposed of currency altogether, the tangible asset can still be envisioned as a fiat instrument held as a reserve by commercial banks or, in a futuristic scenario, as "units" imposed on spaceship owners (Fama, 1980, p. 56). On purely theoretical grounds, the shape or outer form of the means of payment – whether checks or electronic signals – is of course irrelevant. In fact, Wicksell inquired into the "ideal banking system" (1906, pp. 87 ff.) well before the present breakthrough in communications and computation, simply analyzing the diffusion of checking accounts. And Mill more than glimpsed the same idea, which he referred to as the "ideal case" (1848, p. 524), half a century earlier. Substantial progress in payment technology would foster the optimal solution by further limiting the use of currency and by lowering the costs of managing the monetary system. Indeed, the evolution of monetary arrangements has been stimulated by the search for less costly ways of executing transactions. The introduction of non-tangible money can be a key institutional change in the next century, much as the gradual development of fiat money has been a central feature of the present one, with far-reaching implications for monetary policy and the international monetary system.

Concluding remarks
This discussion illustrates the relevance of the institutional element for monetary theory. Without going so far as Hicks' relativistic standpoint, according to which the historical and institutional set-up decisively shapes the theory itself (1967, ch. 9), monetary arrangements can be thought of as a further dimension of monetary analysis[8]. With regard to the notion of equilibrium in a monetary economy, a tangible medium of exchange involves the command of a liquidity premium which necessarily binds from below the rate of return of any other asset. This relates to Keynesian liquidity preference but also to the modern analysis of the essential properties of an exchange economy as contrasted with a Walrasian economy. The interest rate differential between currency and financial or real assets reflects the services of money and suggests that such services are indeed conspicuous since, at the other end of the scale, the differential can go to hundreds of percentage points, as in hyperinflations in which currency is still used in transactions. The implementation of the optimum quantity of money, therefore, can be ultimately related to the effectual design of the Wicksellian pure credit system.

Notes
1. These external effects have been described by Wicksell, who ingeniously relates them to the main idea behind the overlapping generations model. "Anyone who saves a part of his income and locks it away, thereby withdrawing it from circulation, to that extent exercises a depressing influence on prices, even though it may be infinitesimal as regards each individual. Other individuals thereby obtain more for their money; in other words they

divide among themselves that part of consumption which is renounced by those who save. The subsequent use of these savings, say in old age, involves sharing in the consumption of others. The total effect may thus be compared with a sort of consumption loan which those who save give to their contemporaries and of which they subsequently claim the capital (though without interest), from the same generation or from the next" (1906, p. 11).

2. An early critique of satiation in money balances is owing to Mélitz (1972) who approaches the issue from the production side and questions the possibility that the marginal revenue product of money falls to zero.

3. The opening paragraphs of Ostroy and Starr discuss the functions of money exactly in line with the classical approach. "Of the three commonly acknowledged roles that money plays – unit of account, store of value and medium of exchange – it is in the last role as a facilitator of transactions, or essential lubricant to the mechanism of exchange, that money first comes to our attention. The transactions' role of money cannot be separated from its function as a store of value. If after the sale of one commodity for money, but before the purchase of another commodity with it, money perished, it could hardly serve as a medium separating purchase from sale. Though a medium of exchange must necessarily be a store of value, stores of value are not necessarily money. What distinguishes money from other stores of value is its liquidity, and what underlines the liquidity of money is the fact that it is the common medium through which other commodities are exchanged ... The transactions role of money can be readily separated from its usage as a unit of account by observing that the unit of account might be pounds of salt or a more stable foreign currency without being a medium of exchange" (1990, p. 3). In this connection, Wicksell's analysis must again be recalled: "Of the three main functions[measure of value, store of value, and medium of exchange], only the last is in a true sense characteristic of money; as a measure of value any commodity might serve ... Similarly, the function of acting as a *store of value* is not essentially characteristic of money ... the object in view [by those who hoard money] is nearly always that of procuring *something else* for it at a future time. In other words, it is the exchange value which it is desired to preserve; it is money as a future medium of exchange which is hoarded" (1906, pp. 7-8, italics in the original).

4. Keynes defines the liquidity premium as follows. "[T]he power of disposal over an asset during a period may offer a potential convenience or security, which is not equal for assets of different kinds, though the assets themselves are of equal initial value. There is, so to speak, nothing to show for this at the end of the period in the shape of output; yet it is something for which people are ready to pay something. The amount (measured in terms of itself) which they are willing to pay for the potential convenience or security given by this power of disposal (exclusive of yield or carrying cost attaching to the asset), we shall call its liquidity-premium *l*" (1936, p. 226).

5. Nobody would ever plan his receipt and expenditure flows in such a way as to be short of cash, as this celebrated passage of Adam Smith suggests. "In order to avoid the inconveniency of such situations, every prudent man in every period of society, after the first establishment of the division of labour, must naturally have endeavoured to manage his affairs in such a manner, as to have at all times by him, besides the peculiar produce of his own industry, a certain quantity of some one commodity or other, such as he imagined few people would be likely to refuse in exchange for the produce of their industry" (1776, pp. 26-7).

6. This term is due to Hall (1982). The main contributions include Black (1970), Fama (1980), Greenfield and Yeager (1983). Critical reviews are White (1984), McCallum (1985), Hoover (1988) and Cesarano (1995). Moreover, the whole July 1983 issue of the *Journal of Monetary Economics* is dedicated to this topic.

7. In Lecture I of his *Critical Essays*, Hicks lucidly explains this proposition with reference to a clearing system. "There must, however, be some level of money prices in such a market; and there must be something that causes it. We may perhaps get a hint from that

Journal of
Economic
Studies
25,6

448

alternative expression of Wicksell's which I quoted: instead of saying 'unit of account' he says 'measure of value'. It is inevitable, even in a market of the kind we are discussing, that the seller, when he is deciding whether or not to sell (or how much to sell) at a particular price, should implicitly consider what that price may be worth in terms of other goods; he must have some idea about other prices before he can say whether or not a particular price-offer is acceptable" (1967, p. 10).

8. Angela Redish (1990) argues that the successful development of the gold standard was in fact enhanced by the introduction of steam-driven stamping presses, a substantial technological advancement of the end of the eighteenth century.

References

Barro, R.J. and Fischer, S. (1976), "Recent developments in monetary theory", *Journal of Monetary Economics*, Vol. 2, April, pp. 133-67.

Black, F. (1970), "Banking and interest rates in a world without money: the effects of uncontrolled banking", *Journal of Bank Research*, Vol. 1, Autumn, pp. 9-20.

Cesarano, F. (1995), "The new monetary economics and the theory of money", *Journal of Economic Behavior and Organization*, Vol. 26, May, pp. 445-55.

Clower, R.W. (1970), "Is there an optimal money supply?", *Journal of Finance*, Vol. 25, May, pp. 425-33.

Fama, E.F. (1980), "Banking in a theory of finance", *Journal of Monetary Economics*, Vol. 6, January, pp. 39-57.

Friedman, M. (1969), "The optimum quantity of money", in Friedman, M., *The Optimum Quantity of Money and Other Essays*, Aldine, Chicago, IL, pp. 1-50.

Grandmont, J.M. and Younès, Y. (1973), "On the efficiency of a monetary equilibrium", *Review of Economic Studies*, Vol. 40, April, pp. 149-65.

Greenfield, R.L. and Yeager, L.B. (1983), "A laissez-faire approach to monetary stability", *Journal of Money, Credit and Banking*, Vol. 15, August, pp. 302-15.

Hahn, F.H. (1965), "On some problems of proving the existence of an equilibrium in a monetary economy", in Hahn, F.H. and Brechling, F. (Eds), *The Theory of Interest Rates*, Macmillan, London, pp. 126-35.

Hahn, F.H. (1971), "Professor Friedman's views on money", *Economica*, Vol. 38, February, pp. 61-80.

Hall, R. (1982), "Monetary trends in the United States and the United Kingdom: a review from the perspective of new developments in monetary economics", *Journal of Economic Literature*, Vol. 20, December, pp. 1552-6.

Hicks, J.R. (1967), *Critical Essays in Monetary Theory*, Oxford University Press, Oxford.

Hoover, K.D. (1988), "Money, prices and finance in the new monetary economics", *Oxford Economic Papers*, Vol. 40, March, pp. 150-67.

Keynes, J.M. (1936), *The General Theory of Employment, Interest and Money*, Macmillan, London.

McCallum, B.T. (1985), *Bank Deregulation, Accounting Systems of Exchange, and the Unit of Account: A Critical Review*, Carnegie-Rochester Conference Series on Public Policy, Vol. 23, pp. 13-46.

Mélitz, J. (1972), "On the optimality of satiation in money balances", *Journal of Finance*, Vol. 27, June, pp. 683-98.

Mill, J.S. (1909), *Principles of Political Economy*, Ashley, W. (Ed.), (First published in 1848), Longmans, Green & Company, London.

Niehans, J. (1978), *The Theory of Money*, The Johns Hopkins University Press, Baltimore, MD.

Ostroy, J.M. and Starr, R.M. (1990), "The transactions role of money", in Friedman, B.M. and Hahn, F.H. (Eds), *Handbook of Monetary Economics*, North-Holland, Amsterdam, pp. 3-62.

Patinkin, D. (1961), "Financial intermediaries and the logical structure of monetary theory. A review article", *American Economic Review*, Vol. 51, March, pp. 95-116.

Redish, A. (1990), "The evolution of the gold standard in England", *Journal of Economic History*, Vol. 50, December, pp. 789-805.

Smith, A. (1976), *An Enquiry into the Nature and Causes of the Wealth of Nations*, Cannan, E. (Ed.), (First published in 1776), The University of Chicago Press, Chicago, IL.

Tsiang, S.C. (1969), "A critical note on the optimum supply of money", *Journal of Money, Credit and Banking*, Vol. 1, May, pp. 266-80.

White, L.H. (1984), "Competitive payments systems and the unit of account", *American Economic Review*, Vol. 74, September, pp. 699-712.

Wicksell, K. (1935), *Lectures on Political Economy*, (First published in 1960), Vol. II, Routledge, London.

Woodford, M. (1990), "The optimum quantity of money", in Friedman, B.M. and Hahn, F.H. (Eds), *Handbook of Monetary Economics*, North-Holland, Amsterdam, pp. 1067-1152.

The optimum
quantity of
money

449

[10]

Journal of
Economic
Studies
26,3

188

Competitive money supply: the international monetary system in perspective

Filippo Cesarano
Banca d'Italia, Rome, Italy

Keywords *Economics, Money supply*

Abstract *This paper inquires into monetary standards, focusing on the characteristics of money instead of the exchange rate regime. The transition from commodity to fiat money, a major break in monetary evolution, has led to international arrangements that represent an application of the competitive money supply model (section 1), which is consistent with various optimality criteria and has far-reaching implications for the future development of the monetary system (section 2).*

The state of the art in international monetary economics relates primarily to exchange rates. In the main, both theory and policy issues involve the choice of the optimal exchange rate regime[1]. This research strategy, quite appropriate to tackling the subject from an abstract viewpoint, is less promising and may even be misleading when dealing with policy questions and the design of institutions. In this respect, the characteristics of money and of the rules governing the monetary system are an essential factor independent of the exchange rate regime. To give just one example, the EMS and the gold standard are considered to be much alike from an analytical standpoint, both being fixed exchange rate regimes. Hence, inflation convergence in Europe during the 1980s was predicated on the discipline of the EMS and the credibility of its core country, Germany. In contrast with the smooth operation of the gold standard, however, the EMS has experienced recurrent crises even in the absence of major shocks. The EMS's troubled existence is explained by its being a fixed exchange rate agreement linking several fiat monies, quite distinct from a commodity-money system with all the attendant rules of the game and implications for credibility (Bordo and Kydland, 1995). The nature of the money-object, therefore, bears heavily on the working of monetary arrangements regardless of the exchange rate regime. In the study of monetary standards, this is patent; and it remains true for understanding theoretical issues like the time consistency of policy rules.

In this connection, the transition from commodity to fiat money represents an epoch-making change, ending a system that had prevailed since the very beginning of coinage. It was the result of a gradual process begun in the wake of the First World War and culminating with the dollar's inconvertibility

Journal of Economic Studies,
Vol. 26 No. 3, 1999, pp. 188-200.
© MCB University Press, 0144-3585

Thanks are due to Jacques Mélitz and two anonymous referees for their usual comments. The usual caveat applies. The views expressed herein are those of the author and not necessarily those of the Banca d'Italia.

declaration on 15 August 1971. Milton Friedman has thus observed: "The world's current monetary system is, I believe, unprecedented. No major currency has any link to a commodity" (1986, p. 643). Expanding on Friedman's remark, the present paper looks at the characteristics of money, instead of the exchange rate regime, to analyze monetary arrangements. Our point of departure is the observation that the difference between today's institutional framework and those of the past is one of kind, not of degree. This break in monetary evolution has led to international arrangements that represent the application of the competitive money supply model, since each country issues its own fiat instrument, distinguishable from the others and linked to them by floating exchange rates (section 1). The present competitive set-up is consistent with various optimality criteria and has far-reaching implications for the future development of the monetary system (section 2).

Competitive
money supply

189

1. Fiat money and competitive money supply
In the course of the twentieth century, different exchange rate regimes have followed one upon the other. The explanation is rather elusive[2]; but, from the money-object perspective, the alternation of fixed and flexible exchange rates can be viewed as a succession of ephemeral attempts to hold to a commodity standard, against the fundamental transition to fiat money. Underlying this transition was the rejection of two basic principles of classical monetary theory. One was metallism, which relates the purchasing power of money to the value of the money-commodity. Metallism, which provided the foundation of knowledge about money since Aristotle and prevailed to the early twentieth century (Schumpeter, 1954, pp. 62-3), had a policy counterpart in the norm of maintaining parity. Also rejected was the equilibrium hypothesis, which posited the self-adjusting property of the economy. These tenets precluded from the outset any idea of improving the economy's welfare path through changes in the quantity of money. The state of the art was reflected in the "rules of the game", which tightly constrained the authorities' behavior. In particular, the restoration rule (McKinnon, 1993, pp. 6-10), which mandated reestablishing the mint parity after a period of suspension, made the commitment to discipline highly credible, thus fostering long-run price level predictability.

The change in this centuries-old analytical framework was triggered by the events of the inter-war period. The welfare costs of the disinflation that was pursued after the First World War with a view to restoring the gold standard revealed the strains produced by metallic money (Eichengreen, 1992) and sowed the seeds of the Great Depression. These developments paved the way for advocating the severance of the metal link altogether and assigning the objective of stabilizing the price level to the central bank[3]. Keynes's General Theory eventually disposed of the equilibrium hypothesis, assigning economic policy the task of driving the economy towards equilibrium. For the first time, therefore, the performance of the monetary system would rely not on rules but on the behavior of the authorities. This was an epochal break in that the abandonment of rules proved to be an irreversible phenomenon. Reflecting the

Journal of
Economic
Studies
26,3

190

intellectual climate of the time, the Bretton Woods negotiators sought to leave sufficient maneuvering room for domestic policies while allowing for exchange rate changes[4]. Instead of forcing the economy to adjust to monetary rules, the quantity of money would be controlled in order to improve economic performance. Hence, the reversal of the closely intertwined tenets of classical theory, metallism and the equilibrium hypothesis, set off the greatest monetary transformation in recorded history, putting policy-makers in charge of attaining social welfare targets.

In a world of fiat money, reforms aiming at reestablishing fixed exchange rates have an element of artificiality insofar as there is no longer any compelling rationale for such rules. When there was such a rationale, the existence of national monies was referred to as a "barbarism" (Mill, 1848, p. 615) that, albeit reflecting political geography, was at odds with the theoretical paradigm underlying commodity money. Historically, various stages can be observed in which the money issued by the nation with the greatest political and military strength dominated world monetary affairs (Mundell, 1972). Once a country had acquired a hegemonic position, it was able to retain it for a very long period, even spanning centuries.

In today's fiat money scenario, this monopolistic power is more difficult to maintain, as the system has shifted from the commodity money principle to a competitive market for money in which each country issues its own, perfectly distinguishable money and manages it with a view to certain welfare targets. This is an exact application of Klein's (1974) competitive money supply hypothesis, which disputes the case for monopoly, showing that the latter is based on the implicit assumption of indistinguishability between currencies. In a world of incomplete information but distinguishable products, if product quality cannot be evaluated by the commodity's physical characteristics, consumers rely on brand name. This is especially so in the case of fiat money, whose visible features are perfectly irrelevant, in the absence of counterfeiting. Quality and brand name relate, respectively, to price stability and predictability. The brand name, therefore, is a capital asset for the issuer who invests resources optimally to increase the present discounted value of its profit stream. Since future money supply paths are not known (otherwise brand names would be mere identification marks with no value), agents estimate the probability of deception on the part of issuers and increase the quantity of brand-name capital demanded accordingly. The agents' estimate of the possible gain to issuers from deception determines the equilibrium value of the brand-name capital (Klein, 1974, pp. 432-8).

Klein's article, together with Hayek's essay on the denationalization of money (1976), has been critically discussed in a domestic context (Fischer, 1984; Friedman and Schwartz, 1986), with reference to the historical experiences of free banking in Scotland and the USA. The subject, however, has drawn attention more as an intellectual curiosity than as a concrete proposal, given the skepticism surrounding its realization. For, besides currency distinguishability, a necessary condition for a viable competitive money supply scheme is the flexibility of exchange rates between currencies in order to make Gresham's Law inoperative. This condition, which is patently hard to satisfy within a country[5], is fulfilled by the current international monetary set-up. In fact, the emergence of fiat money, in the presence of domestic monopoly in currency issue, has given rise to competition at the international level. The theory of the competitive money supply, therefore, becomes a useful analytical tool in examining today's international monetary arrangements.

In his seminal paper, Klein recognized the applicability of his hypothesis to the international monetary system "where different countries supplying distinguishable monies can usefully be thought of as analogous to competing firms in an unregulated money industry" (1974, pp. 444-5). Writing in 1970, however, he had viewed the system as a fixed exchange rate dollar standard based on the dollar's brand name. A quarter of a century later, with the benefit of hindsight, we can appreciate the effects of competition following the breakdown of Bretton Woods. The international role of the dollar, though still dominant, has gradually declined to the advantage of both mark and yen. Undoubtedly, the desired use of an international money increases its actual use (Krugman, 1984, p. 179). There is, in fact, an element of resilience in the use of a vehicle currency due to the informational foundation of money, witness the long-time dominance of certain monies in the course of the centuries. Compared with a commodity standard, however, fiat money dramatically widens the scope for policy, leaving the monetary authority quite free to pursue targets through continuous rather than once-and-for-all changes in money supply.

In a competitive money scenario, any country can raise seignorage revenue, but at the cost of a depreciation of its brand-name capital. Issuers thus face a dynamic optimization problem. The country's objective function may well include arguments that go beyond the strictly economic sphere, such as political hegemony. Nowadays, the maintenance of stable purchasing power is not devolved to rules but is left to the interplay of competitive issuers. Furthermore, the quantum leap in communication technology together with deregulation has given rise to a global financial market. Hence, while informational considerations limit the number of vehicle currencies, the huge expansion of financial markets has widened the asset role of money. These developments have tended to make the world "money" or currency market a perfectly contestable one where the characteristics of the "products" are strictly related to the quality and brand name of the unit of account in which they are denominated, which in turn depend on the issuer's behavior.

The quality and brand name of fiat money can hardly remain constant; variations are reflected in the exchange rate, whose flexibility is thus a natural outcome of the system's main features. In this respect, the return to fixed exchange rates is quite widely viewed as a "mirage" (Obstfeld and Rogoff, 1995), but one related to the exceptional expansion of world capital markets. However, the dimension of capital flows is neither a necessary nor a sufficient condition for the prevalence of flexible exchange rates. Capital mobility was very high under the gold standard and in fact contributed greatly also to the

Journal of
Economic
Studies
26,3

192

viability of a system regarded as the epitome of fixed exchange rates. Once again, the different nature of the money-object is crucial to explaining these seeming incongruities. The credibility of the gold standard, embodied in the restoration rule, was such that capital flows respond to small interest rate variations (McKinnon, 1993, p. 8), because the whole panoply of economic policy tools was deployed in order to maintain parity. In a fiat money scenario, by contrast, there is no monetary anchor that makes the goal of exchange rate stability credible. Hence, capital flows may well exacerbate rather than quell exchange rate variability in view of short-run gains. Successfully reestablishing fixed exchange rates in a world of high capital mobility would require a new, theoretically founded, welfare-maximizing rule that bound economic policy to an overriding exchange rate target.

2. Optimality and future monetary arrangements
Our present-day monetary institutions are often described as a "non-system", emphasizing "the unstructured nature of the current international monetary system" (Kenen *et al*, 1994, p. 1) in contrast to Bretton Woods or the gold standard. Yet it is hardly proper to call a competitive money supply set-up "unstructured", in that the absence of rules does not imply the lack of a system, just as unfettered individual behavior does not entail chaos but the coordination of economic activity through the market. The relevant question, instead, is whether competitiveness leads to optimality. The theory of competitive money supply suggests that high confidence money will drive out low confidence money because consumer demand takes the predictability of money's future exchange value into account. A competitive market, therefore, incorporates an incentive for achieving a non-inflationary scenario even in the absence of rules. The disinflation of the 1980s is a case in point. Moreover, some consideration of more precise notions of optimality is in order. First, optimum currency areas provide an analytical framework for social welfare maximization. Second, the concept of optimum quantity of money builds on Pareto optimality to attain an efficient solution. These notions will be examined in turn.

Prima facie, the traditional approach to optimum currency area runs counter to the competitive money supply, in that only by sheer chance could the actual configuration of countries meet any of the optimality criteria, i.e. labor mobility (Mundell, 1961), openness to trade (McKinnon, 1963) and degree of product differentiation (Kenen, 1969). But this is a hasty conclusion, based on a received view of the subject that presents a number of weaknesses. The traditional approach is essentially static and assumes rigidity of prices and wages. Furthermore, the standard theory treats the optimizing criteria as if they were exogenous features of the economy unrelated to individual maximizing behavior. These defects are not overcome by the attempt to go beyond a single optimizing criterion to consider the overall costs and benefits of a common currency (Ishiyama, 1975; Tower and Willett, 1976). Indeed, Krugman has recently criticized the "loose-jointed theory of optimum currency areas that stresses the tension between these hypothesized benefits of fixity and the more measurable costs of lost monetary autonomy" (1993, p. 3). Krugman's dissatisfaction with the state of the art is shared by many. Niehans notes that "optimum currency areas are still a concept in search of a theory" (1984, p. 294) and Mélitz (1995) calls attention to the "impasse" in research on the subject. The point is that the traditional approach is simply an application of the theory of economic policy (Tinbergen, 1952) in which the country's border is the instrument used to attain the optimal solution. In the context of the new classical macroeconomics, this view is hardly tenable. The policy-maker's maximization problem, unlike the engineer's, is not amenable to optimal control theory, so it cannot be considered in a vacuum leaving agents' response out (Lucas, 1976). This research program suggests an equilibrium approach to currency areas (Cesarano, 1997). While the traditional theory looks at the currency area as the solution to a policy problem, in an equilibrium model agents take into account the effects of fixing the border and, as for any other policy measure, modify their behavior accordingly. The equilibrium approach, therefore, turns the theory of optimum currency areas upside down inasmuch as the attainment of equilibrium hinges on, and is not independent of, individual behavior.

The country border influences agents' decisions in various respects. To give the flavor of the argument, labor mobility may well be much higher between Seattle and Miami than between Seattle and Vancouver, close by but over the border. The existence of nations not only gives rise to legal and institutional barriers to trade and factor movement but increases uncertainty affecting individual choice. More particularly, the information set is much larger for domestic decision making in that knowledge of institutions, market regulations, language and the like substantially increases both the available data and the explanatory power of the model into which the data are fed. This clearly affects the decision to migrate underlying the Mundellian optimality criterion. The uncertainty and non-pecuniary costs of international migration can be much higher than those of internal migration, thus requiring a much larger wage differential to trigger the decision to move out. Labor mobility, therefore, may well enhance currency area optimality, but it is the outcome of rational behavior rather than an exogenous characteristic of the economy.

Several empirical studies on European monetary integration have found a greater degree of labor mobility in the USA than in Europe but this may simply reflect the long-standing status of the USA as a nation-state rather than an external feature. This finding actually corroborates the equilibrium hypothesis, since it would be hard to maintain that the USA became a currency area because it possessed high labor mobility, just as, in Lucas's words, "no one argues that the anticipation of sixteenth-century inflation sent Columbus to the New World to locate the gold to finance it" (1977, p. 232). The traditional theory is at odds with the stylized fact that countries do not experience cumulative disequilibria and do not frequently join or leave currency areas. The

Competitive
money supply

193

Journal of
Economic
Studies
26,3

194

coincidence between political and monetary sovereignty throughout history corroborates the equilibrium hypothesis of currency areas: once borders are set, the adjustment mechanism sees to maintaining a stable equilibrium position.

As shown in section 1, exchange rate flexibility is a natural implication of a fiat money world in which the introduction of rules of the game is undermined by the lack of theoretical foundations. This conclusion squares with the equilibrium approach to optimum currency areas, which stresses the role and impact of rational behavior in maintaining internal balance. Hence, a competitive money supply setting does not contrast with optimality of currency areas.

Beside the macroeconomic notion of optimality underlying optimum currency areas, there is the microeconomic one based on the optimum quantity of money. The latter, though seemingly unrelated to monetary arrangements, bears on the characteristics of the money-object assuring the optimality solution. The argument for the optimum quantity of money (Friedman, 1969) is well known. While it is costless to society to increase real cash balances by engineering a fall in the price level, individuals wishing to accumulate real money holdings perceive the cost of foregone interest on non-monetary assets. Hence, the discrepancy between private and social cost leads to the non-optimality of cash balances. The socially optimal solution, the Friedman Rule or Chicago Rule, involves a rate of deflation equal to the rate of time preference which brings the nominal interest rate down to zero and real money balances to the satiation level.

Friedman's theory, though widely accepted[6], has been subject to criticism. In particular, the Chicago Rule would make the bond market disappear: with money and bonds yielding the same return, agents would hold money alone, given its superior liquidity characteristic (Tsiang, 1969, p. 267; Hahn, 1971, p. 71; Barro and Fischer, 1976, p. 144). Far from satiating people with cash balances, the Rule would make the demand for money insatiable. This is formally shown by Sargent (1987, pp. 145-6) in a money-in-the-utility-function model. Furthermore, in other models of monetary economies, the Chicago Rule leads to the indeterminacy of stationary equilibrium, since agents would accumulate money balances beyond the minimum needed for transactions (Grandmont and Younès, 1973; Niehans, 1978, p. 79). To account for these strictures, it can be noted that, while it is costless to raise real money balances by pushing down the price level, the marginal flow utility of money, i.e. the utility of an additional dollar spent, can never be zero. In fact, no one would refuse an additional dollar unless the purchasing power of money were zero or resources were not scarce as in a state of perfect bliss (Niehans, 1978, pp. 74-5). Satiation of real balances thus relates to the stock marginal utility of money, i.e. the increase in utility from holding a unit of real cash balances. By driving the nominal interest rate down to zero in order to have a zero stock marginal utility of money, the Chicago Rule puts a wedge between the stock and the flow marginal utility of money, since the latter is strictly positive (Cesarano, 1998, p. 442).

The peculiar implications of the Rule – namely the disappearance of the bond market, the insatiability of cash balances, and price level indeterminacy – stem from the application of general equilibrium theory to a monetary economy. The Rule considers money as a free good in the Walrasian model, like air in an unpolluted environment. But while it would never cross anyone's mind to pay a price for air, everyone eagerly accepts a dollar bill insofar as it can purchase scarce commodities. This outcome ultimately rests on the distinctive informational role of money, which can be performed by a valueless instrument like paper money. The medium for transmitting information is irrelevant on abstract grounds but becomes crucial with regard to monetary arrangements. In particular, the development of non-tangible exchange media suggests a proposal that mends the Chicago Rule (Cesarano, 1998, pp. 444-5).

Dwelling on Fischer Black's pioneering paper (1970), Fama (1980) has contrasted a tangible medium of exchange with an accounting system of exchange in which cash does not exist and payments are managed by a deregulated system of commercial banks[7]. In such an arrangement individuals earn interest on "bonds", i.e. on the banks' portfolio assets minus the cost of running the banks. Since currency does not exist, there is no perfectly liquid asset which commands a liquidity premium and there is no interest rate differential between bonds and money. In fact, the absence of a physical medium of exchange does away with a claim on commodities that has strictly positive flow marginal utility. The viable implementation of the optimum quantity of money, therefore, is strictly dependent on the nature of the money-object, as an accounting system of exchange devoid of tangible money would dispose of those strictures undermining the Chicago Rule.

There is an important caveat, however, because the accounting system of exchange runs into the Wicksellian problem of price level indeterminacy. The solution (Patinkin, 1961, pp. 113-16) is to have the central bank control a nominal quantity, and accordingly, Fama (1980, p. 55) argues for the introduction of currency[8].

This institutional setting may not seem very different from the current one except for its higher degree of efficiency. But this is to miss the significance of the innovation. In an accounting system of exchange, a constant stock of currency serves only and exclusively to make the price level determinate and it is therefore a technical requirement, like fixing the unit of account in the gold standard. As such, it would be less subject to tampering since, as in the case of the gold parity, any interference would be immediately spotted. Indeed, John Stuart Mill (1848, pp. 545-6) considered simplicity a key feature of rules in that it enhanced detectability of misbehavior, thus increasing credibility. More important, the requirement of a constant supply of currency, being dictated by theory, further strengthens credibility insofar as rules imposed by law but not based on widely accepted tenets are likely to be infringed.

The introduction of non-tangible exchange media may paradoxically turn the evolution of the monetary system back to the past, reestablishing the main characteristics of the commodity standard. Each country would issue a constant quantity of a fiat instrument to anchor the price level, linked to other currencies by perfectly fixed exchange rates without oscillating margins in the manner of the gold points. Just as in the commodity standard the unit of account could be varied, or the rules of the game suspended, providing an escape clause for exceptional events (Bordo and Kydland, 1995), in the non-tangible money set-up the quantity of currency could be varied once and for all in extraordinary circumstances.

As is shown in section 1, theory plays a crucial role in the outside money set-up, while innovation and growth in the field of inside money are triggered by market forces. Outside and inside money may be viewed as, respectively, the core and the surrounding belt of the monetary system, but they are of course not watertight compartments. Technical progress in the banking and financial industry poses new problems for theoretical inquiry and stimulates original approaches. Advances in monetary economics, however, have often widened the area of disagreement rather than leading to a settled body of knowledge. When knowledge was scanty, attempts to reform monetary arrangements ended in disaster, witness John Law's experience in France in the early 1700s. Although far more advanced than in Law's time, monetary theory is still a highly controversial subject. New Classicals and New Keynesians are but the latest in a long line of duelists stretching back at least to the English monetary controversies of the 1800s. The state of the art bears heavily on the accounting system of exchange in that the ultimate test for its implementation is the widespread, unconditional acceptance of the equilibrium hypothesis, which precludes driving the economy onto a superior welfare path through discretionary monetary policy. However, the rejection of active monetary management is open to question. Only if the equilibrium hypothesis is unequivocally accepted, as in the age of metallic money, can a constant quantity of fiat money be maintained inside each country.

3. Conclusion
Inquiring about the monetary system from a money-object perspective is suggestive since it raises questions that do not emerge or are unanswered in a more abstract context. The criticism and eventual demise of the classical tenets, i.e. metallism and the equilibrium hypothesis, brought about the epochal transition from commodity to fiat money. The present international scenario, then, is an application of the competitive money supply model in which countries are like firms issuing their own distinguishable money. Hence, the performance of the system is not determined by rules but by the countries' competitive behavior. Moreover, exchange rate flexibility is not the outcome of reform but the natural implication of a competitive set-up based on fiat money.

Besides impinging on the design of monetary arrangements, the approach centered on the money-object also bears on optimality. In this respect, two aspects can be distinguished relating to optimum currency areas and the optimum quantity of money. In an equilibrium model, currency areas do not pose a macro-optimality issue in that, if the country border is likened to a policy measure, agents' rational behavior will account for its effects enhancing the domestic adjustment mechanism. The actual geographical configuration, coincident with the set of competitive money issuers, is thus compatible with social welfare maximization. The nature of the money-object also has relevance for the optimum quantity of money problem, since the transition from tangible money to an accounting system of exchange disposes of some strictures of the Chicago Rule.

Competitive money supply

197

This approach to monetary institutions calls into play and connects different and apparently unrelated topics, namely the competitive money supply, optimum currency areas, the optimum quantity of money and the new monetary economics. The analysis of the monetary system centered on the money-object shows that these strands of literature are indeed linked, thus contributing to a deeper understanding of monetary economics.

Notes

1. For recent surveys of the literature, see van der Ploeg (1994, parts III and IV) and Grossman and Rogoff (1995, part 2).

2. Eichengreen notes: "Although the literature contains many illuminating studies of particular episodes in the history of the international monetary system (the rise of the gold standard or the breakdown of Bretton Woods, for example), it shows few attempts to develop general explanations for shifts between fixed- and flexible-rate regimes. Similarly, although the discipline of international economics contains many models of the collapse of fixed-rate regimes and of the transition from floating to pegged rates, few of the models attempt to endogenize the factors responsible for these shifts" (1995, pp. 3-4). He then puts forward six hypotheses – leadership, cooperation, intellectual consensus, behavior of the macroeconomy, fiscal policy and monetary rules, and distributional politics – and finds that none of them alone provides a general explanation.

3. In the early 1920s, Keynes, in a well-known passage of the *Tract*, already included employment and the business cycle among the policy targets and emphasized the silent demise of commodity money: "In truth, the gold standard is already a barbarous relic. All of us, from the Governor of the Bank of England downwards, are now primarily interested in preserving the stability of business, prices, and employment, and are not likely, when the choice is forced on us, deliberately to sacrifice these to the out-worn dogma, which had its value once, of £3:17:10½ per ounce. Advocates of the ancient standard do not observe how remote it now is from the spirit and the requirements of the age. A regulated non-metallic standard has slipped in unnoticed. *It exists*" (1923, pp. 172-73, italics in the original).

4. Presenting the Bretton Woods plan to the House of Lords on 23 May 1944, Keynes noted: "In fact, the plan introduces in this respect an epoch-making innovation in an international instrument, the object of which is to lay down sound and orthodox principles. For instead of maintaining the principle that the internal value of a national currency should conform to a prescribed *de jure* external value, it provides that its external value should be altered if necessary so as to conform to whatever *de facto* internal value results from domestic policies, which themselves shall be immune from criticism by the Fund. Indeed, it is made the duty of the Fund to approve changes which will have this effect. That is why I say that these proposals are the exact opposite of the gold standard. They lay down by international agreement the essence of the new doctrine, far removed from the old orthodoxy" (1944, pp. 18-19).

5. Examining the US historical experience, Klein (1974, p. 439-41) notes the incentive to overissue and relates it to fixed exchange rates between the circulating monies since each

Journal of
Economic
Studies
26,3

198

money denoted, and was convertible into, a particular weight of gold. However, the
presence of several currencies inside a country involves a sizeable loss of information
inasmuch as each commodity will have as many quoted prices as there are currencies.
Incidentally, this point is often raised in an international context in order to underline the
microeconomic costs of flexible exchange rates (Cooper, 1995). Considering this problem,
Klein (1974, pp. 443) argues that the predictability of exchange rates rather than their
stability is the notion relevant to information costs. But this leaves open the question of
accounting costs minimization related to money's unit-of-account function. which argues
against the presence of several currencies.

6. This statement is subject to some qualifications. In his thorough survey, Woodford (1990,
pp. 1070-73) distinguishes between a weak and a strong form of Friedman's proposition
and argues for the general validity of the former, since the latter, which requires
superneutrality, only holds in special cases.

7. Classical economists had already imagined a cashless payment system based on bank
deposits. Besides Wicksell, whose analysis of an "ideal banking system" is well known
(1906, p. 87 ff.), John Stuart Mill clearly envisaged a situation in which all payments were
made by check. "We just now made the imaginary supposition that all persons dealt with a
bank, and all with the same bank, payments being universally made by cheques. In this
ideal case, there would be no money anywhere except in the hands of the banker: who
might then safely part with all of it, by selling it as bullion, or lending it, to be sent out of
the country in exchange for goods or foreign securities. But though there would then be no
money in possession, or ultimately perhaps even in existence, money would be offered, and
commodities bought with it, just as at present. People would continue to reckon their
incomes and their capitals in money, and to make their usual purchases with orders for the
receipt of a thing which would have literally ceased to exist. There would be in all this
nothing to complain of, so long as the money, in disappearing, left an equivalent value in
other things, applicable when required to the reimbursement of those to whom the money
originally belonged" (1848, pp. 524-5).

8. Illustrating a different way of achieving the optimum, as an alternative to deflation,
Friedman (1969, pp. 38-9) proposed issuing a fixed amount of fiat money which commercial
banks would be required to hold as reserves. Competition among banks would compel
them to pay interest on deposits at a rate below the bond rate in order to cover running
costs. Although it fails to consider a cashless system, Friedman's proposal anticipates the
key feature of a welfare optimizing, deregulated banking system.

References

Barro, R.J. and Fischer, S. (1976), "Recent developments in monetary theory", *Journal of Monetary
Economics*, Vol. 2, April, pp. 133-67.

Black, F. (1970), "Banking and interest rates in a world without money: the effect of uncontrolled
banking", *Journal of Bank Research*, Vol. 1, Autumn, pp. 9-20.

Bordo, M.D. and Kydland, F.E. (1995), "The gold standard as a rule: an essay in exploration",
Explorations in Economic History, Vol. 32 No. 4, pp. 423-64.

Cesarano, F. (1997), "Currency areas and equilibrium", *Open Economies Review*, Vol. 8 No. 1,
pp. 51-9.

Cesarano, F. (1998), "Providing for the optimum quantity of money", *Journal of Economic Studies*,
Vol. 25 No. 6, pp. 441-9.

Cooper, R.N. (1995), "One money for how many?", in Kenen, P.B. (Ed.), *Understanding
Interdependence*, Princeton University Press, Princeton, NJ.

Eichengreen, B. (1992), *Golden Fetters. The Gold Standard and the Great Depression*, Oxford
University Press, Oxford.

Eichengreen, B. (1995), "The endogeneity of exchange-rate regimes", in Kenen, P.B. (Ed.), *Understanding Interdependence*, Princeton University Press, Princeton, NJ.

Fama, E.F (1980). "Banking in a theory of finance", *Journal of Monetary Economics*, Vol. 6, January, pp. 39-57.

Fischer, S. (1984), "Friedman versus Hayek on private money. Review essay", *Journal of Monetary Economics*, Vol. 17, May, pp. 433-9.

Friedman, M. (1969), "The optimum quantity of money", in Friedman, M., *The Optimum Quantity of Money and Other Essays*, Aldine, Chicago, IL, pp. 1-50.

Friedman, M. (1986), "The resource cost of irredeemable paper money", *Journal of Political Economy*, Vol. 94 No. 3, pp. 642-7.

Friedman, M. and Schwartz, A.J. (1986), "Has government any role in money?", *Journal of Monetary Economics*, Vol. 17, January, pp. 37-62.

Grandmont, J.-M. and Younès, Y. (1973), "On the efficiency of a monetary equilibrium", *Review of Economic Studies*, Vol. 40, April, pp. 149-65.

Grossman, G.M. and Rogoff. K. (Eds) (1995), *Handbook of International Economics*, Vol. III, Elsevier, Amsterdam.

Hahn, F.H. (1971), "Professor Friedman's views on money", *Economica*, Vol. 38, February, pp. 61-80.

Hayek, F.A. (1976), *Denationalisation of Money*, The Institute of Economic Affairs, London.

Ishiyama, Y. (1975), "The theory of optimum currency areas", *IMF Staff Papers*, Vol. 22, July, pp. 344-83.

Kenen, P.B. (1969), "The theory of optimum currency areas: an eclectic view", in Mundell, R.A. and Swoboda, A.K. (Eds), *Monetary Problems of the International Economy*, The University of Chicago Press, Chicago, IL, pp. 41-60.

Kenen, P.B. (Ed.) (1995), *Understanding Interdependence*, Princeton University Press, Princeton, NJ.

Kenen, P.B., Papadia, F and Saccomanni, F. (Eds) (1994), *The International Monetary System*, Cambridge University Press, Cambridge.

Keynes, J.M. (1923), *A Tract on Monetary Reform*, Macmillan, London.

Keynes, J.M. (1944), *Activities 1941-1946. Shaping the Post-War World: Bretton Woods and Reparations, The Collected Writings of John Maynard Keynes*, Moggridge, D. (Ed.), Vol. XXVI. Macmillan, London, 1980.

Klein, B. (1974). "The competitive supply of money", *Journal of Money, Credit and Banking*, Vol. 6, November, pp. 423-53.

Krugman, P.R. (1984), "The international role of the dollar: theory and prospect", in Bilson, J.F.O. and Marston, R. (Eds), *Exchange Rate Theory and Practice*, The University of Chicago Press, Chicago, IL, reprinted in Krugman (1992).

Krugman, P. (1992), *Currencies and Crises*, The MIT Press, Cambridge, MA.

Krugman, P. (1993), *What Do We Need To Know About the International Monetary System? Essays in International Finance No. 193*, Princeton International Finance Section, Princeton. NJ.

Lucas, R.E. (1976), "Econometric policy evaluation: a critique", *Carnegie-Rochester Conference Series on Public Policy*, Vol. 1, pp. 19-46, reprinted in Lucas (1981).

Lucas, R.E. (1977), "Understanding business cycles", *Carnegie-Rochester Conference Series on Public Policy*, Vol. 5, pp. 7-29, reprinted in Lucas (1981).

Lucas, R.E. (1981), *Studies in Business Cycle Theory*, The MIT Press, Cambridge, MA.

McKinnon, R.I. (1963), "Optimum currency areas", *American Economic Review*, Vol. 53, September, pp. 717-24.

McKinnon, R.I. (1993), "The rules of the game: international money in historical perspective", *Journal of Economic Literature*, Vol. 31 No. 1, pp. 1-44.

Mélitz, J. (1995), "The current impasse in research on optimum currency areas", *European Economic Review*, Vol. 39, April, pp. 492-500.

Mill, J.S. (1848), *Principles of Political Economy*, Ashley, W. (Ed.), Longmans, Green & Company, London, 1909.

Mundell, R.A. (1961), "The theory of optimum currency areas", *American Economic Review*, Vol. 51, September, pp. 657-64.

Mundell, R.A. (1972), "The future of the international financial system", in Acheson, A.L.K., Chant, J.F. and Prachowny, M.F.J. (Eds), *Bretton Woods Revisited*, Macmillan, London.

Niehans, J. (1978), *The Theory of Money*, The Johns Hopkins University Press, Baltimore, MA.

Niehans, J. (1984), *International Monetary Economics*, The Johns Hopkins University Press, Baltimore, MD.

Obstfeld, M. and Rogoff, K. (1995), "The mirage of fixed exchange rates", *Journal of Economic Perspectives*, Vol. 9 No. 4, pp. 73-96.

Patinkin, D. (1961), "Financial intermediaries and the logical structure of monetary theory. A review article", *American Economic Review*, Vol. 51, March, pp. 95-116.

van der Ploeg, F. (Ed.) (1994), *The Handbook of International Macroeconomics*, Blackwell, Oxford.

Sargent, T.J. (1987), *Dynamic Macroeconomic Theory*, Harvard University Press, Cambridge, MA.

Schumpeter, J.A. (1954), *History of Economic Analysis*, Oxford University Press, Oxford.

Tinbergen, J. (1952), *On The Theory of Economic Policy*, North-Holland, Amsterdam.

Tower, E. and Willett, T.D. (1976), *The Theory of Optimum Currency Areas and Exchange-rate Flexibility*, Special Studies in International Economics No. 11, Princeton International Finance Section, Princeton, NJ.

Tsiang, S.C. (1969), "A critical note on the optimum supply of money", *Journal of Money, Credit and Banking*, Vol. 1, May, pp. 266-80.

Wicksell, K. (1906), *Lectures on Political Economy*, Vol. II, Routledge, London, 1935.

Woodford, M. (1990), "The optimum quantity of money", in Friedman, B.M. and Hahn, F.H. (Eds), *Handbook of Monetary Economics*, Vol. II, North-Holland, Amsterdam.

[11]

The Bretton Woods Agreements: A Monetary Theory Perspective

Filippo Cesarano

The Bretton Woods monetary system is a highly controversial topic in international economics. During the quarter of a century after the Second World War, the largest industrialized countries experienced high growth accompanied by stable exchange rates and prices, constituting the best overall macroeconomic performance since the inception of the gold standard.[1] On the other hand, the Bretton Woods regime displayed a number of weaknesses – an inadequate adjustment mechanism, controls on capital movements, the adjustable peg and a possible incoherence between liquidity provision and gold convertibility – that eventually proved to be fatal. Acknowledging this contrasting evidence, Barry Eichengreen wittily remarked: 'Even today, more than three decades after its demise, the Bretton Woods international monetary system remains an enigma'.[2]

Viewed from the broader perspective of the evolution of monetary institutions, the Bretton Woods construction was part of the epoch-making transition from commodity money to fiat money. This was a momentous transformation that was gradually completed over the period stretching from the outbreak of the First World War to the suspension of the dollar's convertibility on 15 August 1971. Bretton Woods was the final stage of this lengthy process, a last, ephemeral attempt to maintain a link with commodity money. In fact, the very origin of the post-war monetary setting displays a peculiar feature. Distinguishing between a monetary *system* and a monetary *order*, Mundell[3] identified only three instances of a monetary order: the Roman-Byzantine,

---

1   M.D. Bordo, 'The Bretton Woods International Monetary System: A Historical Overview', in M.D. Bordo and B. Eichengreen (eds), *A Retrospective on the Bretton Woods System* (Chicago, 1993), p. 27.

2   B. Eichengreen, *Globalizing Capital. A History of the International Monetary System* (Princeton, 1996), p. 93.

3   'A system is an aggregation of diverse entities united by regular interaction according to some form of control. When we speak of the international monetary system we are concerned with the mechanisms governing the interaction between trading nations, and in particular between the money and credit instruments of national communities in foreign exchange, capital, and commodity markets. The control is exerted through policies at the national level interacting with one another in that loose form of supervision that we call co-operation. An *order*, as distinct from a system, represents the framework and setting in which the system operates. It is a framework of laws, conventions, regulations, and mores that establish the setting of the system and the understanding of the environment by the participants in it.

spanning almost 1,200 years from Julius Caesar to the fall of Constantinople; the gold standard; and Bretton Woods, with each displaying rather different characteristics. The Roman-Byzantine order was the product of imperialistic power, whereas the gold standard emerged from an historical process. In contrast, the Bretton Woods monetary order was a project elaborated by experts, an unprecedented event in monetary history that made the Bretton Woods architecture unique.

An immediate implication of this distinctive feature is the central role of theory. Drawing up a monetary plan requires knowledge of the principles underlying a monetary economy, and although political interests may come to bear, the end product reflects the designers' theoretical framework. In fact, owing to the early appropriation of the issuing function by a monopolist, namely the government, monetary thought exerted a strong influence upon both the design and the management of monetary institutions, even in ancient times when knowledge was rudimentary and rather scanty.[4] This influence was constrained by the commodity standard, but after the diffusion of fiduciary payment media and the advance of monetary economics from the mid eighteenth century, the impact of theory progressively increased. In the late nineteenth century, leading economists suggested innovative monetary schemes and, in the aftermath of the First World War, the quest for monetary reform gained momentum. In general, theory helps to shape the rules of the game, which in turn define the distinctive properties of a given monetary set-up.

Analysing the main theoretical contributions made during the inter-war years is essential for understanding both the origin and the basic characteristics of the Bretton Woods monetary order. From a theoretical perspective, the interpretation of Bretton Woods as the final stage of the transition from commodity money to fiat money clearly emerges. In fact, the various factors put forward to account for the end of Bretton Woods can be reduced to just one: the influence of monetary theory upon the development of the monetary system. In this respect, the Great Depression can be viewed as the 'defining moment'[5] in that it marks a watershed in the evolution of the state of the art. The different approaches to the subject before, and after, 1929 are examined here, showing their relationships with the key features of the Bretton Woods monetary order and the determinants of its demise.

A monetary order is to a monetary system somewhat like a constitution is to a political or electoral system. We can think of the monetary system as the *modus operandi* of the monetary order.' R.A. Mundell, 'The Future of the International Financial System', in A.L.K. Acheson, J.F. Chant and M.F.J. Prachowny (eds), *Bretton Woods Revisited* (London, 1972), p. 92, italics in the original.

4   F. Cesarano, 'Monetary Systems and Monetary Theory', *Kredit und Kapital*, 32, 2, 1999, pp. 192–208.

5   A recent collection of papers bearing this title, M.D. Bordo, C. Goldin and E.N. White (eds), *The Defining Moment. The Great Depression and the American Economy in the Twentieth Century* (Chicago, 1998), analyses the main changes brought about by the crisis of the 1930s, focusing, however, on economic policy rather than theory.

The critique of the gold standard

After the First World War, policymakers' overriding concern was to re-establish the gold standard. In 1918, the Cunliffe Committee called for Britain's return to gold to restore sound monetary and financial conditions, the prerequisite for economic stability. This recommendation was grounded on two basic principles of classical monetary theory: metallism, which considered it a necessary requisite of money to consist of, or be 'covered' by, a commodity;[6] and the equilibrium hypothesis, which assumed the self-adjusting property of the economy and, particularly, of the international monetary mechanism. With regard to the latter, Hume's specie-flow model is the *locus classicus*, but has continuously given rise to controversies since its publication and even before, witness Oswald's critical assessment.[7]

From a theoretical viewpoint, Hume's analysis is commonly thought to violate the law of one price, a key assumption of the modern monetary approach. From an empirical standpoint, the absence of large price differentials and the presence of conspicuous gold flows between countries each allegedly falsifies Hume's hypothesis. Both criticisms, however, are based on the traditional, textbook version of his model, which misinterprets it. On closer examination, Hume's essay maintains the law of one price, and rather than analysing the dynamics of the adjustment process, shows that market forces prevent a departure from long-run equilibrium.[8] This alternative interpretation portrays the gold standard as a homeostatic system hinging on a highly credible fixed parity, quite consistent with the empirical evidence.

The smooth functioning of the gold standard corroborated the hypothesis that it was an optimal monetary system, the crowning achievement of repeated efforts to dispose of centuries-long tampering with the currency by government. Essential to its successful operation were three 'implicit rules'.[9] First, the restoration rule – that is, the re-establishment of parity after a period of suspension in application of the escape clause to overcome major shocks[10] – solved the time-inconsistency problem of monetary policy, thus enhancing the system's credibility. Second, Bagehot's rule efficaciously tackled an incipient gold drain with an interest rate increase since, given highly credible fixed parities, very small interest rate differentials were sufficient to trigger substantial capital inflows. Third, the common price level was determined by the demand for, and supply of, gold, making the system entirely symmetrical because no country could affect the purchasing power of money. All in all, the successful performance of the gold standard stemmed from the efficacy of its implicit rules,

---

6   J.A. Schumpeter, *History of Economic Analysis* (Oxford, 1954) p. 288.

7   D. Hume, 'Of The Balance of Trade', in E. Rotwein (ed.), *David Hume. Writings on Economics* ([1752], Madison, 1970). J. Oswald of Dunnikier, 'Letter to Hume, 10 October 1750', in E. Rotwein (ed.), *David Hume. Writings on Economics* ([1750], Madison, 1970).

8   F. Cesarano, 'Hume's Specie-Flow Mechanism and Classical Monetary Theory: An Alternative Interpretation', in *Journal of International Economics*, 45, June 1998, pp. 173–86.

9   R.I. McKinnon, 'The Rules of the Game: International Money in Historical Perspective', in *Journal of Economic Literature*, 31, March 1993, pp. 1–44, here pp. 3–4.

10   M.D. Bordo and F.E. Kydland, 'The Gold Standard As a Rule: An Essay in Exploration', in *Explorations in Economic History*, 32, October 1995, pp. 423–64.

which were closely interrelated in that the enforcement of one of them enhanced the effectiveness of the others. In fact, the implicit rules were the basis of the chief properties of the gold standard – credibility, stability and symmetry – although this link was more complex than a simple one-to-one correspondence.

However, during the last quarter of the nineteenth century, economists had cast serious doubts on the optimality of the gold standard. On the one hand, advances in price theory exploded the notion of the value of gold as a natural phenomenon and, instead, made it depend on demand and supply forces in the same way as any other price.[11] On the other, the undesirable effects of deflationary pressure stimulated various proposals aimed at price-level stabilization.[12] Although coming from eminent economists, these proposals had hardly any impact on policymakers, whose attitude was rather adverse to innovation in monetary arrangements. Indeed, the cultural lag separating theorists from central bankers is a constant feature of the evolution of the monetary system, with far-reaching implications for its design.

The major problems inherited from the First World War – huge public debts, substantial and differentiated price-level increases, a fall in gold production[13] and war reparations – made the rapid reinstatement of the gold standard, particularly of the restoration rule, hardly sustainable by most countries. The Genoa Conference, April 1922, was an attempt to solve these problems through the gold-exchange standard, which called for coordination between central banks to stabilize the value of gold.[14] Yet only a few policymakers conformed to the Genoa Resolutions, whereas many continued to abide by the gold-standard model. This discrepancy between innovative arrangements and central bank behaviour was one of the chief factors that eventually undermined the monetary system.

---

11   D. Laidler, 'Rules, Discretion and Financial Crises in Classical and Neoclassical Monetary Economics', ms., April 2001, p. 19.

12   To mention just a few representative examples: Jevons suggested the tabular standard introduced earlier by Lowe. Marshall, instead, argued for symmetallism, defining the unit of account as a weighted basket of gold and silver. Walras proposed issuing a divisionary money (billon régulateur) in order to stabilize the money stock. Finally, Wicksell deserves to be mentioned because, in contrast with the other schemes that were all variations on the commodity standard theme, he argued for cutting the link with gold altogether, a 'first step towards the introduction of an ideal standard of value.', K. Wicksell, *Interest and Prices* ([1898], New York, 1965), p. 193.

13   According to R. Nurkse, *International Currency Experience. Lessons of the Inter-War Period* (Geneva, 1944), p. 27, gold output decreased by a third between 1915 and 1922.

14   'These steps [balancing of budgets; adoption of gold as a common standard; fixing of gold parities; cooperation of central banks, etc.] might by themselves suffice to establish a gold standard, but its successful maintenance would be materially promoted [...] by an international convention to be adopted at a suitable time. The purpose of the convention would be to centralize and coordinate the demand for gold, and so avoid those wide fluctuations in the purchasing power of gold which might otherwise result from the simultaneous and competitive efforts of a number of countries to secure metallic reserves. The convention should embody some means of economizing the use of gold by maintaining reserves in the form of foreign balances, such, for example, as the gold exchange standard or an international clearing system.', Ibid., p. 28.

In the academic world, several aspects of commodity money were criticized on theoretical grounds, although the policy argument stressing the barrier against government interference proved an ultimate defence. Inconvertible paper money, therefore, was usually discarded, with the notable exception of Wicksell.[15] In any case, the goal of price stability became the starting-point of the analysis.[16] It led to consideration of a monetary-setting alternative to the gold standard, a 'managed' money instead of a 'natural' money. However, the state of the art presented a rather variegated picture and no common view of the monetary system emerged. Resorting to a heroic simplification, three main strains of thought can be distinguished. The prevailing idea was to shift to managed money while simultaneously maintaining a link with gold. At each side of this middle-of-the-road position, there were two extreme approaches. The radical, chiefly represented by Keynes, favoured the abandonment of commodity money, assigning to the central bank wide discretionary powers to stabilize prices and employment. The conservative, mainly followed by Austrian economists like Mises and Hayek, stuck firmly to the gold standard.

Ralph Hawtrey, a noted exponent of the mainstream and a protagonist of the Genoa Conference, stressed the necessity of resorting to fiduciary media to satisfy the demand for money. He referred to the gold-exchange standard as 'the favourite of currency theorists'.[17] The danger of over-issuing was pointed out, but eventually it was the deflationary pressure produced by the conspicuous accumulation of gold by the United States and France that proved fatal to the monetary system. Central bankers, not deeming the gold-exchange standard as credible as the gold standard, remained faithful to the latter's paradigm. Consequently, while cooperation was essential for stabilizing the value of gold, the necessary meeting of central banks to undertake it never took place.[18] Indeed, from the very beginning, the gold-exchange

---

15   In his classic on quantity theory, I. Fisher, *The Purchasing Power of Money* ([1911], New York, 1963), ch. 13, recognizes the theoretical soundness of fiat money, but rejects it because of the likelihood of government's meddling with monetary stability. Anticipating Friedman's simple rule, he critically considers a 'simple way' of stabilizing the price level. 'It is true that the level of prices might be kept almost absolutely stable merely by honest government regulation of the money supply with that specific purpose in view. One seemingly simple way by which this might be attempted would be by the issue of inconvertible paper money in quantities so proportioned to increase of business that the total amount of currency in circulation, multiplied by its rapidity, would have the same relation to the total business at one time as at any other time. If the confidence of citizens were preserved, and this relation were kept, the problem would need no further solution. But sad experience teaches that irredeemable paper money, while theoretically capable of steadying prices, is apt in practice to be so manipulated as to produce instability', Ibid., p. 329.

16   A.C. Pigou, *Industrial Fluctuations* (London, 1927), pp. 251–7; D.H. Robertson, *Money* ([1928], Cambridge, 1970), p. 116; G. Cassel, *The Theory of Social Economy* ([1932b], New York, 1967), p. 510.

17   R.G. Hawtrey, 'The Gold Standard', in *Economic Journal*, 29, December 1919, pp. 428–42, here p. 437.

18   Montagu Norman's testimony before the Macmillan Committee is, in this respect, rather eloquent. 'It always appeared impossible, during those years when we were waiting, to summon such a conference for the excellent reason that the people would not come. They would not come, not because they were unwilling to co-operate, but because they were

standard was considered 'with misgiving and suspicion as an academic proposal of doubtful practicability'.[19] Such widespread scepticism can be understood since the introduction of an activist policy in place of an 'automatic' mechanism involved such a momentous mutation that even those favouring the new system displayed a great deal of caution. The novel tasks given to central banks marked the birth of modern monetary policy, whose implementation raised complex theoretical questions that are still debated.[20] Moreover, there was great concern about losing the shield against government interference provided by the gold standard.[21] Both theoretical and political difficulties heightened central bankers' conservative attitude, which contrasted with the change in behaviour required by the Genoa Resolutions. Initially, the policies of the United States and the United Kingdom were coherent

---

unwilling to face the publicity and the questionings in their own countries, which would arise if they attended any such conference, and all the attempts that I made to that end failed.', quoted in R.G. Hawtrey, *The Gold Standard in Theory and Practice* ([1927], London, 1947), p. 102. According to Hawtrey, the meeting of central bankers would have had a meaning quite different from the preceding ones. 'Another international conference! What, will the line stretch out to the crack of doom? But here there is a difference. The calling in of the central banks is a recognition of the principle that currency policy is ultimately credit policy, for the direction of credit policy is the special function of a central bank', R.G. Hawtrey, 'The Genoa Resolutions on Currency', in *Economic Journal*, 32, September 1922, pp. 290–304, here p. 291.

    19 Ibid., p. 295.

    20 'Stabilisation cannot be secured by any hard-and-fast rules. The central banks must exercise discretion; they must be ready to detect and forestall any monetary disturbance even before it has affected prices. The policy can only be perfected by long experience. Nor can it be assumed that perfect stabilisation of internal purchasing power is always reconcilable with perfect stabilisation of the foreign exchanges. The maintenance of the exchanges within a small fraction of parity, which is of the essence of the scheme, may involve a small departure of the internal purchasing power of the unit from the norm in one or more countries. A suitable compromise must be arrived at by the central banks among themselves, but it is no use to under-estimate the difficulty of preserving an even course under such conditions.', Ibid., p. 300. In this regard, Keynes too shows a prudent attitude. '[A]n internal standard, so regulated as to maintain stability in an index number of prices, is a difficult scientific innovation, never yet put into practice.', J.M. Keynes, *A Tract on Monetary Reform* (London, 1923), p. 156.

    21 'We must remember the enormous impetus to which any banking system is subject, both from within and without, towards increasing continually the volume of its loans, and the formidable difficulty of so regulating the supply of money as really to meet the legitimate needs of trade. We must remember, too, the pressure exerted upon Governments in the name of the consumer to provide this and that – coal or railway-transport or house-room – by some means or other below its economic cost. It is not surprising if both bankers and Governments in their more responsible moments desire to have some charm more potent than a mere metaphysical index-number both to elevate before the people and to contemplate in the privacy of their own cells. There are the same arguments against disturbing the simple faith of the banker and the City journalist (the politician perhaps has none) as against disturbing that of the pious savage. If a gold standard had never existed, it might be necessary to invent something of the kind for their benefit', Robertson, *Money*, pp. 121–2. Recalling the peculiar experience of stone money on the island of Yap, Robertson remarks: 'Just so gold is a fetish, if you will, but it does the trick', Ibid., p. 123.

with the gold-exchange standard. However, in the late 1920s, the gulf between the innovative model that had emerged at Genoa and central bankers' lack of adaptation or downright hostility to the new mode of thought increased. This brought about the subsequent monetary turmoil.

The goal of purchasing-power stability, which contrasted with price-level determination in the gold market, broke the third implicit rule and, therefore, opened a fissure in the gold standard. A further, more conspicuous, crack followed from the critique of the restoration rule. Its enforcement would have produced a substantial deflation in most countries, thus raising the real value of public debt and depressing output and employment. *Prima facie*, going back to the pre-war parity entailed a once-and-for-all adjustment of monetary equilibrium. Yet, from a modern point of view, it also affected monetary policy as a continuous process since it prevented the time-inconsistency problem. Hence, the critique of the restoration rule undermined the credibility of the gold standard, as well as the stabilizing role of capital movements stemming from Bagehot's rule. Thus, all the implicit rules of the gold standard were impaired, as were their related properties – stability, credibility and symmetry – not easily reproduced in another monetary setting. In fact, the attempt to compensate for the loss of credibility of the gold-exchange standard by increased cooperation failed, simply because cooperation under the gold standard resulted from a high degree of credibility. Once the rules of the gold standard were called into question, the very characteristics of the system were spoiled, and it was hard to reinstate them by other devices.

Departing from the mainstream, Keynes interpreted monetary reform in a radical way, arguing for a bending of the rules of the monetary system with a view to stabilizing prices and employment.[22] This approach, turning upside down the gold-standard model, characterized his research programme on the subject. Clearly, the theoretical framework supporting this idea changed as Keynes's monetary thought progressed from the *Tract* to the *Treatise*, to the *General Theory* and beyond, but the leitmotiv remained the same. Instead of constraining the policymaker's behaviour by means of rigid rules, modify the latter in order to implement activist economic policy. The resort to debasement during the Middle Ages was, thus, considered positively 'as a method of carrying into effect a preference for stability of internal prices over stability of external exchanges'.[23] The chief advantages of the gold standard, that is long-run purchasing-power stability and insulation from political interference, were rejected simply by acknowledging the existence of a 'managed' currency in place of a 'natural' one.[24] Considering a 'pious hope'[25] the possibility of successfully carrying out the cooperation required by the gold-exchange standard, Keynes refused half-way solutions, which he deemed inferior to either the gold standard or fiduciary money, and embraced a modern conception of monetary policy, not, however, based

---

22   Keynes, *Tract*.
23   Ibid., p. 163.
24   Ibid., pp. 172–3.
25   Ibid., p. 174.

on 'a precise, arithmetical formula'.[26] Taking a radical position, Keynes called for cutting the link with gold altogether and allowing substantial discretion in monetary policy.[27]

At the other end of the academic spectrum, Austrian economists such as Mises and Hayek opposed any degree of discretion in monetary management and staunchly defended the gold standard. Albeit sharing the target of stable prices, Mises stressed the difficulty of attaining it, owing to the lack of knowledge of the monetary transmission mechanism – the argument, together with long and variable lags, for Friedman's 'simple rule'. Furthermore, it was argued that discretionary monetary policy led to government abuses and, thus, much higher costs than those deriving from the lack of money stock controllability in the gold standard.[28] Interestingly, Mises,[29] starting from a diametrically opposite position, arrived at the same conclusions as Keynes, namely that the two extreme models, the gold standard and fiat money, were to be preferred to the hybrid gold exchange standard. This is also Milton Friedman's opinion in his classic essay on flexible exchange rates.[30]

---

26   Ibid., p. 186. '[S]ince I regard the stability of prices, credit, and employment as of paramount importance, and since I feel no confidence that an old-fashioned gold standard will even give us the modicum of stability that it used to give, I reject the policy of restoring the gold standard on pre-war lines. At the same time I doubt the wisdom of attempting a "managed" gold standard jointly with the United States, on the lines recommended by Mr. Hawtrey, because it retains too many of the disadvantages of the old system without its advantages, and because it would make us too dependent on the policy and on the wishes of the Federal Reserve Board.', Ibid., p. 176.

27   'It is desirable, therefore, that the whole of the reserves should be under the control of the authority responsible for this, which, under the above proposals, is the Bank of England. The volume of the paper money, on the other hand, would be consequential, as it is at present, on the state of trade and employment, bank-rate policy and Treasury Bill policy. The governors of the system would be bank-rate and Treasury Bill policy, the objects of government would be stability of trade, prices, and employment, and the volume of paper money would be a consequence of the first (just – I repeat – as it is at present) and an instrument of the second, the precise arithmetical level of which could not and need not be predicted. Nor would the amount of gold, which it would be prudent to hold as a reserve against international emergencies and temporary indebtedness, bear any logical or calculable relation to the volume of paper money; – for the two have no close or necessary connection with one another. Therefore I make the proposal – which may seem, but should not be, shocking – of separating entirely the gold reserve from the note issue', Ibid., pp. 195-6.

28   L. von Mises, *The Theory of Money and Credit* ([1912], Indianapolis, 1980), pp. 268–71. The 1934 English translation of von Mises is based on the second German edition published in 1924.

29   Ibid., p. 432.

30   M. Friedman, 'The Case for Flexible Exchange Rates', in M. Friedman, *Essays in Positive Economics* (Chicago, 1953), p. 164; also M. Friedman, 'Real and Pseudo Gold Standards', in *Journal of Law and Economics*, 4, October 1961, reprinted in M. Friedman, *Dollars and Deficits. Inflation, Monetary Policy and the Balance of Payments* (Englewood Cliffs, N.J, 1968), pp. 150–1.

Hayek's case for the gold standard rested on the analysis of business cycles[31] and of monetary policy.[32] He underscored the notion of neutral rather than stable money,[33] so that money should not disturb optimal resource allocation as determined in the general equilibrium model. The neutrality principle, however, is hard to translate into a policy norm, given price rigidity and unpredictability. While price stability would tamper with general equilibrium, a declining price level stemming from productivity increases entailed no costs and avoided distortions in factor allocation. Criticizing Cassel's and Pigou's call for an elastic currency, Hayek, like Mises, emphasized the lack of knowledge of the monetary transmission mechanism, and argued for a constant money stock, albeit with changes allowed to compensate for velocity variations.[34]

The difficulties inherited from the First World War led to a rethinking of the basic features of the monetary system along the lines discussed at the Genoa Conference. The gold exchange standard was assumed to maintain the essential properties of the gold standard, but in reality impaired credibility. Hawtrey's conjecture to offset this credibility loss with more intensive cooperation was at odds with both the innovations introduced into monetary arrangements and central bankers' cultural background. In fact, the suggestion of stabilizing the price level sowed the seeds of spoiling the properties of the pre-war monetary system irremediably. Accordingly, the reformed gold standard eventually collapsed, leaving no common view about the optimal design of monetary institutions. A protagonist of this transformation in the state of the art was Keynes. Explaining these developments with the diffusion of managed money, Hayek traced its origins back to the transition from the gold-specie standard to the gold-bullion standard. The main point was the role of the monetary authority, that is whether or not it could regulate the quantity of money. In this regard, the United Kingdom's abandonment of the gold standard in September 1931 was a watershed in monetary history and the product of a new theoretical paradigm, chiefly due to Keynes.[35]

---

31   F.A. von Hayek, *Monetary Theory and the Trade Cycle* ([1933b], New York, 1966).

32   ·F. A. von Hayek, *Prices and Production* ([1931], New York, 1967).

33   F. A. von Hayek, 'On "Neutral Money"', in R. McCloughry (ed.), *Money, Capital & Fluctuations* ([1933a], London, 1984).

34   Hayek, *Prices*, pp. 121–4.

35   'This abandonment of the gold standard undoubtedly implies a final break with the unique tradition of more than two hundred years, on the basis of which Britain has repeatedly returned to the gold standard at the cost of great sacrifices, even after periods of temporary shock to its currency unit. This time the sacrifices which had been made since 1921 were in vain, because the responsible authorities were unwilling or unable to exact what probably would have been the smaller sacrifices necessary to ensure the long-term position of the pound. The greatest responsibility for this, however, must be borne by those who initially opposed the return to the gold standard. For although their position was justifiable at that time, they did not abandon it even when the gold standard had been restored at its former parity, and fought with the utmost vigour against all the measures necessary if that standard were to be finally consolidated. It is beyond all doubt that they found an increasingly more receptive hearing within the management of the Bank. If one wanted to describe the abandonment of the gold standard in Britain as "the economic consequences of Mr Keynes", and there

The Great Depression and the search for an alternative monetary system

The Great Depression had a major impact upon the economics profession, and led to a general rethinking of the monetary system. The critical assessment of the gold standard after the shock of the First World War weakened the metallist doctrine, one of the two foundations of the classical model. The length and severity of the 1930s depression undermined the second, viz. the equilibrium hypothesis, thus enhancing the acceptance of managed money.

During the 1930s, while support for the gold standard faded, economists were divided over the equilibrium hypothesis. Keynes was the most notable exponent of the critical view, taking, as during the previous decade, a radical position on both economic theory and monetary reform. The mainstream, instead, stuck to the classical model, and arrived at a monetary explanation of the Great Depression, anticipating Milton Friedman's 'inescapable [conclusion]: ... monetary contraction or collapse is an essential conditioning factor for the occurrence of a major depression'.[36] In his Rhodes Memorial Lectures, Gustav Cassel, stressing the different nature of the 1929 crisis with respect to pre-war business cycles, identified its basic characteristic in the price level's sharp fall, which was a monetary phenomenon and, therefore, admitted only a monetary explanation.[37] Following this line of thought, Hawtrey emphasized the dynamic aspect of central bank policy, and thus the danger of disturbing equilibrium through untimely action. Starting from the relationship between the quantity of money and nominal income, Hawtrey put the case for stabilizing the money supply on more solid ground, referring to both assumptions underlying Friedman's simple rule: the presence of lags and the lack of knowledge of the transmission mechanism.[38] Hawtrey also stressed the depression's international character, showing how, in the absence of monetary cooperation, mistaken monetary policies were transmitted to other countries. In particular, the absence of concerted action to implement monetary expansion proved fatal to the gold-exchange standard.[39] The accumulation of gold by the United States and France stopped the adjustment process from the very outset and set off a deflationary process.[40] At the basis of such behaviour was central bankers' distrust of innovations in monetary arrangements departing from the gold standard, thus showing the permanence of a cultural divide between policymakers and economists.[41] In any case, monetary mismanagement, owing to either a violation

are many reasons to do so, I believe that even today J.M. Keynes would still regard such a statement not as criticism but as praise.', F.A. von Hayek, 'The Fate of the Gold Standard', in R. McCloughry (ed.), *Money, Capital and Fluctuations* ([1932], London, 1984), pp. 132–3.

36 M. Friedman, 'Why the American Economy is Depression-Proof', in M. Friedman, *Dollars and Deficits. Inflation, Monetary Policy and the Balance of Payments* ([1954], Englewood Cliffs, N.J, 1968), pp. 82–3.

37 G. Cassel, *The Crisis in the World's Monetary System* (Oxford, 1932a), pp. 41–9.

38 R.G. Hawtrey, *The Art of Central Banking* ([1932], London, 1970), pp. 280–2.

39 R.G. Hawtrey, *Economic Destiny* (London, 1944), pp. 88–9.

40 Cassel, *Crisis*, pp. 63–72.

41 David Williams gives a good description of central bankers' conservative attitude in the 1920s. 'Once the chief results of the gold exchange standard had been achieved – stabilization of exchange rates and the strengthening of monetary reserves – there was

of the gold standard rules or a failure to cooperate and stabilize the money stock, accounted for major downturns in economic activity which, coherently with the equilibrium hypothesis, required a monetary therapy.

In the mid-1930s, this analysis became widely accepted, witness the contributions to Irving Fisher's Festschrift volume.[42] The starting-point was the necessity of reducing the amplitude of cyclical fluctuations since a sharp increase in output caused a subsequent recession and an unstable growth path.[43] The policy recipe was to stabilize the money supply, which, though not eliminating income fluctuations entirely, could reduce them to within small limits.[44] Accordingly, monetary arrangements, in contrast with the commodity standard, must allow control of the money stock.[45] However, while the departure from the rigid rules of the gold

---

increasing pressure by some important countries to revert to a gold bullion standard. The gold exchange standard was never accepted as anything but a temporary palliative by France; Germany and the smaller countries of West and Central Europe had a strong desire to hold as much gold as was possible. The gold exchange standard in the 'twenties was regarded not only as an expedient, but as a temporary expedient', D. Williams, 'The 1931 Financial Crisis', *Yorkshire Bulletin of Economic and Social Research*, 15, November 1963, pp. 92–110, reprinted in M. Thomas (ed.), *The Disintegration of the World Economy Between the World Wars*, vol. 2 ([1963], Cheltenham and Brookfield, 1996), p. 95.

42   A.D. Gayer (ed.), *The Lessons of Monetary Experience* (London, 1937).

43   In this regard, the Fed chairman, Marriner Eccles, notes: 'Those who believe in nature taking its course argue that there are forces that tend to restore the flow of income when it is disturbed. ... The answer to this argument is that it is true as far as it goes, but it does not go far enough. It assumes a condition of stable national income, and this is precisely the condition that is absent during a general downswing. ... Similarly, in depressions, when incomes are falling, a reduction in prices may fail to stimulate demand. This is particularly likely to happen if a further continued fall in prices is generally expected. Thus a departure from stability, although it may set in motion corrective forces, also unfortunately produces intensifying and aggravating ones. Our recent experience is grim witness to the fact that these latter forces may far outweigh the corrective forces for an impossibly long period. Before the self-generating forces of deflation in the last depression were exhausted or were offset by positive government action, the national income had been cut in half, and a sixth of our population was being supported out of public funds. Now that we are on the upswing, the self-generating forces of revival might carry us into another boom unless we are prepared to take corrective action in time', M.S. Eccles, 'Controlling Booms and Depressions', in A.D. Gayer (ed.), *The Lessons of Monetary Experience* (London, 1937), pp. 7–8. See J.W. Angell, 'The General Objectives of Monetary Policy', in A.D. Gayer (ed.), *The Lessons of Monetary Experience* (London, 1937), pp. 52–3; A.H. Hansen, 'Monetary Policy in the Upswing', in A.D. Gayer (ed.), *The Lessons of Monetary Experience* (London, 1937), p. 89; J.H. Williams, 'International Monetary Organization and Policy', in A.D. Gayer (ed.), *The Lessons of Monetary Experience* (London, 1937), p. 26.

44   Angell, 'Objectives', p. 83.

45   'The criminal characteristic of the money and banking systems that have hitherto existed in nearly all modern countries is that they have been inherently unstable within wide limits, and that they have usually worked to *intensify* fluctuations in both directions rather than to damp them down. In so-called good times, when the total money volume of economic activity is increasing, most money and banking systems also greatly increase the quantity of circulating money; indeed, this is one of the favorite ways of augmenting the current volume

standard, suggested by Keynes much earlier,[46] was generally accepted,[47] there was no unanimous opinion about the design of a new monetary setting, a daunting task after the monetary gyrations following the 1929 crisis. Various suggestions were put forward to improve the working of the gold-exchange standard – cancel war debts, re-establish freedom in international trade and capital movements and reduce the demand for gold reserves[48] – but an essential condition remained the stabilization of the value of gold through cooperation. The scepticism surrounding the accomplishment of this objective prevented the formulation of detailed proposals for reconstructing the monetary system. Wide credence was given, instead, to the conception of monetary policy as a continuous process aimed at preventing major cyclical fluctuations in order to maintain price and output stability.[49]

As during the 1920s, the range of opinions remained highly variegated,[50] but the state of the art's centre of gravity permanently shifted away from an 'automatic'

---

of new private investment rapidly. But the increase in the quantity of money, if regarded by the business community as 'normal,' is itself likely to intensify the changes which are already under way. ... All this taken alone might not be a conclusive condemnation. But if expansion does at last cease, and gives way to the beginning of contraction, the money and banking system suddenly turns about, and now intensifies the general *fall*. As bank investments are sold and as bank loans are called or allowed to run off, the quantity of money declines; this decline and the circumstances out of which it arises engender new fear, and accentuate the fall in expectation and the rise in idle balances of cash which are developing anyway; the growing struggle for business solvency compels many liquidations of inventories and other holdings, which further increases the banks' desire to reduce their commitments, and thus further contracts the quantity of money; and thus a downward spiral of interactions is initiated. Once well under way, as is only too familiar, the decline can go to disastrous lengths before it is checked', Angell, 'Objectives', pp. 83–5, italics in the original.

46   Keynes, *Tract*.

47   Mlynarsky clearly describes the change in the state of the art. 'The classical doctrine of the automatic standard was thus opposed by the conception of a managed currency. More and more economists were accepting the principles of the new school. Today Keynes appears to have the greatest number of adherents; according to him the gold parity should be changed from time to time. Foreign-exchange quotations should fluctuate within limits broader than those of the gold points, for instance within 5 per cent of a given parity. The issue of bank notes should be severed from gold movements and controlled only from the point of view of stabilizing the purchasing power of money as the most important consideration. Without going into technical details, and without discussing the shortcomings or advantages of the new doctrine, it can be stated that it is a complete reversal of the Ricardian theory and hence quite revolutionary with regard to the classical doctrine', F. Mlynarsky, 'Proportionalism and Stabilization Policy', in A.D. Gayer (ed.), *The Lessons of Monetary Experience* (London, 1937), p. 272.

48   Cassel, *Crisis*, pp. 89–92.

49   Angell, 'Objectives', pp. 52–3.

50   Viner makes this point. 'In the late 1930's probably no country was wholly satisfied with the existing monetary situation. But there was no agreement as to the directions in which improvement was to be sought. Some wished for a return to the rigid pre-1914 gold standard, without fundamental change therein. Others dreamed of a new kind of gold standard – an internationally managed one designed to produce both stability of the exchanges and stability of world price levels, so as to cure the great defect of the traditional gold standard, that it made

monetary mechanism. However, the pursuit of domestic targets through a managed money might conflict with the maintenance of a fixed parity,[51] eventually leading to the link with gold being cut. This conclusion, once regarded as seemingly 'shocking', was accepted a decade later by all economists arguing for a viable managed money. As Cassel remarked: 'Clearly, the only way to a permanent stabilization of the world's monetary system is to make the supply of credit entirely independent of the gold reserves of central banks'.[52] This question may be viewed as the origin of the policy 'trilemma'[53] – also called the inconsistent trinity, or irreconcilable trilogy, or eternal triangle. In this, only two of the following three elements can be included in choosing a policy regime: fixed exchange rates, free capital movements and independent monetary policy aimed at domestic goals. This is indicative of the complex problems, both theoretical and institutional, that arose from the abandonment of the gold standard during the early 1930s. To give a cursory example: while Cassel fully grasped the one-way bet offered by a gold parity that was not credible,[54] thus anticipating Friedman's criticism of the Bretton Woods system,[55] several other problems remained unsolved. Economists, venturing into uncharted waters, did not arrive at a clear idea for the design of future monetary arrangements.[56]

Following the impact of the Great Depression, the mainstream moved towards the position taken by Keynes roughly a decade before. However, Keynes was now proposing more innovative monetary schemes. His *Treatise on Money*, although widely criticized from a theoretical point of view, suggested a monetary setting

---

the world subject to sustained deflationary or inflationary price trends resulting from fortuitous developments in the discovery of gold fields and in the technology of gold mining. Still others, and especially the totalitarian countries, sought a permanent and complete divorce of their monetary systems from gold and a further extension and intensification of exchange controls administered on a national basis and with narrowly nationalistic and indeed, in some cases, openly aggressive objectives.', J. Viner, 'Two Plans for International Monetary Stabilization', in J. Viner, *International Economics* ([1943], Glencoe, Ill., 1951), p. 194. See also Angell, *Objectives*, pp. 53–4.

51　Keynes, *Tract*, ch. 4.

52　G. Cassel, *The Downfall of the Gold Standard* ([1936], New York, 1966), p. 229.

53　M. Obstfeld and A.M. Taylor, 'The Great Depression as a Watershed: International Capital Mobility over the Long Run', in M.D. Bordo, C. Goldin and E.N. White (eds), *The Defining Moment. The Great Depression and the American Economy in the Twentieth Century* (Chicago, 1998), pp. 354–5.

54　Cassel, *Downfall*, pp. 240–1.

55　Friedman, 'Case', pp. 163–4.

56　Two specific proposals, though subject to various criticisms, may be an exception: Fisher's 100 per cent reserve requirement: I. Fisher, 'The Debt-Deflation Theory of Great Depressions', in *Econometrica*, 1, October 1933, pp. 337–57, and I. Fisher, *100 per cent Money* ([1935], New Haven, 1945), pp. 133–4, with a view to dampening fluctuations in the money multiplier, and thus in the money supply, and Benjamin Graham's and Frank Graham's commodity reserve currency, substituting a basket of commodities for a single one as the standard in order to avoid the defects of the gold standard and preserve all its advantages, B. Graham, *Storage and Stability* (New York, 1937), and F.D. Graham, 'The Primary Functions of Money and Their Consummation in Monetary Policy', in *American Economic Review. Papers and Proceedings*, 30, March 1940, part 2, pp. 1–16.

consistent with the implementation of autonomous economic policy and the maintenance of stable exchange rates.[57] Widening the gold price fluctuation band to 2 per cent would discourage capital movements, and make it possible to manoeuvre short-term interest rates for internal purposes. The high capital mobility of the gold standard had to be avoided because, in an economy characterized by rigidities, it would produce serious imbalances.[58] The control of capital movements provided a solution to the policy trilemma that was to be part of the British position during the Bretton Woods negotiations. In the final chapter of the *Treatise*, two plans were proposed: a more limited one, mostly tracking the Resolutions of the Genoa Conference, and a more radical one, based on the establishment of a supranational central bank.

After the Great Depression, Keynes's main contributions were to economic theory, not monetary institutions. In contrast with the received view that identified the cause of the crisis with monetary mismanagement in an equilibrium model, he rejected the equilibrium hypothesis.[59] The foundations of this approach were

---

57   J.M. Keynes, *A Treatise on Money* (London, 1930), vol. 2, pp. 300–6.

58   'If we deliberately desire that there should be a high degree of mobility for international lending, both for long and for short periods, then this is, admittedly, a strong argument for a fixed rate of exchange and a rigid international standard. What, then, is the reason for hesitating before we commit ourselves to such a system? Primarily a doubt whether it is wise to have a Currency System with a much wider ambit than our Banking System, our Tariff System and our Wage System. Can we afford to allow a disproportionate degree of mobility to a single element in an economic system which we leave extremely rigid in several other respects? If there was the same mobility internationally in all other respects as there is nationally, it might be a different matter. But to introduce a mobile element, highly sensitive to outside influences, as a connected part of a machine of which the other parts are much more rigid, may invite breakages', Keynes, *Treatise*, vol. 2, pp. 334–5.

59   In a radio broadcast with the eloquent title 'Poverty in Plenty: Is the Economic System Self-Adjusting?', Keynes divides economists into two groups according to their positive or negative answer to the question. Including himself in the second one, he claims to have found a basic weakness in the orthodox model. 'Now *I* range myself with the heretics. I believe their flair and their instinct move them towards the right conclusion. But I was brought up in the citadel and I recognize its power and might. A large part of the established body of economic doctrine I cannot but accept as broadly correct. I do not doubt it. For me, therefore, it is impossible to rest satisfied until I can put my finger on the flaw in that part of the orthodox reasoning which leads to the conclusions which for various reasons seem to me to be unacceptable. I believe that I am on my way to do so. There is, I am convinced, a fatal flaw in that part of the orthodox reasoning which deals with the theory of what determines the level of effective demand and the volume of aggregate employment; the flaw being largely due to the failure of the classical doctrine to develop a satisfactory theory of the rate of interest', J.M. Keynes, 'Poverty in Plenty: Is the Economic System Self-Adjusting?', in D. Moggridge (ed.), *The Collected Writings of John Maynard Keynes, vol. 13* ([1934], London, 1973), p. 489, italics in the original. In a previous passage, Keynes lucidly expounds the main principles of the classical position underlying the malfunctioning of the monetary system. 'Professor Robbins [...] stresses the effect of business mistakes under the influence of the uncertainty and the false expectations due to the faults of post-war monetary systems. These authorities do not, of course, believe that the system is automatically or immediately self-adjusting. But

developed in the *General Theory* which, given its policy implications, was to play a key role in shaping the design of monetary institutions. He dealt with the latter topic in two essays reflecting the vision of his *magnum opus*. The scheme outlined in *The Means to Prosperity* is the institutional counterpart of an analysis investigating the conditions for economic recovery, and anticipates many features of the Bretton Woods system. Besides providing abundant credit and maintaining a low long-run interest rate, a public expenditure programme must be implemented to trigger output expansion.[60] In the monetary proposal, an international authority issues gold notes, obtainable by countries against gold bonds according to quotas determined on the basis of gold reserves. Voting power is proportional to quotas. The main aim is to stabilize the price level by fixing the interest rate and controlling the creation of gold notes. In Keynes's words, the plan involved 'a qualified return to the gold standard',[61] allowing parity variations and a widening of the gold points up to 5 per cent to discourage capital movements. In a subsequent paper,[62] two kinds of problems were distinguished: short-run fluctuations and a persistent disequilibrium. The former could be tackled with the policies indicated in the *Means to Prosperity*. The latter, mainly related to either a divergence between wage and efficiency increases, or more general causes – such as a lack of confidence or the possibility of war – required a parity change. The article's message was to eschew credit contraction to cure a 'fundamental international maladjustment'.[63] This was a concept analogous to the 'fundamental disequilibrium' of the Bretton Woods agreements because, in the absence of a decrease in nominal wages, monetary restriction would raise unemployment.

The Great Depression was indeed a turning point because it delivered a fatal blow to the theoretical model underlying the gold standard. Before 1929, criticism of the latter was confined to the academic world in its search for a more stable monetary set-up, but had little or no impact on policymakers. In fact, as has been shown, central bankers' unwavering trust in the gold-standard model was a main factor in the monetary gyrations of that period. After 1929, the state of the art's centre of gravity definitely moved towards managed money, and even policymakers began to distance themselves from gold-standard orthodoxy. In this regard, there are striking differences between the results of the Cunliffe Committee in 1918 and those of the Macmillan Committee in 1931. The former stressed the benefits of the gold standard and the necessity of the return to gold, whereas the latter argued for a managed money aimed at not only maintaining parity but also stabilizing prices and employment, thus revealing a fracture in the approach to monetary arrangements. Clearly, such a major paradigm shift occurred at different speeds according to

---

they do believe that it has an inherent tendency towards self-adjustment, if it is not interfered with and if the action of change and chance is not too rapid', Ibid., p. 487.

60   J.M. Keynes, 'The Means to Prosperity', in D. Moggridge (ed.), *The Collected Writings of John Maynard Keynes, vol. 9* ([1933], London, 1972), pp. 353–5.

61   Ibid., p. 362.

62   J.M. Keynes, 'The Future of the Foreign Exchanges', in D. Moggridge (ed.), *The Collected Writings of John Maynard Keynes, vol. 21* ([1935], London, 1982).

63   Ibid., p. 367.

the relative degree of conservatism of the protagonists.[64] Even abstracting for a moment from both Keynes's downright rejection of the equilibrium hypothesis and the message of the *General Theory*, mainstream economists definitely rejected the 'automatic' gold standard, although they did not have a unanimous view about how to reform the monetary system.

The Bretton Woods agreements: designing the post-war monetary order

After the unsuccessful attempt of the Tripartite Agreement in September 1936, the objective of reconstructing the monetary system was pursued by the major powers from the outbreak of war. Germany's *Neuordnung*[65] was intended to replace the gold standard and London as the main financial centre by introducing a clearing mechanism in continental Europe. The Keynes Plan and the White Plan, issued respectively in April and July 1943, countered the German project. They eventually led to the Joint Statement of April 1944, the document that constituted the basis of the Bretton Woods conference.

The British Ministry of Information contacted Keynes as early as November 1940 to criticize the German proposal. However, he appreciated this scheme, built on Schacht's idea of a clearing system, and argued in the first draft of his Plan for 'a refinement and improvement of the Schachtian device'.[66] The starting-point was to eliminate the dysfunctionality of the inter-war monetary system by doing without an international money altogether through the 'banking principle', that is bank

---

64 Contrasting the results of the Genoa and London conferences, respectively influenced by the Cunliffe and Macmillan Committees, Clarke stresses this point. 'Although both the Genoa and London conferences must be classed as failures, the records of the negotiations and the memoirs of participants provide a fascinating account of the interaction between economic developments and international monetary thought. At Genoa the traditional gold-standard view, as formulated by British thinkers, was accepted almost without question. Eleven years later this view was championed primarily by the French and other continental Europeans but was rejected in practice by the United States, Britain, and the countries that were to comprise the sterling area. With this shift in monetary views came two other crucial changes. At Genoa the aim was a unified monetary system based on parities fixed in terms of gold – a system in which domestic economies would have to adjust in order to maintain international equilibrium. By 1933 only the inflation-scarred Continental Europeans were clinging to the traditional order of priorities, while Britain and the United States gave domestic recovery precedence over external stability. The further outcome of London was to accelerate international monetary disintegration, with the sterling area, the European gold bloc, and the United States each dealing as best it could with its special regional problems', S.V.O. Clarke, *The Reconstruction of the International Monetary System: The Attempts of 1922 and 1933*, Princeton Studies in International Finance, no. 33 (Princeton, 1973), p. 2.
65 W. Funk, *Wirtschaftliche Neuordnung Europas* (Berlin, 1940).
66 *CW* 25, p. 24, References to Keynes's *Collected Writings* are indicated as *CW* followed by the volume number. According to R.E. Lüke, 'The Schacht and the Keynes Plans', *Banca Nazionale del Lavoro Quarterly Review*, March 1985, pp. 65–76, the central idea of the Keynes Plan goes back to a monetary reform presented by Schacht at an international conference in February 1929.

clearing. The Keynes Plan, reflecting Mill's 'ideal case'[67] and Wicksell's 'organized credit economy',[68] extended a main tenet underlying monetary evolution, that is the development of less costly payment media, to an international context, while searching for optimal macroeconomic solutions.

The Plan opens with a quest for autonomous domestic policy, thus calling for a monetary system, managed by a supranational central bank, consistent with this objective. In order to avoid competitive devaluations and favour a return to multilateral trade, exchange rates are fixed but can be varied in the event of external imbalances. Furthermore, the money stock is independent of the vagaries of the gold market, and creditor countries are involved in the adjustment process to assure symmetry. Credit facilities prevent the monetary mechanism from causing a fall in economic activity, and controls on capital movements create sufficient room for manoeuvre to implement domestic policies.

The kernel of the Plan is best illustrated by Keynes himself in a comment on Hayek's revival of the commodity reserve currency. The Clearing Union solved the two main problems of the gold standard, namely the lack of control over the money supply and the unemployment effects of the adjustment mechanism, by, respectively, working through the velocity, not the quantity, of money, and allowing autonomous price and wage policies to maintain employment. An external disequilibrium requires a change in domestic policies and, if this proves unfeasible, an exchange rate variation. With respect to the gold standard, therefore, the Keynes Plan turned the design of the monetary system upside down in that the latter, instead of being a constraint, allowed economic policy to pursue domestic targets.[69]

The Keynes Plan, albeit original and radical like his previous proposals, contained various weaknesses. The most delicate aspect was the independence of economic policy in the presence of the adjustable peg, which was to be reconciled by capital controls. Their efficacy is, however, disputable. Moreover, the establishment of a supranational central bank raises the problem of apportioning the decision-making power, which is likely to be concentrated in one or just a very few countries. This limitation is of a political nature but also has economic implications. In a context of waning monetary discipline and discretionary policies in a fixed-exchange rate regime, it creates a gap in the scale of sovereignty, thereby undermining credibility

---

67   J.S. Mill, *Principles of Political Economy*, W. Ashley (ed.), ([1848], New York, 1987), p. 524.

68   Wicksell, *Interest*, [1898], pp. 62–101.

69   'The fundamental reason for thus limiting the objectives of an international currency scheme is the impossibility, or at any rate the undesirability, of imposing stable price-levels from without. The error of the gold-standard lay in submitting national wage-policies to outside dictation. It is wiser to regard stability (or otherwise) of internal prices as a matter of internal policy and politics. Commodity standards which try to impose this from without will break down just as surely as the rigid gold-standard', J.M. Keynes, 'The Objective of International Price Stability', in *Economic Journal*, 53, June–September 1943, pp. 185–7, here p. 187; F.A. von Hayek, 'A Commodity Reserve Currency', in *Economic Journal*, 53, June–September 1943, pp. 176–84.

and the system's other properties.[70] At the country level, the sanctioning power of the International Clearing Union may prove insufficiently effective to keep the system viable, given the pursuit of full employment policies. The inflationary potential of the Keynes Plan thus does not derive from an intrinsic defect of its rules,[71] but rather from the lack of an adequate disciplining mechanism squaring the adjustable peg with activist economic policies.

The innovative character of the Keynes Plan contrasted with the conservative approach of the White Plan. An International Stabilization Fund supplies financing facilities to member countries, which contribute their quotas in gold, currencies and government bonds. The monetary unit is the unitas, equivalent in value to $10 of fine gold. The excessive accumulation of credit balances is met by the scarce currency clause instructing the Fund to purchase and distribute the scarce currency among member countries. A variation in the exchange rate is admitted in the event of a 'fundamental disequilibrium'.

The objectives of the two Plans were analogous – trade multilateralism, stable exchange rates, activist stabilization policies and symmetry in the adjustment process – but the instruments to attain them differed. The Keynes Plan aimed to overcome the slow and costly adjustment of the gold standard with a clearing system making overdraft facilities available to debtor countries. Quotas fixed the limit of debt and credit positions, whereas in the White Plan, quotas were effectively deposited. Underlying the American position, there was an adversity to all potentially inflationary features, such as overdraft facilities and the introduction of an international money – the bancor – too radical an innovation to pass the politicians' approval.[72] The White Plan, in fact, reflected a more conservative vision, stressing the principle of free trade and capital movements, and trying to maintain a role for gold in the system. These objectives were consistent with America's huge gold reserves, strong competitiveness and high net credit position.

After their publication, both proposals were critically reviewed. In general, the White Plan was considered similar to the gold-exchange standard, and thus inadequate for overcoming inter-war problems, while the Keynes Plan was deemed inflationary. According to Lutz, neither had a mechanism to prevent policies from

---

70   In the concluding section of the Plan, Keynes is aware of this criticism but plays it down, deeming the surrendering of sovereignty by member countries 'no greater ... than in a commercial treaty', J.K. Horsefield, *The International Monetary Fund 1945–1965: Twenty Years of International Monetary Cooperation, vol. 3, Documents* (Washington, 1969b), p. 36. This argument, however, does not fully consider the implications of establishing a supranational monetary authority, particularly on the consistency of the rules of the game of the International Clearing Union and their enforcement.

71   After the circulation of the first draft in a restricted circle, Hawtrey objected to the mild penalties against persistent debtors (*CW* 25, pp. 40–2). In the final version, therefore, a series of rigid limits is set for debtors, including a generalized reduction of quotas in the event of 'an excess of world purchasing power', Horsefield, *Monetary Fund*, vol. 3, p. 25.

72   J.K. Horsefield, *The International Monetary Fund 1945-1965: Twenty Years of International Monetary Cooperation, vol. 1, Chronicle* (Washington, 1969a), p. 30.

leading to a fundamental disequilibrium.[73] Though based on gold, its role was 'quite unnecessary or even a nuisance under both schemes',[74] whose viabilities were doubtful, given the contrast of activist policies with a fixed-exchange-rate regime.[75] On the contrary, Viner took a positive view and, albeit pointing out some limitations, was favourable to a monetary reform including the best elements of each proposal.[76] The Joint Statement carried out such a melding in a way that was heavily biased towards the American position. This widely held view, however, neglects the influence of Keynes's thought on economic policy design and on post-war monetary arrangements.

Albeit recognizing the predominance of the United States in the negotiations, Keynes worked hard to assure the success of the reform. In his House of Lords speech, he considered the Joint Statement to be 'a considerable improvement on either of its parents', though lacking 'certain features of elegance, clarity and logic' of the Clearing Union plan.[77] After pointing out several advantages of the joint proposal, he emphasized the primacy of domestic targets *vis-à-vis* exchange rate stability, so that economic policy was not directed at maintaining parity as in the gold standard but at full employment.[78] This change in policy perspective stands out in Article I of the Bretton Woods Articles of Agreement acknowledging the epoch making paradigm shift produced by the *General Theory.*

The architects of the Bretton Woods monetary order sought to re-establish a symmetrical adjustment mechanism, as well as multilateral trade, in a fixed-exchange-rate regime, while allowing the pursuit of independent domestic policy. The policy trilemma was solved by maintaining capital controls and, in the long

73   F.A. Lutz, *The Keynes and White Proposals*, Essays in International Finance, no. 1 (Princeton, 1943), p. 17.

74   Ibid., p. 20.

75   Concluding his article, Lutz remarks: 'It is interesting to step back and to look at the plans as a whole. Unlike the classical economists, most modern economists do not favor solutions of economic problems which are based on principles. Instead they advocate, in each concrete instance, measures devised ad hoc which, if ingenious from a technical point of view, may contradict other measures devised in other fields. The result is that the pattern of economic policy of modern governments is far from being a model of logical consistency', Ibid., pp. 20–21.

76   Viner, 'Plans', p. 215.

77   *CW* 26, p. 10.

78   'The plan not merely confirms the de-thronement [of gold] but approves it by expressly providing that it is the duty of the Fund to alter the gold value of any currency if it is shown that this will be serviceable to equilibrium. In fact, the plan introduces in this respect an epoch-making innovation in an international instrument, the object of which is to lay down sound and orthodox principles. For instead of maintaining the principle that the internal value of a national currency should conform to a prescribed *de jure* external value, it provides that its external value should be altered if necessary so as to conform to whatever *de facto* internal value results from domestic policies, which themselves shall be immune from criticism by the Fund. Indeed, it is made the duty of the Fund to approve changes which will have this effect. That is why I say that these proposals are the exact opposite of the gold standard. They lay down by international agreement the essence of the new doctrine, far removed from the old orthodoxy.' (*CW* 26, pp. 18–9).

run, by resorting to changes in parity, when the reversal of policies proved unable to correct external imbalances. Hence, in the spirit of the treaty, exchange rates were kept stable in the short run to avoid the beggar-thy-neighbour policies of the 1930s, and flexible enough in the longer term to square with autonomous domestic policies.

However, after the 1949 devaluations, the game began to be played with fixed exchange rates, giving rise to the fixed-rate dollar standard of 1950–70.[79] This development, arising from the necessity of both facilitating the operation of the European Payments Union and enhancing the credibility of post-war anti-inflation policies, made the system much more similar to the gold-exchange standard. Not only were parity variations regarded as exceptional, but gold had far from lost its role. This was not just a mere legislative matter regarding the Bretton Woods rules,[80] but characterized policymakers' behaviour.

Major countries came to accumulate substantial gold reserves, something that continued until the early 1960s. Indeed, the very idea of a fiat-money standard was somewhat alien to central bankers, as shown by the deep concern for the dollar convertibility constraint and the related Triffin dilemma. However, since the United States controlled the home price level, the growth of demand-determined reserves held by other countries, mainly in United States Treasury bonds, was not a threat to the American gold stock. Hence, one can agree with McKinnon's conjecture that the fixed-rate dollar system could have continued indefinitely, had the United States maintained a stable purchasing power and demonetized gold.[81] Yet, neither condition was met, again due to the determining influence of economic theory.

First, at the heyday of Keynesian economics, no country would have renounced the pursuit of domestic targets other than the price level. Certainly not the United States, which, playing the role of the *nth* country in Mundell's redundancy problem,[82] could hardly have been expected to renounce the extra degree of freedom in order to uphold the viability of the international monetary system. Second, the decision to demonetise gold would have been difficult for the holder of the largest gold reserve to take. There was no schizophrenic attitude, therefore, on the part of the centre country, whose behaviour simply reflected the prevailing state of the art and the overwhelming strength of its economy *vis-à-vis* the rest of the world.

Bringing all these factors together, it appears that the post-Second-World-War monetary order was doomed, since the rules by which the game was eventually played were inconsistent. Keeping a link with gold while concurrently pursuing

79 McKinnon, 'Rules', sections 2–3.
80 'Bretton Woods ratified the gold-exchange standard, it did not legislate a dollar standard', J. Williamson, 'On the System in Bretton Woods', in *American Economic Review. Papers and Proceedings*, 75, May 1985, pp. 74–9, here p. 75.
81 McKinnon, 'Rules', p. 39. The implicit assumption underlying McKinnon's hypothesis is that the seignorage gained by the US was considered by other countries as a price to pay in exchange for the service of guaranteeing the system's stability.
82 R.A. Mundell, 'The Redundancy Problem and the World Price Level', in R.A. Mundell, *International Economics* (New York, 1968).

autonomous domestic policies necessarily led to the system's collapse.[83] It is not by chance that increasing concern about the viability of monetary arrangements dates from the early 1960s, when capital movements began to be liberalized, and official dollar liabilities held by foreign central banks exceeded, in 1964, the United States' gold reserve. The policy trilemma, then, had no solution, and seeking refuge in the convertibility constraint was as illusory as it was erroneous.

The central role of theory, thus, comes out once more in the epilogue of the Bretton Woods story. Not only was there a repeat of the divide between policymakers' conservative thinking and economists' more progressive analytical framework, but also the latter was not sufficiently advanced to fully grasp the problem of the international monetary system in its entirety. As McKinnon rightly remarked in connection with the failure of the post-Second World War monetary setting: 'Understanding what the rules actually are, and the obligations of the various players, can be extremely important'.[84] And, in the case in point, it was precisely an incomplete understanding of the Bretton Woods viability conditions that brought about the demise of the system. In fact, Friedman's far-sighted suggestion to introduce flexible exchange rates and treat gold like any other commodity was regarded as a curiosity. With the possible exception of the United Kingdom, the fiscal and monetary discipline followed by countries other than the United States reflected a traditional habit of mind and was coherent with the system's stability. On

---

83   The possible inconsistency between fixed exchange rates and domestic economic policy had already been pointed out immediately after the Bretton Woods conference. In the symposium published by the *Review of Economic Statistics* in November 1944, Halm remarks: 'It will be one of the most delicate tasks of the Fund to arbitrate the conflict between the principle of exchange stability and the principle of non-interference with domestic policies. Since these two principles characterize the positions of the gold standard and of Lord Keynes respectively, one cannot be surprised to find the Fund Agreement rather obscure in this respect and inclined to leave it to the Board and the Executive Directors gradually to solve by experience and according to given circumstances what cannot be crystallized in unequivocal formulae right at the beginning', G.N. Halm, 'The International Monetary Fund', in *Review of Economic Statistics*, 26, November 1944, pp. 170–5, here p. 172. Frank Graham's comment is more caustic: 'It would seem that, after all this, we might have learned that we cannot both have our cake and eat it. We should know that we must either forgo fixed exchange rates *or* national monetary sovereignty if we are to avoid the disruption of equilibrium in freely conducted international trade or the system of controls and inhibitions which is the only alternative when the internal values of independent currencies deviate – as they always tend to do – from what was, perhaps, a correct relationship when the fixed rates of exchange were set up. Yet the old error was, to all intents and purposes, again repeated in the International Monetary Organization which did not much curtail national monetary sovereignty. It is true that some concessions were made to the consequent demand for flexibility in exchange relationships. But there is, nevertheless, a strong bias in the statute toward the ideal of rates maintained unchanged for an indefinitely lengthy period, and not even the slightest provision for the adoption, by the various participating countries, of the congruent monetary policies without which a system of fixed exchange rates simply does not make sense', F.D. Graham, *The Cause and Cure of 'Dollar Shortage'*, Essays in International Finance, no. 10 (Princeton, 1949), p. 6, italics in the original.

84   McKinnon, 'Rules', p. 39.

the contrary, the centre country failed to provide an effective anchor. However, even the most virtuous policies might not have been sufficient to assure viability, given the inadequacies of the prevailing analytical view of sticking to gold convertibility and to the Triffin dilemma.[85]

Finally, an answer can be given to the Bretton Woods enigma posed by Eichengreen, raised in this article's opening paragraph. Initially, economic growth was sustained by trade expansion and domestic policies that did not create instability, given pervasive capital controls and huge American gold reserves. When both these factors faded away, the constraints of the system – fixed exchange rates and gold convertibility – became binding. Furthermore, they clashed with the policy design of the centre country, which was no longer in line with the function of anchoring the system. Enhanced by a laggard state of the art, irresolvable inconsistencies eventually emerged and caused the end of the post-war monetary setting.

Conclusions

The Bretton Woods monetary order had the unique characteristic of being a project designed by experts and, therefore, lends itself to examination from a monetary theory perspective. However, the advance of monetary economics is not continuously and promptly translated into monetary reform. The state of the art can either fall behind or be ahead of the actual institutional framework. Such temporal discrepancies are often eliminated by the impact of exogenous shocks on the received view. Hence, the aftermath of the First World War enhanced the critique of the gold standard, and subsequently the effects of the Great Depression produced a decisive step towards managed money and the search for an innovative monetary system.

This challenging task became a priority after the outbreak of the Second World War. The ruling paradigm of Keynesian economics, which emphasized activist economic policy in pursuit of full employment, influenced the approach of the Bretton Woods negotiators, though the institutional structure of the new setting maintained some of the features of the traditional gold-exchange standard. Indeed, central bankers' conservative attitude, lagging behind theoretical advances, was the cause of the inertia in monetary arrangements throughout the twentieth century. The asynchronous evolution of theory and institutions brought about the inconsistencies that plagued the Bretton Woods system and eventually led to its collapse. In fact, most of the factors commonly put forward to account for the end of Bretton Woods – the structural flaws in its design, namely the gold-exchange standard and the adjustable peg, the failure of the United States to stabilize the price level after 1965 and the pursuit of domestic policy targets by other industrial countries[86] – mainly reflected the major shift in the state of the art during the inter-war period and the related contrast with conservative modes of thought.

All things considered, the influence of monetary theory on the evolution, and viability, of monetary arrangements was decisive. The properties and the success

---

85   The EMS, lacking any link to gold and allowing frequent exchange-rate realignments, worked somewhat better than Bretton Woods, at least until September 1992.

86   Bordo, 'Bretton Woods', p. 83.

of the gold standard were founded on the metallist doctrine and the equilibrium hypothesis of the classical model. The rejection of both inverted the principles underlying the monetary system and paved the way for the epoch-making transition to fiat money. The Bretton Woods monetary order was the last stage of this process, a last ephemeral attempt to maintain a link with commodity money while stressing the role of activist economic policies.

PART IV

MONETARY UNIONS

[12]

Journal of International Economics 19 (1985) 367–374. North-Holland

ON THE VIABILITY OF MONETARY UNIONS

Filippo CESARANO*

Banca d'Italia, 00184 Roma, Italy

Received February 1984, revised version received April 1985

This paper contrasts the notion of optimality with that of viability of monetary unions and attempts to provide a positive analysis of the latter by dwelling upon Herbert Simon's work on models of bounded rationality. A macro model developed by Frenkel and Aizenman is appended to the above theoretical framework and it is shown that viability is strictly related to certain specific properties of the economy.

1. Introduction

Monetary union was not of much interest to economists until fairly recent times. In the early fifties, the analyses of the subject, with the exception of the works by Meade (1953, 1957) and Scitovsky (1957, 1958), were of a cursory character and enclosed in essays mainly concerned with other themes of international economics such as flexible exchange rates [Friedman (1953)] and interregional adjustment [Ingram (1959)]. Subsequently, the focus of research shifted to the optimal domain of a currency area up to the late sixties when political developments in Western Europe drew an increasing attention to the topic, witness the publication of no less than three collections of essays in a single year [Johnson and Swoboda (1973), Krause and Salant (1973), Krauss (1973)]. Despite this outburst of literature, however, the important issue regarding the viability of a monetary union has been largely neglected. Indeed, while normative pronouncements have abounded, a positive analysis is still lacking.[1]

*A first draft of this paper was presented several years ago at the International Trade Workshop of the University of Chicago; thanks are due to Jacob Frenkel, Harry Johnson and other participants for their useful criticism. Ignazio Angeloni, Rainer Masera and Giuseppe Tullio also made helpful comments on this early draft. The present version has benefited from the important suggestions of Stanley Fischer and an anonymous referee. The usual disclaimer applies.

[1]As Ingram aptly puts it:

A curious reversal of roles is apparent in this discussion of monetary union. Economists seem to be saying that monetary union will not work because sufficient political will is lacking and because the politicians never do what they say they will do. But I wonder whether we, as economists, are qualified to make such a political judgment. It seems to me that the economists' interest should be focused on how such a system would work if it once got started. They should specify *what are the minimum requirements for a workable system of monetary union and then let the politicians decide whether those minimum requirements are tolerable or not* [Ingram (1973b, p. 184), italics added].

The purpose of the present paper is to provide a positive analysis of viability, attempting to identify the conditions under which a monetary union will survive.

2. Viability of a monetary union

A monetary union involves the adoption of a common currency by a *given* number of countries or regions. Hence, its essential implication is the loss of monetary sovereignty by each member. Several questions arise from this single feature. The point in time of the introduction of the common currency makes it possible to distinguish between two classes of problems, regarding the period before and the one after the circulation of the common currency respectively: those relating to the *transition* towards the establishment of the monetary union and those pertaining to the *operation* of the monetary union. The very notion of viability relates to the latter class of problems since it generally concerns the feasibility of maintaining the circulation of a common currency for an indefinite period of time. Hence, while analysing this notion, it is appropriate to assume that the transition stage has been successfully completed.[2] The discussion of viability will then refer to a monetary union which has already been established and is isolated from the rest of the world.[3]

The traditional approach to the subject has focused upon the notion of optimality, involving the search for a specific feature — factor mobility [Mundell (1961)], proportion in the production of 'tradables' [McKinnon (1963)], product diversification [Kenen (1969)] — which, following payments imbalances due to demand disturbances, would make the adjustment process consistent with the maximization of the social welfare function of the single countries.[4] Viability, instead, relates to the possibility of survival of a common currency circulating within a specific area. Hence, with respect to

[2]Each country assesses the decision to join the union according to the 'calculus of participation'.

The rational theory of participation indicates that an individual decision unit decides to participate in a collective action if the anticipated benefit is larger than the cost. The rational decision for a country contemplating membership in a monetary union is to join if the benefits from participation, such as the use of common currency, reduction in uncertainty and the increase in the bargaining power as a group, are larger than the costs, such as the sacrifice of independent monetary policy and the wider variation in the unemployment rate [Hamada (1977, p. 18)].

[3]Kenen and Allen (1980) and Canzoneri (1982) thoroughly examine various aspects of the operation of a monetary union open to the rest of the world.

[4]An immediate objection to the traditional approach concerns its lack of generality since it makes optimality dependent upon various criteria, each providing a sufficient but not a necessary condition. As more criteria are introduced, different notions of optimality obtain. This poses the further question of selecting among the various definitions. Most plausibly the choice is not unconditional since different notions may be relevant in different situations, thus blurring the very concept of optimality.

optimality, the setting of the problem is analogous but the way of solving it is exactly reversed: the geographical dimension of the currency area is already given and what is to be determined is the value of the arguments of the regions social welfare function resulting from the adjustment process. This difference in approach notwithstanding, it is useful to contrast optimality with viability in order to pin down the latter more elusive concept. The fundamental feature which characterizes viability regards its less restrictive nature inasmuch as it does not involve a unique solution but a set of solutions which satisfy a minimum requirement for maintaining the circulation of a common currency. The solution that maximizes the social welfare function defines the optimum. Therefore, the relationship between the two notions is such that one contains the other: an optimal currency area must necessarily be viable, but the contrary does not hold.

2.1. A theoretical framework for the analysis of viability

The arguments shown in the foregoing paragraph can be rigorously treated by means of some analytical tools introduced by Simon in a different context. In a series of influential papers, Simon analysed models of behaviour which postulate a lower level of abstraction with respect to traditional economic theory, thereby making it possible to explain 'all-or-none' types of choice hardly accounted for by maximization processes. Initial works dealt with topics such as employment relationships (1951) and organization theory (1952–53). The latter, as contrasted with the theory of the firm, has '*been concerned not so much with optimality as with the conditions necessary for organisational survival, that is, the conditions under which the participants will continue to participate*' (1952, p. 42).[5]

Following Simon (1955), each decision unit in the system faces a set of alternatives open to choice and maximizes a satisfaction or pay-off function which depends upon the set of outcomes or future states of affairs. Provided that an ordering relation on pairs of elements of the set of outcomes can be made, necessary and sufficient conditions for viability can be derived. This viability solution involves a boundary or critical value of the satisfaction function, sometimes called the 'aspiration level' or the 'acceptance price', defining a threshold at which the agent is indifferent as to the choice of withdrawing or not from the organization (an opportunity cost concept). Any pay-off higher or equal to such a threshold is a viable solution.

This analytical framework can be readily applied to the subject of the present paper. The decision units are the *n* member countries facing the

---

[5]This approach was generalized in a subsequent essay (1955) in which the limited access to information leads to the search for models of behaviour which depart from the traditional hypothesis of 'global rationality'. It must be stressed that Simon's analytical frameworks do rest on an optimizing behavioural hypothesis, albeit constrained by incomplete information [Simon (1955, pp. 99–101)].

alternative of maintaining or not their membership of the monetary union. The set of alternatives includes the whole range of exchange-rate regimes: irrevocably fixed exchange rates (i.e. participation in the monetary union), fully flexible exchange rates, and, between the two, the 'continuum' of managed floating rates. The countries behaviour is described by a rational decision process which rests upon the boundary value of the pay-off function that the agent regards as the acceptance price. All the values of the pay-off function which are higher or equal to the acceptance price define the set of 'satisfactory' or viable pay-offs. The latter, if the *n* countries minimize a loss function *H* defined for all elements *s* of the set of outcomes *S*, can be expressed as:

$$H_i(s) \leqq \bar{H}_i \quad (i = 1, \ldots, n), \tag{1}$$
$$s \in U$$

where *U* is the subset of *S* for the *i*th country participating in the monetary union and $\bar{H}_i$ is the acceptance price, i.e. the highest value of the loss function which the *i*th country is prepared to accept.[6] According to the decision rule, then, each country chooses the alternative of maintaining membership as long as (1) is not violated. Thus, a monetary union is viable if and only if (1) holds for all the *n* regions at every point in time.[7]

In general, if a viable solution exists, there will be a set of outcomes satisfying the condition for viability. When the problem can be represented graphically — e.g. Simon (1951, p. 296) — there will be a whole region in which the relevant inequalities are satisfied and only in exceptional cases will this region degenerate into a single point. Viability, as distinguished from optimality, does not involve a unique solution but refers to all possible equilibrium states which do not violate the critical boundary value.[8]

2.2. Determinants of the decision rule

The most recent literature on the choice of the exchange-rate regime has stressed that optimality, in general, will obtain under neither perfectly fixed

---

[6]To simplify notation, subscript *i* will later on be suppressed.

[7]As regards the benefits of joining the union, it should be noted that most of them [see the analyses by Mundell (1973) and Hamada (1977)] are related to once-and-for-all structural changes occurring at the introduction of the common currency and, thus, pertain to the transition stage.

[8]It should be emphasized that, in previous studies, the failure to recognize this characteristic feature has often determined a pessimistic attitude with regard to projects of monetary unification, even on the part of authoritative scholars. Meade's scepticism for example (1953, ch. 2: 1957), was founded upon the hypothesis according to which member countries would look only at the optimum value of the social welfare function. In the light of the foregoing exposition, this hypothesis seems rather weak. Given incomplete information, the countries may well be willing to depart from optimality up to the point where the boundary value $\bar{H}$ is not violated, as dictated by the decision rule.

nor fully flexible exchange rates, but in the presence of an optimal managed float [Boyer (1978), Roper and Turnovsky (1980), Frenkel and Aizenman (1982), Turnovsky (1982)]. However, the possibility of arriving at the optimal solution, call it H^*, may be severely limited by incomplete information on the part of the policy-maker. This assumption is a common one in the literature on economic policy and is germane to Simon's theoretical framework. In this connection, the sub-optimal solution that the country can aim at is just the acceptance price $\bar{H}$. This is the boundary value of the objective function that the country is willing to accept for retaining membership of the monetary union and, thus, it is equal to the best attainable value of the objective function (the lowest level of loss) outside the union. It represents the opportunity cost of participation.

In order to examine the subset of solutions defined by participation in the union, an explicit model is needed showing the behaviour of the economy under different exchange-rate regimes.[9] Assume that the country seeks to minimize the quadratic loss function:

$$H \equiv \mathrm{E}[c_t - \mathrm{E}(Y_t)]^2, \qquad (2)$$

where c_t is real consumption and Y_t is the supply of output. The economy is subject to random shocks of different nature: real (μ), monetary (ε and δ, stochastic disturbances to the demand for and supply of money respectively), and foreign (χ) which disturb income from its permanent level y. The relationships of the model [see Frenkel and Aizenman (1982) for details] allow us to approximate the discrepancy between consumption and expected income by the first two terms of a Taylor expansion. Thus

$$c_t - \mathrm{E}(Y_t) \simeq [\mu - (1-\gamma)\alpha k \theta] y, \qquad (3)$$

where γ is the coefficient of managed float[10] varying from 0 (in the case of perfectly fixed rates) to 1 (in the case of fully flexible rates), α is the speed of portfolio adjustment in the demand for money function, k is the Cambridge k defining the desired ratio of money to income, and θ is the global shock ($\theta \equiv \mu + \chi + \varepsilon - \delta$). The policy-maker optimizing behaviour involves the choice of the intervention index γ in (3) so as to minimize the squared discrepancy

---

[9]For the sake of the argument, the model developed by Frenkel and Aizenman (1982) is referred to in the following pages so that the length of the paper can be kept within reasonable limits. Indeed, it is not the specific approach employed to model the economy but rather the attempt to give a rigorous content to the analysis of viability that represents the main message of the present article.

[10]'The coefficient γ may be viewed as indicating the fraction of money market disequilibrium that is allowed to be eliminated through changes in the exchange rate' [Frenkel and Aizenman (1982, p. 235)].

between μ and $(1-\gamma)\alpha k\theta$.[11] It can be shown that when the shocks are only of a monetary nature $(\sigma_\mu^2=0)$ freely flexible exchange rates give the optimal solution $(\gamma^*=1)$; at the other extreme, when the disturbances are entirely of a real character $(\sigma_{(\chi+\varepsilon-\delta)}^2=0)$, the optimal regime is that of fixed rates $(\gamma^*=0)$. In the more general case, disturbances are of both monetary and real origin $(0<\gamma^*<1)$ and optimal behaviour will be characterized by intervention in the exchange market.[12] As the value of γ for the member countries is equal to zero, it may be inferred that the closer to zero is γ^* the more likely is viability to hold. This conclusion, however, neglects a crucial element. By withdrawing from the union the policy-maker can achieve a higher value of the objective function but the magnitude of the gain can be quite different depending on the properties of the objective function.

Taking again the Frenkel and Aizenman model as an example, the difference between the loss under fixed rates H^0 and the loss at the optimum H^* is

$$H^0 - H^* = \sigma_\theta^2 \left[\alpha k - \frac{\sigma_\mu^2}{\sigma_\theta^2} \right]^2 . \tag{4}$$

This result shows that the loss from joining the union is directly related to αk — the propensity to save out of transitory income[13] — and to σ_θ^2, the variance of the global shock, and varies inversely as the weight of the real shock on the global shock. Thus, while the determination of the optimal solution essentially depends on the relative strength of the variance of the real shock as compared to the variance of the effective monetary shock [Frenkel and Aizenman (1982, pp. 239–240)], the satisfaction of the viability condition also depends, for a given value of αk, on the absolute size of the variance of the global shock.

More generally, the issue of viability involves a judgement on the part of the country on the performance of the economy subject to the rules of the monetary union, on the one side, and free to pursue a policy of managed

---

[11]This exercise gives the optimal solution γ^*:

$$\gamma^* = 1 - \frac{\mathrm{cov}(\mu, \theta)}{\alpha k \sigma_\theta^2}.$$

When all shocks are independent of each other the solution becomes:

$$\gamma^* = 1 - \frac{\sigma_\mu^2}{\alpha k [\sigma_\mu^2 + \sigma_{(\chi+\varepsilon-\delta)}^2]}.$$

[12]In accordance with the approach of the present paper, in this model the policy-maker does not possess complete information: he knows only the value of the global shock θ but not its individual components and, thus, cannot attain the optimal solution.

[13]An increase in αk, for any given value of the real shock, produces a stronger impact on the excess flow demand for money thereby increasing the desirability of exchange rate flexibility.

floating on the other. Whether the country will be better off by choosing the former or the latter course of action is basically related to the factors contained in eq. (4). The interplay of these factors will determine the choice of each country as dictated by the decision rule.

3. Concluding remarks

In this paper a positive analysis of viability has been provided dwelling upon Simon's work on models of rational choice. An explicit model of the economy, developed by Frenkel and Aizenman, has been appended to the above theoretical framework showing that viability is strictly related to certain specific properties characterizing the member country and particularly, to the overall stability of the economy.

References

Aliber, R.Z., ed., 1977, The political economy of monetary reform (MacMillan, London).
Allen, P., 1976, Organization and administration of a monetary union, Princeton studies in international finance No. 38, Princeton, N.J., Princeton University.
Balassa, B., 1961, The theory of economic integration (Irwin, Homewood, Ill.).
Balassa, B. and Resnick, S.A., 1974, Monetary integration and the consistency of policy objectives in the European common market, Weltwirtschaftliches Archiv 110, 564–579.
Basevi, G. and De Grauwe, P., 1978, Vicious and virtuous circles and the optica proposal: A two-country analysis, in M. Fratianni and T. Peeters, eds., One money for Europe (MacMillan, London) 144–157.
Boyer, R.S., 1978, Optimal foreign exchange market intervention, Journal of Political Economy 86, 1045–1055.
Canzoneri, M.B., 1982, Exchange intervention policy in a multiple country world, Journal of International Economics 13, 267–289.
Corden, W.M., 1972, Monetary integration, Essays in international finance, No. 93, Princeton, N.J., Princeton University.
Corden, W.M., 1973, The adjustment problem, in Krause and Salant (1973) 159–184.
De Grauwe, P., 1975, Conditions for monetary integration — A geometric interpretation, Weltwirtschaftliches Archiv 111, 634–645.
Fischer, S., 1977, Stability and exchange rate system in a monetarist model of the balance of payments, in Aliber (1977) 59–73.
Fleming, J.M., 1971, On exchange rate unification, Economic Journal 81, 467–488.
Flood, R.P. and Marion, N.P., 1982, The transmission of disturbances under alternative exchange-rate regimes with optimal indexing, Quarterly Journal of Economics 96, 43–66.
Frenkel, J.A. and Aizenman, J., 1982, Aspects of the optimal management of exchange rates, Journal of International Economics 13, 231–256.
Friedman, M., 1953, The case for flexible exchange rates, in: Essays in positive economics (The University of Chicago Press, Chicago) 157–203.
Grubel, H.G., 1970, The theory of optimum currency areas, Canadian Journal of Economics 3, 318–324.
Grubel, H.G., 1973, The theory of optimum regional associations, in Johnson and Swoboda (1973) 99–113.
Hamada, K., 1977, On the political economy of monetary integration: A public economics approach, in Aliber (1977) 13–31.
Helpman, E. and Razin, A., 1979, Towards a consistent comparison of alternative exchange rate systems, Canadian Journal of Economics 12, 394–409.

Ingram, J.C., 1959, State and regional payments mechanisms, Quarterly Journal of Economics 73, 619–632.

Ingram, J.C., 1973a, The case for European monetary integration, Essays in international finance. No. 98, Princeton, N.J., Princeton University.

Ingram, J.C., 1973b, Comments to Corden (1973), in Krause and Salant (1973) 184–191.

Ishiyama, Y., 1975, The theory of optimum currency areas: A survey, Staff Papers 22, 344–383.

Johnson, H.G. and Swoboda, A.K., eds., 1973, The economics of common currencies (Harvard University Press, Cambridge, Mass.).

Kenen, P.B., 1969, The theory of optimum currency areas: An eclectic view, in R.A. Mundell and A.K. Swoboda, eds., Monetary problems of the international economy (The University of Chicago Press, Chicago) 41–60.

Kenen, P.B., and Allen, P.R., 1980, Asset markets, exchange rates and economic integration, (Cambridge University Press, Cambridge).

Krause, M.B., ed., 1973, The economics of integration (Allen & Unwin, London).

Krause, L.B. and Salant, W.S., eds., 1973, European monetary unification (The Brookings Institution, Washington, D.C.).

Laffer, A.B., 1973, Two arguments for fixed rates, in Johnson and Swoboda (1973) 25–34.

Magnifico, G., 1973, European monetary unification (John Wiley & Sons, New York).

Masera, R.S., 1974, A 'stylized' model of a highly open economy under a system of fixed exchange rate and its implications for the establishment of currency areas, Oxford Bulletin of Economics and Statistics 37, 211–225.

McKinnon, R.I., 1963, Optimum currency areas, American Economic Review 53, 717–725.

Meade, J.E., 1953, Problems of economic union (The University of Chicago Press, Chicago).

Meade, J.E., 1957, The balance-of-payments problems of a European free-trade area, Economic Journal 67, 379–396.

Mundell, R.A., 1961, A theory of optimum currency areas, American Economic Review 51, 657–665.

Mundell, R.A., 1973, Uncommon arguments for common currencies, in Johnson and Swoboda (1973) 114–132.

Roper, D.E. and Turnovsky, S.J., 1980, Optimal exchange market intervention in a simple stochastic macro-model, Canadian Journal of Economics 13, 296–309.

Scitovsky, T., 1957, The theory of the balance of payments and the problem of a common European currency, Kyklos 10, 18–44.

Scitovsky, T., 1958, Economic theory and western European integration (Stanford University Press, Stanford).

Simon, H.A., 1951, A formal theory of employment relationship, Econometrica 19, 293–305.

Simon, H.A., 1952–53, A comparison of organization theories, Review of Economic Studies 20, 40–48.

Simon, H.A., 1955, A behavioral model of rational choice, Quarterly Journal of Economics 69, 99–118.

Turnovsky, S.J., 1982, Exchange market intervention in a small open economy: An expository model, typescript, University of Illinois.

[13]
Monetary Union:
A Theoretical Perspective *

1. Introduction

According to the absolutist approach to the history of economic analysis (Pantaleoni 1898; Schumpeter 1954; Stigler 1969), changes in institutions and in the structure of the economy may give rise to a demand for theories, although such factors do not shape the theories themselves as the relativist approach maintains. Monetary union seems a case in point, since the research on the subject has been stimulated by various proposals for monetary unification in Europe in the last half-century. In fact, the present outgrowth of literature is but the last stage of a debate which goes back to the end of the Second World War when the spread of federalist ideals prompted early analyses of the implications of supranational institutions and of an extended currency area (Einaudi 1945; Hartland 1949; Meade 1953, 1957; Scitovsky 1957, 1958). In 1970, the Werner Report gave new momentum to these studies after the contributions to the theory of optimum currency areas in the 1960s, pioneered by Robert Mundell (1961). However, despite the number of publications of the last three decades, no consensus has been reached and, as Niehans puts it, "optimum currency areas are still a concept in search of a theory" (1984, p. 294). This is reflected in today's debate among academic economists on EMU, widely echoed in the financial press. Indeed, the controversial nature of the effects of monetary union does not allow

---

* Paper presented at the Conference on Medium Term Economic Assessment organized by the Bundesbank in Frankfurt, 28-30 September 1992. Thanks are due to L. Bini Smaghi and G. Galli for their useful comments on a first draft of this paper. The usual caveat applies.

BNL Quarterly Review, no. 182, September 1992.

any hard and fast answer to the sundry questions it raises. The present paper revisits the issues at stake and sets them in the perspective of monetary theory. Monetary unification is just a case study in the theory of money so that its treatment is intimately related to the state of advancement of the latter. In the absence of substantial progress in the field, different emphasis on certain assumptions brings contrasting results, especially with regard to the basic question of the welfare implications of participation.

2. Effects of Monetary Union

The introduction of a common currency poses problems that fall into two main classes, concerning respectively the transition towards monetary union and the operation of monetary union. While the former come to an end once the common currency starts to circulate, the latter span the entire life of the union. Transition is thus a once-and-for-all type of process which brings about a variation in the rate of growth of high-powered money in the countries involved. The effects of these changes in money, whose magnitude is related to the initial range of the base growth rates, are strongly debated especially with regard to the timing of transition. The dispute between the gradual and the immediate approach mirrors, albeit hinging on different arguments, the controversy of the 1970s between the so-called "economists" and "monetarists" (Giovannini 1990, pp. 217-18). The problems of transition are momentous from a policy standpoint. Yet, on theoretical grounds, their analysis is closely related to the key assumptions that also explain the smooth operation of a monetary union, *e.g.* the rationality of expectations and the absence of frictions in macroeconomic adjustment.

The factual implication of monetary union is the loss of monetary sovereignty, and thus of the conduct of monetary policy, by each member country. This proposition can also be viewed from an international economics perspective since monetary union is analogous to the adoption of irrevocable and perfectly fixed exchange rates. In such a monetary regime, the single country cannot pursue an independent monetary policy insofar as it does not control the total size of the monetary base but only its composition. This statement is of course purely abstract since a currency area and a fixed exchange rate system differ in kind rather than in degree. Indeed, however narrow is the exchange rate band, a system of fixed rates is, as it were, an agreement that sovereign states may break at any moment. Hence, the current argument according to which the EMS is already a *de facto* monetary union should be handled with the greatest caution.

In his seminal paper on the theory of optimum currency areas, Mundell (1961) identified labor mobility as the criterion which maximizes social welfare. Other factors, *i.e.* the share of tradables (McKinnon 1963) and product diversification (Kenen 1969), were also put forward to account for optimality. The immediate objection to these approaches is their lack of generality, since they make optimality depend on different criteria, thus posing the question of choosing between them. In order to overcome these difficulties, a more general approach (Ishiyama 1975) considers the overall welfare costs and benefits of a monetary union. The benefits essentially stem from the savings in transaction costs involved in the enlargement of the area where the same means of payment is used. The modern literature on the foundations of monetary theory (Ostroy and Starr 1990) views money as an information-producing mechanism which allows the decentralization of exchange and, hence, enables agents to exploit the gains from trade without violating the budget constraint. The establishment of the union brings about sundry welfare gains repeatedly illustrated in the literature. First, the quotation of prices in several units of account is avoided. Second, no resources need to be employed in order to convert the different monies of the formerly independent countries. Third, no forward markets for foreign exchange are necessary within the union. Besides, there will be economies of scale in foreign exchange reserves (Meade 1957). These benefits are closely related to the threefold classification of the functions of money – unit of account, medium of exchange, and store of value – and increase with the openness in trade and capital movements (Corden 1992, pp. 2-3). The welfare benefits must be set against the welfare costs which are mainly related to the adjustment problem. While the nature of the benefits is widely accepted, the analysis of the costs is less straightforward.

In any market, a state of disequilibrium brings about price and/or quantity changes that drive towards a new equilibrium. Monetary union, by fixing the "price of currency" in each member country, puts the burden of adjustment on quantities, *i.e.* on output and employment. Therefore, a key prerequisite for the optimality of a currency area is a high degree of flexibility of certain quantities in the equilibrating mechanism. This is the core of Mundell's theory. The region of a monetary union hit by an asymmetric shock, say a fall in the demand for its product due to a change in tastes, suffers a trade imbalance. In order to restore equilibrium at an unchanged relative price, there must be an upward shift in the supply of the home-produced commodity through labor migration out of the region.

The disequilibrium could in principle be eliminated by a relative price instead of a quantity change. Since in a currency area a variation in the exchange rate is ruled out, the only way to affect relative prices is via a price level fall in the region hit by the adverse shock. Indeed, full price flexibility would do away with disequilibrium problems at once.

These two distinct adjustment mechanisms, which hinge on quantity and price changes respectively, may not operate since labor may not be mobile – owing to a variety of institutional, cultural, and social factors – and prices may be sticky. In that case, disequilibrium is going to persist and the region affected by an adverse shock will experience a drop in employment and output. Adjustment will be slow and entail a high social welfare cost. In such a state of affairs, the outcome of the traditional analysis is the call for flexible exchange rates between regions within which there is high labor mobility.

This sketch of the theory of optimum currency areas shows that Mundell's contribution relates to the solution of the adjustment problem in the particular case of price and wage rigidity. However, a more general approach can be pursued by framing the subject in the theory of monetary policy. Viewed from a broader perspective, the ultimate issues underlying optimum currency areas concern the effects of changes in money on social welfare. Various efforts in this direction seem to characterize the most recent work in the field. Dwelling on contemporary developments in monetary policy, some authors (Giavazzi and Pagano 1988) have emphasized the constraint that fixed exchange rates impose on the monetary authority thus enhancing the credibility of policy conduct and reducing the welfare costs of a deflationary policy. On the other hand, Canzoneri and Rogers (1990) follow a new classical macroeconomic approach and stress the fiscal revenue aspect of inflation. Hence, the possibility of pursuing an independent monetary policy outside the monetary union must be evaluated in an optimal taxation context in which inflation is one of the revenue sources. This provides a further criterion for defining optimum currency areas because the latter would include those countries that impose the same seignorage.

3. Optimum Currency Areas and Monetary Policy

In a well-known passage quoted by Mundell (1961, p. 662) and more recently by Sala-i-Martin and Sachs (1992, p. 1), John Stuart Mill refers to the existence of national currencies as a "barbarism". For the classical economists, the optimum currency area is the world. This is the natural outcome of the main hypotheses of their model. The classics pointed to the welfare benefits of a common currency, related to the savings in transaction costs, and did not even pose the adjustment problem. Indeed, in the frictionless world envisioned by the classics, the economy is self-adjusting and any shocks are equilibrated by market forces, *i.e.* the specie-flow mechanism. Furthermore, classical monetary theory hinged on metallism, relating the value of money to the value of the money commodity (Schumpeter 1954, p. 288), which entirely waved aside the modern conception of monetary policy. In a metallic standard, the unit of account must be kept equal to a given quantity of the money commodity and the principle of free coinage provides both a rule of behavior and a constraint for the monetary authority. Of course, even commodity monetary systems require some management activity by the central bank, but the chief objective remains the maintenance of parity so that those managing activities are quite distinct from the present-day use of policy instruments in a welfare optimizing framework.

Mill's quotation is evocative of Keynes's famous dictum that the gold standard was "a barbarous relic" (1923, p. 172). The clash between these two standpoints perfectly sums up the issues at stake. Keynes's main concern, in the *Tract on Monetary Reform*, was to put the level of economic activity at the center of the stage, and he accordingly called for the demise of the gold standard, whose chief goal was the stability of purchasing power. The crisis of the international monetary system after the First World War paved the way to theoretical developments leading to an "elastic" or "managed currency". In the 1920s, Keynes and several distinguished economists like

Cassel and Pigou overturned the classical stance and pioneered the modern conception of monetary policy.

This brief reference to Mill's and Keynes's viewpoints illustrates the relevance of the key hypotheses of the model of the economy for the role and effectiveness of monetary policy. In this regard, there is as yet no consensus. New classical macroeconomists and new Keynesians are but the last example of dissenting schools that go back centuries. Schumpeter's authoritative account (1954, pp. 281 ff.) shows how the classical approach prevailed and became the orthodox view. Nowadays, there is a resurgence of the classical school and, in the rules *vs.* discretion debate, the pendulum has swung back in the direction of rules. Given the tight relationship between monetary policy and the exchange rate, these developments have reinforced the case for monetary union. A metallic standard or fixed exchange rates in a fiat money system is the institutional counterpart to a monetary policy based on rules. In principle, a rule fixing an equal rate of money growth in a given number of countries is analogous to the introduction of a common currency in those countries. The theoretical foundations of a monetary rule in the new classical macroeconomics, however, are quite distinct from Friedman's (1960) analysis. The latter hinges on the lack of knowledge of the model of the economy and on long and variable lags in the effectiveness of policy actions. The new approach, instead, is based on the rational expectations hypothesis or on the strategic behavior of agents, which in any case incorporates rational expectations, *vis-à-vis* the monetary authority. In fact, the rational expectations hypothesis postulates that the agents know the "true" model of the economy which, together with the relevant data, is an element of the agents' information set. This hypothesis implies monetary policy ineffectiveness even in the short run and, thus, excludes discretion since monetary policy only raises the inflation rate with no impact on output and employment. Hence, while both Friedman and rational expectations theorists favor a policy rule, their arguments differ sharply in that the former stresses short-run policy efficacy as a powerful source of income fluctuations.

The case for rules has been further strengthened by the well-known argument of the time inconsistency of central bank behavior. As mentioned above, the call for flexible exchange rates on the part of new classical macroeconomists may rest on the pursuit of an inflationary policy within an optimal taxation framework (Canzoneri and Rogers 1990). Otherwise, the modern classical approach lends itself to the case for monetary union; for one thing, its reliance on the Walrasian general equilibrium model does away with any concern for permanent disequilibria in the labor market. It is only when rigidities of various types are introduced that the classical paradigm fails to yield an optimum solution. The main rigidity regards prices and wages and has been emphasized in the traditional Keynesian model. The new Keynesians have put forward some original hypotheses, *i.e.* menu costs and efficiency wages, which explain these rigidities in a context of rational behavior. In this theoretical framework, an active monetary policy may play a key role in tackling the adjustment problem.

The efficacy of monetary policy, however, does not necessarily stem from strictly Keynesian assumptions, *i.e.* rigidity of labor contracts (Fischer 1977) or menu costs (Mankiw 1985), but may be equally derived from an alternative hypothesis based on the optimal use of information (Stigler 1961). While Friedman emphasizes the lack of knowledge of the economy, the rational expectations hypothesis assumes that individuals know the "true" model of the economy. Most plausibly, information is neither wholly lacking nor complete but is just a scarce commodity and is then used optimally by rational agents. The resort to monetary policy, then, allows the country hit by an adverse shock to reduce the adjustment cost in terms of employment and output. This policy of course cannot aim to raise income beyond its natural level but may smooth out fluctuations in economic activity. If the magnitude of policy actions is small enough, rational agents do not revise expectations because the net benefit of processing information is negative. Exchange rate flexibility associated with this policy conduct leads to an optimum solution if the area affected by the disequilibrium coincides with the nation. This is, in fact, recognized by Mundell in his discussion of a shock affecting the Eastern regions of both Canada and the United States, which illustrates his original hypothesis.

"The preceding example does not destroy the argument for flexible exchange rates, but it might severely impair the relevance of the argument if it is applied to national currencies. The logic of the argument can in fact be rescued if national currencies are abandoned in favor of regional currencies" (1961, p. 660).

Indeed, if the case for short-run monetary policy effectiveness can be made via either new-Keynesian assumptions or the optimal use of scarce information by rational agents, then monetary policy, and possibly a variation of the exchange rate, may bring about adjustment when shocks hit the entire nation. This is the "flexible price" solution. Alternatively, if the exchange rate is fixed and shocks occur only in a limited area, labor mobility is needed to re-establish equilibrium. This is the "flexible quantity" solution. Therefore, the theory of optimum currency areas can be viewed from a different perspective inquiring about the effects of changes in money on social welfare so that monetary policy efficacy may provide an alternative criterion for defining optimality. In the prevailing intellectual climate of the time, Mundell stressed price rigidity and relied upon quantity variations in order to restore equilibrium. Ultimately, Mundell's main contribution was to point out the possible lack of correspondence between the region hit by shocks and the nation. His suggestion of the need to make the two coincide follows from, or is an application of, the classical assumption of full input mobility within the nation and total absence thereof outside (Mundell 1961, p. 661). Yet research on a general solution of the optimum currency area problem should be directed to the relative effectiveness of the different adjustment mechanisms working their effects through both prices and quantities. Admittedly, there is little to recommend this suggestion on theoretical grounds. But this may after all explain the soundness of Jürg Niehans' skepticism concerning the theory of optimum currency areas (see p. 1).

4. The Role of Fiscal Policy

This analysis of the main issues underlying optimum currency areas suggests some general propositions concerning the process of monetary unification. Member countries maximize a social welfare function subject to a set of constraints which describe the model of the economy and are in turn related to the arguments of the social welfare function. Hence, the country's preferences must be set against the main hypotheses of the model in order to evaluate the net welfare effects of participation. The outcome may not be optimal but can nevertheless give rise to a monetary union if the countries follow a satisficing instead of a maximizing behavior (Simon 1955). Therefore, a currency area, though not optimal, may yet be viable as long as each member's welfare does not go below a given threshold (Cesarano 1985).

In this regard, a most hotly debated issue is the necessity of federal fiscal policy for the success of the monetary union. Economists are divided on this point. In the early literature, Meade (1953, pp. 43, 45; 1957, p. 165), Scitovsky (1957, p. 98) and Lundberg (1972, p. 129) argued the case for federal fiscal policy. The removal of exchange rate variations from the policymaker's weaponry could be made up for other instruments and federal fiscal policy could then play a paramount role. Triffin (1972) and Lutz (1972) held the opposite viewpoint as well as Ingram (1959, p. 631), who stressed the role of capital movements in the adjustment mechanism. Recent works (Eichengreen 1991; Sala-i-Martin and Sachs 1992) have buttressed the case for fiscal union emphasizing not only the tranfers in favor of the countries affected by adverse shocks but also the built-in redistributive mechanism provided by a federal fiscal system. In fact, an income fall in a region automatically triggers a decrease in federal taxes and an increase in transfers, mainly in the form of unemployment benefits, thus helping to smooth out adjustment. According to the estimates by Sala-i-Martin and Sachs (1992) concerning the U.S. economy, a one-dollar drop in income in a state brings roughly a 34-cent decline in federal taxes by residents of that state and a 6-cent increase in federal fiscal tranfers. Besides, Eichengreen (1991) illustrates how the effects of the second oil shock on Michigan's economy were mitigated through the federal fiscal system. Even more telling empirical evidence is documented in Hartland's (1949) early article showing the substantial redistributive effect of the federal fiscal policies implemented in the inter-war period and especially during the Great Depression. Some of the contemporary studies have been critized, and it has also been argued that the fiscal policy of the single states can attain the same redistributive goal (Bini Smaghi and Vori 1992). In any case, the main issue here is the confidence in a self-adjusting economy. Alternatively, the lack of this confidence suggests the use of policy instruments in order to foster the adjustment mechanism. It is worth observing that no less an enemy of government activity than Milton Friedman has emphasized the role of fiscal and monetary policy in a monetary union. In his classic article on flexible exhange rates, he contrasts the sterling area with the United States and, in a footnote, anticipates some essential elements of the theory of optimum currency areas.

> "The key difference for present purposes between the different states of the United States, on the one hand, and the different members of the sterling area, on the other, is that the former are, while the latter are not, all effectively subject to a single central fiscal and monetary authority – the federal government – having ultimate fiscal and monetary powers. In addition, the former have, while the latter have not, effectively surrendered the right to impose restrictions on the movements of goods, people, or capital between one another. This is a major factor explaining why a central monetary authority is able to operate without producing serious sectional strains. Of course, these are questions of economic fact, not of political form, and of degree, not of kind. A group of politically independent nations all of which firmly adhered to, say, the gold standard would thereby in effect submit themselves to a central monetary authority, albeit an impersonal one. If, in addition, they firmly adhered to the free movement of goods, people, and capital without restrictions, and economic conditions rendered such movement easy, they would, in effect, be an economic unit for which a single currency – which is the equivalent of rigid exchange rates – would be appropriate" (1953, p. 193, footnote 16).

5. Conclusions

After a brief survey of the main issues concerning monetary union (section 2), the present paper has attempted to put the subject in a broader perspective, showing that the central questions concerning the optimality of currency areas are strictly related to the theory of monetary policy and, particularly, to the effectiveness of domestic monetary actions (section 3). In fact, participation in a monetary union is tantamount to the loss of monetary sovereignty and thus of the monetary policy instrument. The basic problem, then, is to evaluate the effects of this loss on social welfare. In this regard, federal fiscal policy can play a crucial role in the adjustment mechanism (section 4). Historically, the demise of the metallic standard after the First World War, eventually heading towards a fiat money system, paved the way for the modern conception of monetary policy. Yet, the other side of the coin of this development is the lack of rules which act both as a guideline and as a constraint for the monetary authority. An alternative disciplinary framework may be difficult to set up and enforce. The provision of written rules, *i.e.* a monetary costitution, may not be an adequate substitute for the gold standard mythology if the various forces at work, not only economic ones, do not drive towards an equilibrium path.

Rome

FILIPPO CESARANO

REFERENCES

ALIBER, R.Z., ed. (1977), *The Political Economy of Monetary Reform*, Macmillan: London.

BALASSA, B. (1961), *The Theory of Economic Integration*, Irwin: Homewood, Ill.

BINI SMAGHI, L. and VORI, S. (1992), "Rating the EC as an Optimal Currency Area: Is It Worse Than the U.S.?", mimeo, Banca d'Italia.

CANZONERI, M.B. and ROGERS, C.A. (1990), "Is the European Community an Optimal Currency Area? Optimal Taxation Versus the Cost of Multiple Currencies", *American Economic Review*, 80, 419-33.

CESARANO, F. (1985), "On the Viability of Monetary Unions", *Journal of International Economics*, 19, 367-74.

CORDEN, W.M. (1972), "Monetary Integration", *Essays in International Finance*, No. 93, Princeton, N.J., Princeton University.

CORDEN, W.M. (1992), "The Theory of Monetary Integration Revisited", mimeo, Johns Hopkins University.

DE GRAUWE, P. (1992), *The Economics of Monetary Integration*, Oxford University Press: Oxford.

EICHENGREEN, B. (1991), "Is Europe an Optimum Currency Area?", *NBER Working Paper* No. 3579.

EINAUDI, L. (1945), *I problemi economici della federazione europea*, La Fiaccola: Milano.

FISCHER, S. (1977), "Long-term Contracts, Rational Expectations, and the Optimal Money Supply Rule", *Journal of Political Economy*, 85, 191-205.

FLEMING, J.M. (1971), "On Exchange Rate Unification", *Economic Journal*, 81, 467-88.

FRIEDMAN, M. (1953), "The Case for Flexible Exchange Rates", in M. FRIEDMAN, *Essays in Positive Economics*, The University of Chicago Press: Chicago.

FRIEDMAN, M. (1960), *A Program for Monetary Stability*, Fordham University Press: New York.

GIAVAZZI, F. and PAGANO, M. (1988), "The Advantage of Tying One's Hands: EMS Discipline and Exchange Rate Credibility", *European Economic Review*, 32, 1055-75.

GIOVANNINI, A. (1990), "European Monetary Reform: Progress and Prospects", *Brookings Papers on Economic Activity*, No. 2, 217-74.

GRUBEL, H.G. (1970), "The Theory of Optimum Currency Areas", *Canadian Journal of Economics*, 3, 318-24.

HARTLAND, P. (1949), "Interregional Payments Compared with International Payments", *Quarterly Journal of Economics*, 63, 392-407.

INGRAM, J.C. (1959), "State and Regional Payments Mechanisms", *Quarterly Journal of Economics*, 73, 619-32.

ISHIYAMA, Y. (1975), "The Theory of Optimum Currency Areas: A Survey", *IMF Staff Papers*, 22, 344-83.

JOHNSON, H.G. and SWOBODA, A.K., eds. (1973), *The Economics of Common Currencies*, Harvard University Press: Cambridge, Mass.

KENEN, P.B. (1969), "The Theory of Optimum Currency Areas: An Eclectic View", in R.A. Mundell and A. K. Swoboda eds., *Monetary Problems of the International Economy*, The University of Chicago Press: Chicago.

KENEN, P.B. and ALLEN, P.R. (1980), *Asset Markets, Exchange Rates and Economic Integration*, Cambridge University Press: Cambridge.

KEYNES, J.M. (1923), *A Tract on Monetary Reform*, Macmillan: London.

KRAUSE, M.B., ed. (1973), *The Economics of Integration*, Allen & Unwin: London.

LUNDBERG, E. (1972), "Discussants on Professor Lutz' Paper", in Machlup, Gutowsky and Lutz (1972), 127-31.

LUTZ, F.A. (1972), "Foreign Exchange Policy and European Economic Integration", in Machlup, Gutowsky, and Lutz (1972), 107-23.

MACHLUP, F., GUTOWSKY, A., and LUTZ, F.A., eds. (1992), *International Monetary Problems*, American Enterprise Institute for Public Policy Research, Washington, D.C..

MANKIW, N.G. (1985), "Small Menu Costs and Large Business Cycles: A Macroeconomic Model of Monopoly", *Quarterly Journal of Economics*, 100, 529-39.

MANKIW, N.G. (1991), "The Reincarnation of Keynesian Economics", *NBER Working Paper* No. 3885.

McKINNON, R.I. (1963), "Optimum Currency Areas", *American Economic Review*, 53, 717-25.

MEADE, J.E. (1953), *Problems of Economic Union*, The University of Chicago Press: Chicago.

MEADE, J.E. (1957), "The Balance-of-Payments Problems of a European Free-Trade Area", *Economic Journal*, 67, 379-96.

MUNDELL, R.A. (1961), "A Theory of Optimum Currency Areas", *American Economic Review*, 51, 657-65.

NIEHANS, J. (1984), *International Monetary Economics*, The Johns Hopkins University Press: Baltimore.

OSTROY, J.M. and STARR, R.M. (1990), "The Transactions Role of Money", in B.M. Friedman and F.H. Hahn, eds., *Handbook of Monetary Economics*, North-Holland: Amsterdam.

PANTALEONI, M. (1898), "Dei criteri che debbono informare la storia delle dottrine economiche", *Giornale degli Economisti*, 17, 407-31.

SALA-I-MARTIN, X. and SACHS, J. (1992), "Federal Fiscalism and Optimum Currency Areas: Evidence for Europe from the United States", *CEPR Discussion Paper* No. 632.

SCHUMPETER, J.A. (1954), *History of Economic Analysis*, Oxford University Press: Oxford.

SCITOVSKY, T. (1957), "The Theory of the Balance of Payments and the Problem of a Common European Currency", *Kyklos*, 10, 18-44.

SCITOVSKY, T. (1958), *Economic Theory and Western Economic Integration*, Stanford University Press: Stanford.

SIMON, H.A. (1955), "A Behavioral Model of Rational Choice", *Quarterly Journal of Economics*, 69, 99-118.

STIGLER, G.J. (1961), "The Economics of Information", *Journal of Political Economy*, 69, 213-25.

STIGLER, G.J. (1969), "Does Economics Have a Useful Past?", *History of Political Economy*, 1, 217-30.

TRIFFIN, R. (1972), "Discussants on Prof. Lutz' Paper", in Machlup, Gutowsky, and Lutz (1972), 125-27.

Open economies review **8**: 51–59 (1997)
© 1997 *Kluwer Academic Publishers. Printed in The Netherlands.*

Currency Areas and Equilibrium

FILIPPO CESARANO
Banca d'Italia

Key words: optimum currency areas, monetary union

JEL Classification Number: F40

Abstract

The standard approach to optimum currency areas clashes with both modern monetary theory and empirical evidence. The present paper sets forth an equilibrium hypothesis that views the national border as the analogue of a policy measure impinging on agents' optimizing behavior.

In his Graham Lecture, Paul Krugman refers to optimum currency areas "as the central intellectual question of international monetary economics" (1993, p. 4). Krugman, however, is dissatisfied with the state of the art[1]. He criticizes the "loose-jointed theory" that matches the costs of lost monetary autonomy with the benefits of fixed rates and stresses the lack of a model of the microeconomics of money to analyze the latter. Aside from this inherent difficulty, which goes to the heart of monetary economics itself, the current approach to optimum currency areas is defective on both theoretical and empirical grounds. It is at odds both with the notion of equilibrium and with the available evidence.

Even when countries are extremely unequal in size, geographically or economically, the formation of monetary union is seldom observed. U.S. dollars have not replaced Canadian dollars and are not going to, and German marks do not circulate in Austria. These stylized facts clash with the standard theory, which implies the regrouping of currency areas under the incentive of welfare maximization. Of course, monetary sovereignty coincides with political sovereignty. But this argument, far from offering a defense of the traditional theory, actually begs the question. First of all, countries do surrender sovereignty in various fields, e.g., trade and foreign policy, by signing treaties that do not reduce territorial or political sovereignty in the broader sense. Second, sovereignty has in fact been given up in the monetary sphere, albeit in the special case of tiny states, i.e., Luxembourg, Liechtenstein, and the like. The fact that currency unions are rare and that the countries involved are small is not merely a curiosity but a relevant piece of empirical evidence that falsifies the standard theory. Third, aside from the policy aspect, optimum currency areas are of major interest from a purely theoretical standpoint, given the unsatisfactory state of the field commonly acknowledged by the profession.

The present note adopts an equilibrium approach to the subject in which agents with given tastes adapt their behavior to the policy regime, and emphasizes that the national boundary is an important characteristic of such a regime with regard to both input and output mobility. A prime obstacle to adjustment between countries, the national border nevertheless enhances adjustment inside each country. To give the flavor of the argument, labor mobility may be much greater between Seattle and Miami than between Seattle and Vancouver, just a few miles away but severed by the border. From the standpoint of modern monetary economics, in fact, the national boundary may be assimilated to a policy measure that impinges on agents' behavior (Lucas, 1976). The standard theory, instead, looks at the currency area border as the solution, founded upon exogenous criteria, to a policy problem. It is indeed an oddity of the state of the art that we treat domestic monetary issues on the basis of an equilibrium model but continue to study international monetary economics with the analytical framework of the sixties. Disposing of this schizophrenic attitude would much improve our understanding of currency areas.

Before proceeding further, a disclaimer should be made. There is little in this paper that is not implicit in the literature founded on equilibrium stretching from Hume to Lucas. The main purpose here is simply to show the relevance of this conception for understanding currency areas. After a critical appraisal of the current theory (Section 1), an equilibrium hypothesis is set forth (Section 2) and the relative implications are analyzed (Section 3).

1. The theory of optimum currency areas: An assessment

The traditional approach to optimum currency areas is an application of the theory of economic policy (Tinbergen, 1952). In this specific case, the policy instrument is not the discount rate or the level of government expenditure but the fixing of country boundaries which, according to some predetermined criterion, leads to the optimal solution. Actually, Mundell's seminal contribution (1961) pointed out that the regions hit by shocks do not necessarily coincide with nations and, thus, that exchange rate changes may fail to restore equilibrium. If Canada and the U.S. are divided into two regions, so Mundell's example runs (1961, pp. 659–660), an East producing cars and a West producing lumber goods, an increase in productivity in the automobile industry causes excess demand for lumber products and inflationary pressures in the West and excess supply of cars and unemployment in the East. Monetary policy cannot reestablish equilibrium in both regions because expansion of the money supply will eliminate unemployment in the East but not inflation in the West; and conversely in the event of a restriction. However, if national borders were redrawn so that East and West replaced Canada and the U.S., a depreciation of the Eastern dollar would restore equilibrium. Exchange rate flexibility, then, is an effective equilibrating mechanism between different areas inside each of which the Ricardian assumption of high factor mobility is satisfied.

Mundell's pioneering idea has been developed by stressing other aspects, namely openness to trade (McKinnon, 1963) and degree of product diversification (Kenen, 1969). The entire approach, however, is liable to several objections. Though quite distinct, all the criteria ought to yield the optimal solution. This poses an immediate problem of choice which, especially in case of conflict between different criteria, has no obvious answer. Another weakness of the standard theory is the crucial assumption of rigid prices and wages, which reflects the intellectual climate of the sixties. Besides these particular observations, the received view has more general limitations also related to the prevailing ideas of the time. The analysis is essentially static. It focuses on some exogenous feature of the economy unrelated to individual maximizing behavior which, once it happens to be born out, yields the optimal solution. The solution, as Mundell acknowledges (1961, p. 661), ultimately reduces to the empirical question of the occurrence of the relevant feature, say a high degree of factor mobility. This is hard to accept because it makes optimality depend on outside characteristics and not on the equilibrium properties of the economy. The same critique applies to the literature of the seventies, which in order to go beyond the single optimizing criterion looks at the overall costs and benefits of a common currency (Ishiyama, 1975; Tower and Willett, 1976). But this approach too considers the policymaker's maximization problem *in vacuo* and neglects the impact on individual behavior of fixing the borders of a currency area.

The traditional theory, if taken beyond the short run, has paradoxical implications. In a non-stationary world the policymaker has to solve his welfare optimization problem again and again as initial conditions, type of shock, and the regions affected change. In consequence, the domain of currency areas should be repeatedly reshaped. However, if national boundaries were fixed, as in fact they are, the standard theory would imply everlasting disequilibria in all countries, which we do not observe. On grounds of positive economics, the current approach is a clear case of what Friedman (1946), in his critique of Lange, has called "taxonomic theorizing", or building logically coherent models of abstract worlds upon which several specific characteristics of the economy are superimposed. These models are not generalizations about the real world and are accordingly useless for prediction[2].

2.   An equilibrium hypothesis of currency areas

The received view of optimum currency areas must be turned upside down in accordance with the effects of policies on rational behavior. In the traditional literature, various exogenous criteria—factor mobility, openness to trade, product diversification—solve the optimization problem. In the context of an equilibrium model, however, a given geographical configuration impinges on individual choices, which in turn are essential to the adjustment mechanism. In this regard, national boundaries are important in three distinct respects. Two of these are straightforward and are often mentioned. First, the existence of nations entails the presence of government bodies in charge of economic policy; second, it gives rise to legal and institutional arrangements that act as a barrier to trade and factor movement. Nowadays, the difficulties of effective implementation of the Single European Market, which is supposed to abolish all remaining technical barriers and safety regulations, offers a striking example of the difficulty of overcoming trade obstacles between sovereign countries, the commitment to liberalization notwithstanding[3]. However, there is also a third, momentous implication of the existence of nations that bears on the agents' behavior and on adjustment. Individual choices that extend to the international dimension are subject to a higher degree of uncertainty. This raises the cost of computing the expected values of variables on which agents base their decisions and, *ceteris paribus*, produces friction in the equilibrating mechanism. For choices referring to the domestic economy, by contrast, the agent's information set is much larger. Knowledge of institutions, market regulations, language, and the like substantially increases both the available data and the explanatory power of the "true" model into which those data are fed. Hence, the cost of forming expectations is reduced and agents are more reactive to any given shock.

The existence of nations, besides creating barriers to commodity and factor movement, essentially affects individual behavior, and this is reflected in the contrast between domestic and international adjustment. With regard to labor mobility, for instance, the uncertainty and the non-pecuniary costs of international migration can be considerable as compared with internal migration, so that it takes a much higher wage differential to prompt the former. Inside a country, the effects of interregional money flows are inescapable (Mundell, 1961, p. 660) and speed up the equilibrating mechanism as in the textbook case of the frictionless gold standard. The disequilibrium caused by a permanent shock, say the decline of a major industry like coal mining, is adjusted through price and quantity changes in both commodity and factor markets. The ultimate adjustment, in fact, is microeconomic in nature and entails resource reallocation in both consumption and production (Friedman, 1953a, p. 182). In this regard, the adjustment speed of the variables differs greatly. If the structure of relative prices in the commodity market changes more quickly than in the factor market, it is quantities in the latter that bear the brunt of the equilibrating mechanism, with fiscal policy smoothing out the process[4]. The response of workers and holders of capital, then, becomes crucial. The larger dimension of the information set with reference to the domestic economy makes for faster and less variable calculation of their economic choices. In the very long run, real forces hold sway, so that trade theory offers more detailed answers. Modern developments in this field (Krugman, 1991, ch. 3) show and corroborate the hypothesis of increased polarization of domestic economic activity. This proposition is a direct implication of the equilibrium hypothesis of currency areas. Furthermore, John McCallum offers striking empirical evidence supporting "the fact that even the relatively innocuous Canada-U.S. border continues to have a decisive effect on continental trade patterns [which] suggests that national borders in general continue to matter" (1995, p. 622).

CURRENCY AREAS AND EQUILIBRIUM   55

This note is in the tradition of equilibrium theory, which cuts across several fields of economics and thus mirrors other well-known propositions. The analogy with the Coase Theorem is immediate. Just as the solution of externalities is reached, in the absence of transaction costs, through individual contracting independent of the initial allocation of legal entitlements, so adjustment inside a currency area is ensured by the equilibrium hypothesis based on rational behavior independent of the initial geographical configuration. The analogue of the postulate of no transaction costs is the assumption of no friction in the intranational adjustment process.

The setting of national borders not only increases labor mobility but also enhances the optimality criteria of McKinnon (1963) and Kenen (1969) insofar as impediments to trade stimulate product diversification[5]. Indeed, the triad of criteria introduced in the standard literature provides a clue to optimality because it is the result of maximizing behavior, not an exogenously determined guideline, that gives the optimal solution. Therefore, the traditional analysis should be entirely reversed. In the final section of his Graham Lecture, Krugman concisely describes the state of the field.

"Mundell (1961), McKinnon (1963), and Kenen (1969) gave us a very nice intellectual structure for thinking about the problem of defining an optimum currency area. In all cases, we think of a country as asking whether it prefers the macroeconomic independence that comes with an independent currency and perhaps a floating rate, or whether it prefers the microeconomic benefits of stable rates and perhaps a common currency. We have a fairly good idea of what the macroeconomic tradeoff is: we know that fixed rates cost least when trade is large, when labor mobility is high, when shocks are symmetric, and when there are compensating fiscal transfers. Knowing this, we guess that some index based on these criteria will indicate when and if a country should join a currency area." (1993, p. 20.)

However, as there is no such a thing as a domestic macroeconomic tradeoff, there is no such a thing as an international macroeconomic tradeoff. It is individual behavior that, given the policymaker's choices, determines the adjustment path within the nation, lending substance to the characteristics highlighted by the traditional theory. The coexistence of countries as diverse as the United States and, say, Iceland, whose economy is a thousand times smaller, each issuing its own currency and having no incentive to form a monetary union, corroborates the equilibrium hypothesis upon which the efficacy of the domestic adjustment mechanism is founded.

In the vast literature on European monetary unification, e.g., Eichengreen (1992) and Bayoumi and Eichengreen (1993), the United States is contrasted with Europe as satisfying two main optimality criteria, namely labor mobility and fiscal integration. But this is no more than the outcome of the U.S. longstanding status as nation. As for fiscal integration, this is patent. With regard to

labor mobility, the division of the European Union into fifteen sovereign countries substantially affects long-run adjustment and the decision to migrate. The
higher labor mobility in the U.S., rather than providing evidence for the Mundellian criterion, actually corroborates the equilibrium hypothesis. Upon reflection,
no one would maintain that the United States was set up as an optimum currency
area because it enjoyed high labor mobility, just as, in Lucas's words, "no one
argues that the anticipation of sixteenth-century inflation sent Columbus to the
New World to locate the gold to finance it" (1977, p. 232). Individuals react to the
fixing of national borders as they do to a change in money supply or the discount
rate and, just as it makes no sense to evaluate optimal monetary policy disregarding the agents' rational behavior, it hardly makes sense to assess the optimality of a currency area neglecting the impact of a given geographical set-up.

3. The equilibrium hypothesis and optimality

David Hume (1752a) grounded international monetary theory in the notion of
equilibrium. He showed that forces of equilibrium prevent any country from ac-
cumulating an ever-growing gold stock and bring about a natural distribution of
money supplies. Likewise, it is misleading to design an optimum currency area
since, within any geographical configuration, the domestic adjustment mechanism yields an equilibrium solution. In another celebrated essay, however,
Hume (1752b, pp. 37–38) stressed slow price and wage adjustment to argue
for the effectiveness of variations in the money stock. The predictive power of
the equilibrium hypothesis can be impaired by incomplete information. Agents
change their expectations when the effort to calculate them is more than offset by the prospective benefit. Therefore, a smaller information set raises the
cost of expectation formation and, *ceteris paribus*, slows the revision of expectations. The assumption relating to the varying dimension of the information
set does not affect the logic of the equilibrium hypothesis of currency areas,
though it is relevant to its application. As attrition must be taken into account in
applying the model of classical mechanics, frictions of various kinds entail the
modification of the equilibrium hypothesis, but the latter's analytical coherence
is not weakened by such disturbing factors. The presence of frictions and lags
augments the time and cost of adjustment, and this can eventually be made up
by fiscal transfers.

   The thrust of the present paper is to underscore the momentous implications
of fixing a national border for agents' behavior and the effectiveness of the
intranational, as contrasted with the international, equilibrating mechanism. In
his classic essay on flexible exchange rates, Friedman seizes on the core of the
issue, and does so in a mere footnote, which is worth quoting in full.

"The key difference for present purposes between the different states of
the United States, on the one hand, and the different members of the sterling area, on the other, is that the former are, while the latter are not, all

effectively subject to a single central fiscal and monetary authority—the federal government—having ultimate fiscal and monetary powers. In addition, the former have, while the latter have not, effectively surrendered the right to impose restrictions on the movements of goods, people, or capital between one another. This is a major factor explaining why a central monetary authority is able to operate without producing serious sectional strains. Of course, these are questions of economic fact, not of political form, and of degree, not of kind. A group of politically independent nations all of which firmly adhered to, say, the gold standard would thereby in effect submit themselves to a central monetary authority, albeit an impersonal one. If, in addition, they firmly adhered to the free movement of goods, people, and capital without restrictions, and economic conditions rendered such movement easy, they would, in effect, be an economic unit for which a single currency—which is the equivalent of rigid exchange rates—would be appropriate." (1953, p. 193, footnote 16.)

In his penetrating analysis, Friedman stresses the difference between the regions of a single country and the members of a currency area. This difference, it should be added, crucially conditions agents' behavior and the forces behind adjustment. The very existence of nations represents a discontinuity that is the ultimate basis of international economics. Hence, the intrinsically distinct nature of money circulating in a single nation *vis-à-vis* a fixed exchange rate regime linking several countries relates not only to the greater credibility of the former but especially to the implications of the equilibrium hypothesis for intranational adjustment. Therefore, monetary union among nations that maintain territorial and political sovereignty can be difficult to achieve and, in fact, political unions tend to precede monetary unions[6]. Only tiny countries such as Luxembourg or Liechtenstein join larger currency areas, and they have an incentive to do so, because the non-trivial cost of establishing their own money is not matched by seignorage or by any other advantage. Their objective is not to conform to exogenous welfare maximizing criteria, which in this special case are simply irrelevant.

4. Conclusion

The standard theory of optimum currency areas is falsified by the empirical evidence. Countries do not experience cumulative disequilibria and have no apparent motive to participate in a monetary union. After all, nations do not dissolve because of a failure to adjust to domestic shocks or interregional money flows. These stylized facts corroborate the equilibrium hypothesis, which emphasizes the behavioral implications of fixing the national borders. The various channels of the equilibrium mechanism are enhanced by the very existence of the nation. On strictly theoretical grounds, the coincidence between monetary and political sovereignty is an outcome of the equilibrium hypothesis. Once borders are set, the adjustment mechanism sees to the achievement of a stable equilibrium position. This explains both the viable coexistence of countries of unequal economic size and the lack of incentive to join a monetary union.

Acknowledgments

Thanks are due to Milton Friedman, David Laidler, Jacques Mélitz, and a referee for helpful comments. The usual caveat applies. The views expressed herein are those of the author and not necessarily those of the Banca d'Italia.

Notes

1. Krugman's frustration is shared by many. In his textbook, Niehans remarks: "Optimum currency areas are still a concept in search of a theory" (1984, p. 294). And, in a recent article (1995), Mélitz calls attention to the "current impasse" in research on the subject.
2. "Having completed his enumeration [of all possible economic systems], or gone as far as he can or thinks desirable, Lange then seeks to relate his theoretical structure to the real world by judging to which of his alternative possibilities the real world corresponds. Is it any wonder that "very special conditions" will have to be satisfied to explain the real world? If a physicist or astronomer were to explore all possible interrelations among a variable number of planets, each of which could be of any size, density, or configuration, and possess any possible gravitational properties, he would surely find that only very special conditions would explain the existing universe. There are an infinite number of theoretical systems; there are only a few real worlds" (Friedman, 1946, p. 284). With regard to the subject of the present paper, Genberg notes: "A comprehensive survey ... by Tower and Willett (1976) ... clearly brought out the somewhat bewildering number of structural factors that were offered as criteria for the delineation of optimum currency areas. It also showed that while the analysis supporting these criteria had contributed to our understanding of interdependence and the role of exchange rate changes in the process of adjustments to external and internal shocks, the difficulty in finding empirical counterparts and measures of the theoretical concepts prevented the suggestions from being operational" (1989, p. 443).
3. In his recent booklet on *Geography and Trade*, Krugman refers to this point. "Nations matter— they exist in a modeling sense—because they have governments whose policies affect the movements of goods and factors. In particular, national boundaries often act as barriers to trade and factor mobility. Every modern nation has restrictions on labor mobility. Many nations place restrictions on the movement of capital, or at least threaten to do so. And actual or potential limits on trade are pervasive, in spite of the best efforts of trade negotiators" (1991, pp. 71–72). See also Hartland (1949).
4. According to Hartland's (1949) empirical analysis, the disequilibria following the Great Depression were attenuated through a plurality of channels, mainly fiscal transfers and factor mobility in the short and long run respectively. Hartland emphasizes the role of the U.S. Treasury in alleviating the conditions of the agricultural regions, the most hard hit by the depression, as contrasted with the greater severity of the crisis in smaller countries. "[T]he agricultural sections of the United States were more fortunate than the agricultural countries in South America and the Balkans during the same period. The policies of the federal government implemented by the financial activities of the Treasury caused their reserves to be replenished, making it possible for them to maintain a balance of payments equilibrium and also a certain level of consumption. Without such transfers, the loss of reserves to which they would have been subject, would have forced agricultural districts to undergo a severe deflation of purchasing power and incomes at a time when they were suffering a greater deflationary pressure than the rest of the country. Also, such a decrease in real income would have caused a migration of people from agricultural to industrial regions where real incomes were higher" (1949, p. 406).
5. Empirical evidence in support of this proposition is presented by Krugman (1992, pp. 75–78) with reference to the industrial structures of the U.S. as compared with Europe.
6. On the relationships between political union and monetary union, see Fratianni (1994, pp. 225–227).

References

Bayoumi, Tamin and Barry Eichengreen (1993) "Shocking Aspects of European Monetary Integration." In Francesco Giavazzi and Francisco Torres (eds.), *Adjustment and Growth in the European Monetary Union*. Cambridge: Cambridge University Press, pp. 193–229.

Eichengreen, Barry (1992) "Is Europe an Optimum Currency Area?" In Silvio Borner and Herbert Grubel (eds.), *The European Community after 1992. Perspectives from the Outside*. London: MacMillan, pp. 138–161.

Fratianni, Michele (1994) "What Went Wrong with the EMS and European Monetary Union." In Berhanu Abegaz, Patricia Dillon, David H. Feldman, and Paul F. Whiteley (eds.), *The Challenge of European Integration. Internal and External Problems of Trade and Money*. Boulder: Westview Press, pp. 219–235.

Friedman, Milton (1946) "Lange on Price Flexibility and Employment: A Methodological Criticism." *American Economic Review* 36, 613–631; reprinted in Friedman (1953b), 277–300.

Friedman, Milton (1953a) "The Case for Flexible Exchange Rates." In Friedman (1953b), 157–203.

Friedman, Milton (1953b) *Essays in Positive Economics*. Chicago: The University of Chicago Press.

Genberg, Hans (1989) "Exchange Rate Management and Macroeconomic Policy: A National Perspective." *Scandinavian Journal of Economics* 91, 439–469.

Hartland, Penelope (1949) "Interregional Payments Compared With International Payments." *Quarterly Journal of Economics* 63, 392–407.

Hume, David (1752a) "Of the Balance of Trade." In Eugene Rotwein (ed.), *Writings on Economics*. Madison: The University of Wisconsin Press, 1970, pp. 60–77.

Hume, David (1752b) "Of Money." In Eugene Rotwein (ed.), *Writings on Economics*. Madison: The University of Wisconsin Press, 1970, pp. 33–46.

Ishiyama, Yoshihide (1975) "The Theory of Optimum Currency Areas." *IMF Staff Papers* 22, 344–383.

Kenen, Peter B. (1969) "The Theory of Optimum Currency Areas: An Eclectic View." In Robert A. Mundell and Alexander K. Swoboda (eds.), *Monetary Problems of the International Economy*. Chicago: The University of Chicago Press, pp. 41–60.

Krugman, Paul (1991) *Geography and Trade*. Cambridge, Mass.: The MIT Press.

Krugman, Paul (1992) *Currencies and Crises*. Cambridge, Mass.: The MIT Press.

Krugman, Paul (1993) "What Do We Need To Know About the International Monetary System?" Essays in International Finance No. 193. Princeton, N.J.: Princeton International Finance Section.

Laidler, David (1988) "Taking Money Seriously." *Canadian Journal of Economics* 21, 687–713.

Lucas, Robert E. (1976) "Econometric Policy Evaluation: A Critique." *Carnegie-Rochester Conference Series on Public Policy* 1, 19–46; reprinted in Lucas (1981), 104–130.

Lucas, Robert E. (1977) "Understanding Business Cycles." *Carnegie-Rochester Conference Series on Public Policy* 5, 7–29, reprinted in Lucas (1981), 215–239.

Lucas, Robert E. (1981) *Studies in Business-Cycle Theory*. Cambridge, Mass.: The MIT Press.

McCallum, John (1995) "National Borders Matter: Canada-US Regional Trade Patterns." *American Economic Review* 85, 615–623.

McKinnon, Ronald I. (1963) "Optimum Currency Areas." *American Economic Review* 53, 717–724.

Mélitz, Jacques (1995) "The Current Impasse in Research on Optimum Currency Areas." *European Economic Review* 39, 492–500.

Mundell, Robert A. (1961) "The Theory of Optimum Currency Areas." *American Economic Review* 51, 657–664.

Niehans, Jürg (1984) *International Monetary Economics*. Baltimore, MD: The Johns Hopkins University Press.

Tinbergen, Jan (1952) *On The Theory of Economic Policy*. Amsterdam: North-Holland.

Tower, Edward and Thomas D. Willett (1976) "The Theory of Optimum Currency Areas and Exchange-Rate Flexibility." Special Studies in International Economics No. 11. Princeton, N.J.: Princeton International Finance Section.

[15]

The equilibrium approach
to optimum currency areas *

FILIPPO CESARANO

Robert Mundell's (1961) celebrated contribution to the theory of optimum currency areas has given rise to an extensive literature. His original idea was to show the limitations of exchange rate flexibility in restoring internal balance, thus leading to the optimal solution of reshaping currency areas. This accomplishment, which reflected the state of the art based on Keynesian economics, held sway up to our days, even though the pendulum had swung back towards the classical paradigm since the late 1960s.

In the last decade, however, the traditional approach has been subjected to several criticisms. The sundry optimality criteria introduced in the wake of Mundell's seminal essay are all exogenous, consisting in specific characteristics of the economy, detached from an equilibrium mechanism. Optimality then involves the mere verification of such characteristics and therefore reduces to an empirical question. Dwelling on these criticisms, modern contributions have developed an equilibrium approach, pointing out the efficacy of equilibrium forces in achieving the optimum. This strain of thought, emphasizing the endogeneity of the optimum currency area criteria, has turned the concept of optimality upside down.[1]

From a broader historical perspective, the traditional approach appears as a detour from the evolution of economics dominated by the

☐ Banca d'Italia, Ufficio Ricerche Storiche, Roma (Italy); e-mail: filippo.cesarano @bancaditalia.it.

* Thanks are due to Michael Bordo and Giulio Cifarelli for their useful comments. The usual caveat applies. The views expressed herein are those of the author and do not necessarily reflect the position of the Banca d'Italia.

[1] For a recent survey see De Grauwe and Mongelli (2005).

BNL Quarterly Review, vol. LIX, no. 237, June 2006, pp. 193-209.

notion of equilibrium. In fact, in the post-war discussion of European economic integration, some distinguished economists anticipated Mundell's theory, though taking a different route consonant with the recent equilibrium approach. In a sense, in half a century we have come full circle because contemporary works have brought the subject again into the realm of equilibrium theory after the long intermezzo beginning with Mundell's classic essay.

The purpose of this paper is to examine these developments, drawing attention to the remarkable achievements of today's research. After critically comparing the early literature on monetary unions with Mundell's contribution (section 1), this article analyses the modern equilibrium approach, showing the sharp theoretical and policy differences from the received view (section 2).

1. Monetary unions and optimality

In the post-war literature, the lack of adjusting capacity in the Bretton Woods system and, in particular, the inconsistency between the overriding target of full employment and fixed parities motivated the call for flexible exchange rates, considered the logical counterpart of employment policies. Mundell thought he had spotted a weak point in this position. As he recalls the genesis of his 1961 article, he was investigating whether exchange rate flexibility might solve regional problems, noting also that the floating Canadian dollar did not cushion Canada from the US business cycle.[2] His research strategy of locating production across countries, together with the Keynesian assumption of price and wage rigidity, put the burden of adjustment on quantity changes. Hence, the limitations of floating rates in adjusting a demand shift readily emerged because virtually all channels of adjustment were

---

[2] The starting point of his analysis was the possible failure of flexible exchange rates to ensure full employment and a stable price level, not the optimal design of currency areas. "I was not, however, proposing an independent currency for British Columbia; rather, I was beginning to think of the argument as a qualification, if not a refutation, of the argument for flexible exchange rates" (Mundell 1997, p. 31). In the same essay, Mundell tells in detail how subsequent reflection on the idea underlying optimum currency areas heightened his doubts about the case for flexible exchange rates.

precluded but for the innovative solution of reshaping national borders in accordance with labour mobility.

This optimality criterion, however, had already been put forward by Abba Lerner in his analysis of the gold standard (1944, pp. 370-77) and, subsequently, in a debate on the post-war monetary order (1947).[3] Contrasting the output and employment costs of the gold standard adjustment with the smoothness of adjustment inside a country, he pointed to labour mobility as the key explanatory factor. Undoubtedly, Lerner did not elaborate this argument to arrive at a full-fledged analysis of optimality. In particular, he did not explicitly set the macroeconomic benefits of increasing the number of currency areas against the microeconomic losses in terms of higher transaction and information costs. Yet he anticipated the basic principle underlying Mundell's contribution and, more importantly, arrived at this result by an entirely different route. While Mundell focused on a failure of exchange rate flexibility to re-establish equilibrium *between* countries, Lerner emphasized the efficacy of adjustment *within* a country, where the exchange rate is irrevocably fixed.

These analyses suggest opposite conceptions of currency area optimality. For Mundell (1961, p. 658, n. 6), labour mobility is the solution to inadequate international adjustment, which ultimately hinges on the postulate of interregional factor immobility, with regions spanning the country borders. For Lerner, instead, factors are mobile within a country, which accounts for the effectiveness of interregional adjustment as distinct from the international gold standard.[4] The main point of these contrasting views relates to the meaning and impact of the country border on interregional adjustment, considered to be a barrier dividing two sides of a region in the first interpretation, or the

---

[3] For a detailed reconstruction of the origins of the theory of optimum currency areas see Cesarano (2006).

[4] If all obstacles to trade and factor mobility were removed, Lerner argued, the gold standard would be immune from adjustment costs, thus providing a sound monetary system. "Tariffs and quotas interfere with trade, and the movement of people from country to country is seriously limited. It is only because of these restrictions that a rigid enforcement of fixed exchange rates between the values of the currencies of different countries can be so very harmful. If there were complete freedom of movement of goods, investment, and people, an international currency system would be as sound as a single monetary system for a country within which the three freedoms of movement are realities, and a properly managed gold standard system might be one way of arranging this" (1944, p. 376).

defining factor of efficacious interregional adjustment in the second. This divergence of opinion could not emerge more clearly than from Mundell's argument that, contrary to Lerner's hypothesis, intranational adjustment and international adjustment in the gold standard are alike, involving the same problems and high costs[5] (see the striking contrast between the quotations in footnotes 4 and 5).

Lerner's contribution went unheeded. Indeed, it is never mentioned in the vast literature on the subject. He did not start from a policy problem, but analysed a purely theoretical issue. In the 1950s, however, the process of European economic integration set in motion the debate on monetary unions. Actually, the study of optimum currency areas and of monetary unions displays a dual nature in that it tackles the same class of problems from different perspectives: search for the optimality criteria with a view to redesigning currency areas or, alternatively, given a certain number of countries, deploy those criteria to assess the optimality of circulating a common currency. Not surprisingly, in the latter context the main issues analysed by Mundell had been discussed earlier by other economists.

Independently of Lerner, Meade and Scitovsky pointed out factor mobility as one of the key properties enhancing the effectiveness of intranational *vis-à-vis* international adjustment. Thus, contrasting the gold standard approach with the integration approach to monetary unification, Meade (1957, pp. 384-88) contended that full employment and a stable price level could be achieved only in the latter, involving both a common currency and supranational fiscal policy tantamount to a federal government, because goods, labour and capital could move freely as between the regions of a single country. Likewise Scitovsky, while stigmatizing the impossibility of pursuing full employment in the gold standard, noted

---

[5] "[I]f the arguments against the gold standard were correct, then why should a similar argument not apply against a common currency system in a multiregional country? Under the gold standard depression in one country would be transmitted, through the foreign-trade multiplier, to foreign countries. Similarly, under a common currency, depression in one region would be transmitted to other regions for precisely the same reasons. If the gold standard imposed a harsh discipline on the national economy and induced the transmission of economic fluctuations, then a common currency would be guilty of the same charges; interregional balance-of-payments problems are invisible, so to speak, precisely because there is no escape from the self-adjusting effects of interregional money flows" (Mundell 1961, p. 660).

"that the condition of a common currency is the presence of market forces able automatically and without the aid of deliberate economic policy to obviate balance-of-payments difficulties" (1957, pp. 18-19).

For Scitovsky, such forces include, besides labour mobility, capital market integration and employment policy, both playing a key role in ensuring the effectiveness of intranational adjustment.

These analyses take the geographical extension of the currency area as given and therefore arrive at the optimality principles through a reverse route, stemming from the dual nature of the subject yet yielding the same results as Mundell's seminal paper. Interestingly, these very principles were also expounded by Milton Friedman in a footnote to his classic essay on flexible exchange rates.[6]

The important point is that all these authors ascribe the efficacy of intranational adjustment not only to economic policies but especially to market forces underlying the classical adjustment model. However paradoxical it may appear, in the heyday of Keynesian economics it was a commonplace to consider Hume's specie-flow mechanism the theoretical blueprint of monetary union. Thus Scitovsky, while rejecting the gold standard for its unemployment effects, noted:

"We must beware, however, of throwing the classical theory out altogether. Its mechanism, if limited, is still effective, at least in interregional relations. The flow of funds from one region to another affects the reserve ratios of banks that operate in only one and not both of the regions and causes these banks to contract and expand credit respectively. The influence of this on the balance of interregional payments is similar to that of classical monetary policy on the balance of international payments but much more limited. It is more limited, first of all, because the leverage of commercial-bank expansion and contraction is much smaller than that of central-

---

[6] Discussing the operation of fixed exchange rates between the members of the sterling area as distinct from the different regions of a country, he observed: "The key difference for present purposes between the different states of the United States, on the one hand, and the different members of the sterling area, on the other, is that the former are, while the latter are not, all effectively subject to a single central fiscal and monetary authority – the federal government – having ultimate fiscal and monetary powers. In addition, the former have, while the latter have not, effectively surrendered the right to impose restrictions on the movements of goods, people, or capital between one another. This is a major factor explaining why a central monetary authority is able to operate without producing serious sectional strains" (Friedman 1953, p. 193, n. 16).

bank expansion and contraction; and secondly, because the credit
policy of commercial banks is partly under central-bank direction
and only partly governed by their own reserve position. Furthermore, no such regional expansion or contraction can occur in a
country all of whose banks operate on a national scale, with regional branches that serve merely as collecting stations for deposits and
loan applications" (1957, p. 21).[7]

The essential difference with Mundell's analysis (see footnote 5
above) does not consist in considering the border of the currency area
to be fixed, but in deeming interregional adjustment to be highly effective. As already argued, Mundell's case of disequilibrium is constructed
on the assumption that regions overlap the countries' borders, so that
the solution of labour mobility is an exogenous characteristic depending more on geography than on economics because it is not the outcome of an equilibrium mechanism driven by market forces.[8] This deficiency mars many of the further optimality criteria developed in the
wake of Mundell's essay. All of them represent exogenous features of
the economies considered, resulting from a static analysis removed
from the realm of equilibrium theory. A sheer antinomy therefore
emerges with the theory of monetary unions, based on the classical
model, developed by Lerner and, subsequently, by Friedman, Meade
and Scitovsky. As Scitovsky observed:

> "[T]he classical theory [...] is a dynamic equilibrium theory; dy-
> namic, because it deals with a process of adjustment over time;
> equilibrium, because it asserts the existence of a tendency toward
> balance-of-payments equilibrium" (1957, p. 19).

Besides these criticisms of a general character, several specific
strictures can be levelled against the received view. Mundell's solution
is an application of Tinbergen's (1952) approach to economic policy,
using the instrument of fixing national borders according to some predetermined criterion, and is thus subject to the Lucas critique. Furthermore, the traditional approach arrives at a plurality of optimality criteria, each supposed to yield the optimum, which poses an uneasy prob-

---

[7] Analogous arguments were also used by Meade (1953, pp. 39-41 and 1957, p.
386).

[8] As McKinnon observes: "Mundell demonstrates that it is necessary to ask *what
economic characteristics* determine the optimum size of the domain of a single currency" (1963, p. 717, italics added).

lem of choice, especially in the case of conflict between them. And, even sticking to a single criterion, say labour mobility, the optimum would merely reduce to an empirical question, as Mundell (1961, pp. 661-62) himself recognized. Finally, the fulfilment of a given optimality criterion in a dynamic setting would require a frequent redrawing of the border, which is not only impracticable but also theoretically weak since it would multiply the number of solutions tantamount to a *reductio ad absurdum*.

With the publication of the *Werner Report* in 1970, the revival of European monetary integration again drew attention to monetary unions. Research focused on the counterpoint between the microeconomic benefits of a common currency and the macroeconomic costs of forsaking monetary sovereignty underlying the calculus of participation (Corden 1972, Ishiyama 1975, Tower and Willett 1976, Hamada 1977). However, progress along these lines was scanty because the lack of advancement on the microeconomic front left the only option of investigating the macroeconomic side.[9] Apart from some attempts to define the conditions for viability of monetary unions (Cesarano 1985), a weaker and more slippery concept than optimality, this meant the mere multiplication of optimality criteria,[10] exacerbating the shortcomings of the traditional approach shown in the preceding paragraphs. This development, therefore, made the topic even more elusive, giving the impression of presenting a series of special cases rather than a comprehensive, fully-fledged theoretical framework. Hence Niehans remarked: "Optimum currency areas are still a concept in search of a theory" (1984, p. 294).

The preparation of the *Delors Report* and the signing of the Maastricht Treaty gave a decisive impulse to European monetary unification, propelled by the new classical macroeconomics rather than the slow progressing theory of optimum currency areas. The paradigm shift in macroeconomics – the analysis of expectations formation, ex-

---

[9] As Paul Krugman noted: "We have some suggestive phrases – reduced transaction costs, improvement in the quality of the unit of account – to describe what we think are the benefits of fixed rates and common currencies. We even have a loose-jointed theory of optimum currency areas that stresses the tension between these hypothesized benefits of fixity and the more measurable costs of lost monetary autonomy. What we do not have, however, is anything we can properly call a model of the benefits of fixed rates and common currencies" (1993, p. 3).

[10] Tavlas (1993, pp. 666-67) lists no fewer than nine optimality criteria, from similarity of inflation rates to political willingness to adhere to monetary union.

change rate determination and the time inconsistency problem – cast the subject in a new light, but did not displace the traditional approach. Certainly, the mainstream opinion tilted in favour of currency union, stressing the benefits of "tying one's hands", and the meaning of some important tenets changed: similar inflation rates, interpreted as a condition for optimality in the early literature, were now considered a result of monetary union (Tavlas 1993, p. 673). Nonetheless, the theory of optimum currency areas still pivoted on correspondence of the economies to given, exogenous criteria. Bayoumi and Eichengreen (1997, p. 762) thus observed: "The theory has advanced only minimally since the seminal contributions of Mundell (1961), McKinnon (1963) and Kenen (1969)".

2. Optimum currency areas and equilibrium

That the received view remained so highly influential a quarter of century after the renaissance of classical economics witnesses the momentous and lasting impact of Mundell's seminal article. In this connection, Willem Buiter deems the theory of optimum currency areas "one of the low points of post-World War II monetary economics" (2000, p. 222), pointing out two basic faults – the failure to distinguish between short-run nominal rigidities and long-run real rigidities and the failure to consider capital mobility.[11] Buiter's assessment may appear excessively disparaging, yet his conclusion must be shared:

> "[T]he debate on the merits of monetary union and other exchange rate arrangements in the first decade of the new millennium tends to be conducted with the intellectual apparatus of the 1960s. It is out of date and a misleading guide to policy" (2000, pp. 222-23).

Not all economists, however, were mesmerized by the traditional approach. Beginning in the late 1990s, several contributions shifted the

---

[11] The pre-Mundellian literature was immune from these shortcomings. In relation to the first, Friedman pointed out that "the ultimate adjustment to a change in external circumstances will consist of a change in the allocation of productive resources and in the composition of the goods available for consumption and investment" (1953, p. 182), thus assigning to exchange rate flexibility only the function of absorbing the initial impact of adjustment. As regards the second, Scitovsky (1957) underlined the key role of capital mobility in ensuring the viability of currency union.

analysis in a radically different direction. Although they tackled the subject from various perspectives, these works, as with Robert Merton's independent multiples in scientific discovery, all arrived at the same innovative hypothesis: optimality does not derive from exogenous, pre-existing characteristics of the economy, but is endogenous, i.e. the outcome of an optimizing process. The modern approach stems from the rational expectations hypothesis and its basic corollary, the Lucas critique, underlying the new classical macroeconomics, which not only renders empirical verification of optimality criteria on the basis of historical data quite meaningless, but overturns the very concept of optimum currency area. While in the traditional approach optimality boils down to the empirical question of verifying the existence of factor mobility or other optimality criteria, in the equilibrium approach it is the operation of a common currency that, impinging on the behaviour of agents, sparks the emergence of the optimality criteria.

The notion of endogeneity of optimum currency areas has been developed in various ways. Concentrating on trade integration and cross-country correlation of business cycles, Frankel and Rose (1998) argue that these optimality criteria are not independent, i.e. that an increase in international trade relations is accompanied by more closely correlated business cycles across countries.[12] As the authors themselves recognize, these results are empirically controversial, given a number of previous findings linking trade integration to higher specialization in production. However, the main message is theoretical rather than empirical, because the authors make the important point that the optimality criteria stem from the working of monetary union and are therefore endogenous. Alesina and Barro (2002), besides recognizing the effects of lower transaction costs on trade and output, focus on the benefits of commitment to price stability which, given the difficulty of stepping out of a monetary union, is more credible than in other fixed exchange rate regimes. Once account is taken of the other variables influencing the decision to join a currency union – the size of countries,

---

[12] In a subsequent paper, they show that a currency union triples trade with the other members without creating trade diversion and, in the long run, expands output (every 1 percent increase in total trade, relative to GDP, raises per capita income by one-third of a percent or more; Frankel and Rose 2002, p. 461). They find no evidence, however, that the enhanced monetary stability stemming from currency union has a significant positive effect on output. The reader is also referred to related works by Bayoumi and Eichengreen (1997) and Fatás (1997).

the distances between them, the correlations between shocks, the feasibility of transfers – the country with the strongest incentive to renounce monetary sovereignty is one with a history of high inflation and close, in various respects, to a large country with stable money (Alesina and Barro 2002, p. 435).

This succinct exposition does not do justice to these contributions, but it does show the emergence of a new approach to optimum currency areas grounded in the equilibrium model of the new classical macroeconomics. Like all policy measures, the establishment of a currency area affects individual behaviour in that agents evaluate its implications and adjust their decisions. The endogenous character of optimality stems from this general principle (Cesarano 1997).

In this respect, it is important to distinguish a monetary union among countries that maintain their national borders and sovereignty from a common currency with political unification. In the latter case, the coincidence of monetary union and political union substantially increases the agents' information set, not merely statistical data but the dispersed bits of information referred to by Hayek as "a body of very important but unorganized knowledge [...]: the knowledge of the particular circumstances of time and place" (1945, p. 521). A larger information set sharpens individuals' reactions to changes in circumstances, increasing the efficiency of the price system and reducing the macroeconomic costs of adjustment. The role of information is therefore crucial not only in Hayek's microeconomic argument but also in the new classical macroeconomics. Any obstacles to the availability of information – and national borders are surely a serious impediment as shown in the seminal papers by McCallum (1995) and Engel and Rogers (1996) – would tamper with this communication network, eventually leading to sub-optimal solutions. Hence, while a monetary union between countries severed by borders may be impaired by many kinds of barriers, political union disposes of these interferences, establishing both a common institutional and legal framework that widens agents' information set and a sole economic policy authority with extensive powers. These general principles impinge on a variety of equilibrium mechanisms inside a currency area so that most of the optimality criteria found in the literature are the outcome of an equilibrium model.

First, the absence of a border and deeper knowledge of labour market rules makes the decision to migrate to another region less risky and less costly, thus increasing labour mobility. Moving from Seattle to

Miami, for instance, may well be easier and more advantageous than migrating to Vancouver, just a few miles away but across the border. Second, a common institutional setting has an immediate impact on trade integration; otherwise, regulations and non-tariff barriers constitute substantial obstacles. An eloquent example is the EMU, where despite the completion of the single market program in 1993 market segmentation and price discrimination are still present (Gil-Pareja 2003). Third, the use of fiscal transfers to smooth adjustment and overcome disruptive shocks is patently easier for a central government. Recalling Hartland (1949), factor mobility and fiscal transfers greatly mitigated the impact of the Great Depression in the United States. Fourth, as regards the similarity of shocks and cycles, the evidence is more ambiguous, as output and employment trends seem to diverge more at the regional than at the national level, a stylized fact that has long been theorized (Krugman 1991; De Grauwe and Vanhaverbeke 1993, p. 125, n. 10). Political union would therefore intensify such divergences and the occurrence of asymmetric shocks, seemingly running counter to optimality.

The agglomeration effects and polarization of economic activity relate to the real aspects of regional development, facilitated by the unchecked forces of monetary adjustment. Intranational adjustment, however, is enhanced by labour mobility, trade integration and fiscal transfers, witness the fact that no country in history, even the largest, has ever split its domestic monetary circulation into various currencies. A most conspicuous example is the United States which, Krugman conjectured, "would be better off with a half-dozen regional currencies" (1993, p. 22), yet has never even considered it. The reason is not merely political. That so huge a currency area could thrive for more than two centuries is indicative of the operation of an equilibrium process enhancing optimality. By contrast, designing optimum currency areas on the basis of pre-existing exogenous features, as the traditional approach suggests, is a meaningless exercise in comparative statics: indeed, no one would contend that the United States was set up as an optimum currency area because it had the property of labour mobility or trade integration.

The equilibrium approach does not of course imply that any country is an optimum currency area. In fact, monetary unions have often been established but, until recently, were limited to particularly tiny countries – Andorra, Liechtenstein, Monaco and the like – which invariably adopted the currency of a large neighbour. This stylized fact

simply shows that there is a lower bound below which the costs of setting up a currency are not offset by any advantage from monetary independence. As Mundell (1961, section V) argued, there is an upper
limit on the number of currencies above which the functions of money fade away. Setting the benefits of multiplying the number of currency areas – the stabilization argument – against the increase in transaction costs associated with such multiplication, he recalled that, for
the classics, the stabilization argument was irrelevant and, thus, the optimum currency area was the world.[13]

Actually, the analysis of optimum currency areas, as an applied
topic in the field of money, reflects the state of the art of monetary
theory and, particularly, two fundamental issues: the essential properties of money and monetary policy effectiveness. As put by Mundell,
optimality hinges on the tension between these opposing forces. The
result of course depends on the characteristics of the model and, especially, on the second aspect intimately related to the adjustment problem. The extreme assumptions distinguishing the classical model, envisaging a frictionless economy with a large information set, from the
Keynesian model, featuring various sources of disequilibrium and limited information, lead to polar solutions: a world money and the designing of currency areas according to some exogenous optimality criterion. Yet both hypotheses go to extremes and, above all, disregard
the impact of national borders on the availability of information and,
thus, on agents' maximizing behaviour.

The classical solution highlights the information-producing role
of money, which finds a counterpart, at the macroeconomic level, in
the ineffectiveness of monetary policy under complete information:
monetary autonomy is quite useless and international adjustment is
very smooth. In fact, Hayek (1937) called for the gold standard because
it is a truly international monetary system in which, in contrast with
other arrangements characterized by a developed banking sector and
the presence of central banks, money flows are the result of individual
behaviour as between the regions of a single country. However, if we
do not live in a world of complete information, a one-money world is
not optimal. The modern equilibrium approach, albeit akin to classical

---

[13] This ideal was almost realized under the gold standard which, as Friedman remarked, "came very close to being a unified currency" (1965, p. 268). In his Nobel lecture, Mundell (2000, p. 338), stretching the case for fixed exchange rates, envisaged the
possible introduction of a world money.

thought, does not lead to the one-money solution inasmuch as it high-lights the impact of national borders. Unless borders do not matter at all and the equilibrium model is stretched to the extreme, envisaging a frictionless, perfectly adjusting world economy, the classical solution does not hold.[14] An important stream of literature (McCallum 1995, Engel and Rogers 1996, Helliwell 1998, Laidler 2006) points in this di-rection so that, save for very tiny countries, the viability of monetary unions is enhanced by political union, which triggers several adjust-ment channels. Hence, between the polar cases of a one-money world and monetary unions involving only very tiny countries, optimality may ultimately be related to the fixing of national borders and the consequent emergence of endogenous optimizing criteria, as suggested by the equilibrium approach.

The everlasting "one-country one-money" configuration, there-fore, is not just the outcome of politics but of economics. That throughout three millennia of monetary history sovereign countries have issued and maintained their own currency is a stylized fact ex-plained by economic theory. As nature abhors a vacuum, economics abhors unexploited gains. If, on the one hand, very large countries like the United States did not break down into sundry currency areas or de-liberately decided such a division and, on the other hand, most coun-tries, excepting very small ones, seldom formed successful monetary unions (Bordo 2004), there must have been an equilibrium mechanism grounded in agents' optimizing behaviour, and supported by domestic policies, that ensured the viability of national monies. The recently de-veloped equilibrium approach to optimum currency areas, highlighting the impact of the country's border on individual maximizing behav-iour, points out the role of information and of market forces in en-hancing interregional adjustment, thus upholding this result.

3. Conclusions

The traditional view of optimum currency areas is embedded in the Keynesian paradigm, denying the self-adjusting nature of the economy

---

[14] This argument was clear to Lerner (see footnote 4 above) and provided the basis for his rejection of the gold standard.

and making the case for full employment policies. Introducing specific assumptions, like price and wage rigidity and interregional factor immobility, this view implicitly posits the inherent inefficacy of the economy's equilibrium properties, considering optimality as the outcome of exogenous features.

The paradigm shift brought about by the new classical macroeconomics has recently led to a novel approach, setting the optimality problem in a dynamic equilibrium context, in which agents rationally respond to the extension of the currency area. This is simply an application of the Lucas critique. The notion of optimality is therefore endogenous in that the very operation of a common currency heightens those features underlying the optimality criteria. The equilibrium approach thus turns the received view of optimum currency areas on its head. The areas do not stem from pre-existent optimizing features; rather, the features themselves are the product of an equilibrium process set off by the introduction of the common currency.

Information plays a key role in that a larger information set consequent on the fixing of national borders enhances adjustment and thus the optimality criteria. Monetary unions among sovereign nations may lead to non-optimal solutions since both the adjustment mechanism and the range of policy instruments may be wanting. In this connection, EMU is an interesting experiment, whose success will depend on a high degree of factor mobility and a tight link between trade integration and cross-country cycle correlation, notwithstanding the maintenance of national borders and the lack of a supranational fiscal policy. Otherwise, EMU may be the worst of two worlds, destroying the flexibility of monetary independence without generating the full benefits of a common currency issued by a sovereign state, i.e. a truly single market for goods and factors, a common institutional and legal framework and one fiscal authority, all elements heightening interregional adjustment.

All in all, the equilibrium approach to optimum currency areas can be viewed as an ideal type of equilibrium proposition like the Tiebout hypothesis and the Coase Theorem, whose validity is subject to certain restrictions, the absence respectively of barriers to mobility and of transaction costs. To make an analogy with the Coase Theorem, just as externalities can be solved, in the absence of transaction costs, through individual contracting independent of the initial allocation of legal entitlements, so adjustment within a currency area is attained through an equilibrium model based on rational behaviour independent of the initial geographic set-up (Cesarano 1997, p. 55). Of course, as with all 'pure' equilibrium propositions, applicability must be tested against the actual availability of information. In any case, on theoretical grounds, the equilibrium approach can boast the momentous achievement of having changed the theory of optimum currency areas from the search for exogenous criteria into an endogenous process.

REFERENCES

ALESINA, A. and R.J. BARRO (2002), "Currency unions", *Quarterly Journal of Economics*, vol. 117, no. 2, pp. 409-36.

BAYOUMI, T. and B. EICHENGREEN (1997), "Optimum currency areas and exchange rate volatility: theory and evidence compared", in B.J. Cohen ed., *International Trade and Finance: New Frontiers for Research*, Cambridge University Press, Cambridge, pp. 184-215.

BORDO, M.D. (2004), "The United States as a monetary union and the euro: a historical perspective", *Cato Journal*, vol. 24, nos. 1-2 , pp. 163-70.

BUITER, W.H. (2000), "Optimal currency areas", *Scottish Journal of Political Economy*, vol. 47, no. 3, pp. 213-50.

CESARANO, F. (1985), "On the viability of monetary unions", *Journal of International Economics*, vol. 19, nos. 3-4, pp. 367-74.

CESARANO, F. (1997), "Currency areas and equilibrium", *Open Economies Review*, vol. 8, no. 1, pp. 51-59.

CESARANO, F. (2006), "The origins of the theory of optimum currency areas", *History of Political Economy*, vol. 38, no. 4, forthcoming.

CORDEN, W.M. (1972), *Monetary Integration*, Essays in International Finance, no. 93, Princeton University, International Finance Section, Princeton.

DE GRAUWE, P. and F.P. MONGELLI (2005), "Endogeneities of optimum currency areas. What brings countries sharing a single currency closer together?", *Working Paper Series*, no. 468, European Central Bank.

DE GRAUWE, P. and W. VANHAVERBEKE (1993), "Is Europe an optimum currency area? Evidence from regional data", in P.R. Masson and M.P. Taylor eds, *Policy Issues in the Operation of Currency Unions*, Cambridge University Press, Cambridge, pp. 111-29.

ENGEL, C. and J.H. ROGERS (1996), "How wide is the border?", *American Economic Review*, vol. 86, no. 5, pp. 1112-25.

FATÁS, A. (1997), "EMU: countries or regions? Lessons from the EMS experience", *European Economic Review*, vol. 41, nos. 3-5, pp. 743-51.

FRANKEL, J.A. and A.K. ROSE (1998), "The endogeneity of the optimum currency area criteria", *Economic Journal*, vol. 108, no. 449, pp. 1009-25.

FRANKEL, J.A. and A.K. ROSE (2002), "An estimate of the effect of common currencies on trade and income", *Quarterly Journal of Economics*, vol. 117, no. 2, pp.
437-66.

FRIEDMAN, M. (1953), "The case for flexible exchange rates", in *Essays in Positive Economics*, The University of Chicago Press, Chicago, pp. 157-203.

FRIEDMAN, M. [1965] (1968), "The political economy of international monetary
arrangements", in *Dollars and Deficits: Inflation, Monetary Policy and the Balance
of Payments*, Prentice-Hall, Englewood Cliffs, pp. 266-79.

GIL-PAREJA, S. (2003), "Pricing to market behaviour in European car markets", *European Economic Review*, vol. 47, no. 6, pp. 945-62.

HAMADA, K. (1977), "On the political economy of monetary integration: a public economics approach", in R.Z. Aliber ed., *The Political Economy of Monetary Reform*,
Macmillan, London, pp. 13-31.

HARTLAND, P. (1949), "Interregional payments compared with international payments", *Quarterly Journal of Economics*, vol. 63, no. 3, pp. 392-407.

HAYEK, F.A. VON [1937] (1939), *Monetary Nationalism and International Stability*,
Longmans, Green, London.

HAYEK, F.A. VON (1945), "The use of knowledge in society", *American Economic Review*, vol. 35, no. 4, pp. 519-30.

HELLIWELL, J.F. (1998), *How Much Do National Borders Matter?*, Brookings Institution
Press, Washington.

ISHIYAMA, Y. (1975), "The theory of optimum currency areas: a survey", *IMF Staff Papers*, vol. 22, no. 2, pp. 344-83.

KENEN, P.B. (1969), "The theory of optimum currency areas: an eclectic view", in
R.A. Mundell and A.K. Swoboda eds, *Monetary Problems of the International
Economy*, The University of Chicago Press, Chicago, pp. 41-60.

KRUGMAN, P. (1991), *Geography and Trade*, The MIT Press, Cambridge, Mass.

KRUGMAN, P. (1993), *What Do We Need to Know About the International Monetary System?*, Essays in International Finance, no. 190, Princeton University, International Finance Section, Princeton.

LAIDLER, D. (2006), "Canada's monetary choices in North America and their dubious
parallels with Britain's in Europe", *Current Politics and Economics of Europe*, vol.
17, no. 1, pp. 71-98.

LERNER, A.R. (1944), *The Economics of Control: Principles of Welfare Economics*,
Macmillan, New York.

LERNER, A.R. (1947), "Discussion of 'International monetary policy and the search
for economic stability' by Ragnar Nurkse", *American Economic Review. Papers
and Proceedings*, vol. 37, no. 2, pp. 592-94.

MCCALLUM, J. (1995), "National borders matter: Canada-US regional trade patterns",
American Economic Review, vol. 85, no. 3, pp. 615-23.

MCKINNON, R.I. (1963), "Optimum currency areas", *American Economic Review*, vol.
53, no. 4, pp. 717-25.

MEADE, J.E. (1953), *Problems of Economic Union*, George Allen and Unwin, London.

MEADE, J.E. (1957), "The balance-of-payments problems of a European free-trade area", *Economic Journal*, vol. 67, no. 267, pp. 379-96.

MUNDELL, R.A. (1961), "A theory of optimum currency areas", *American Economic Review*, vol. 51, no. 4, pp. 657-65.

MUNDELL, R.A. (1997), "Updating the agenda for monetary union", in M.I. Blejer, J.A. Frenkel, L. Leiderman and A. Razin eds, in cooperation with D.M. Cheney, *Optimum Currency Areas: New Analytical and Policy Developments*, International Monetary Fund, Washington, pp. 29-48.

MUNDELL, R.A. (2000), "A reconsideration of the twentieth century", *American Economic Review*, vol. 90, no. 3, pp. 327-40.

NIEHANS, J. (1984), *International Monetary Economics*, The Johns Hopkins University Press, Baltimore.

SCITOVSKY, T. (1957), "The theory of the balance of payments and the problem of a common European currency", *Kyklos*, vol. 10, no. 1, pp. 18-44.

TAVLAS, G.S. (1993), "The 'new' theory of optimum currency areas", *The World Economy*, vol. 16, no. 6, pp. 663-85.

TINBERGEN, J. (1952), *On the Theory of Economic Policy*, North-Holland, Amsterdam.

TOWER, E. and T.D. WILLETT (1976), *The Theory of Optimum Currency Areas and Exchange-Rate Flexibility*, Special Papers in International Economics, no. 11, Princeton University, International Finance Section, Princeton.

[16]

Optimum currency areas: a policy view [*]

FILIPPO CESARANO

Robert Mundell's pathbreaking article on the theory of optimum currency areas could nowadays seem an abstract intellectual exercise with no immediate bearing on the policy issues of half a century ago. On rereading his paper, however, this impression soon evaporates. In the introduction, Mundell (1961, p. 657) denies that "the question is purely academic", drawing attention to new projects of economic integration, Canada's experiment with flexible exchange rates and a better understanding of the functions of money in relation to problems of economic policy. Economic theories are often revamped when the issues they deal with become topical. The theory of optimum currency areas is a case in point. Its recent revival in connection with the launching of Economic and Monetary Union is but the latest instance of renewed interest stimulated by the process of European economic integration: in the early post-war years with the establishment of the first European institutions and the Common Market; after the publication of the *Werner Report* in 1970 and, finally, upon the signing of the Maastricht Treaty. A vast literature then grew out of Mundell's seminal paper, introducing further optimum principles.

In the last decade, however, novel theoretical developments have given the subject a new twist. In the traditional approach, optimality depends on exogenous criteria – labour mobility, openness to trade, product diversification and several others – reflecting the once-dominant Keynesian paradigm. The recent equilibrium approach instead emphasizes the endogeneity of optimality criteria, bringing the analysis of the subject into line with the new classical macroeconomics.

□ Banca d'Italia, Ufficio Ricerche Storiche, Roma (Italy); e-mail: filippo.cesarano@bancaditalia.it.

[*] The views expressed in this paper are those of the author and do not necessarily reflect the position of the Banca d'Italia.

BNL Quarterly Review, vol. LIX, no. 239, December 2006, pp. 317-32.

These antithetical views therefore arise from different models, leading to opposite conceptions of currency area optimality. Yet this contraposition does not necessarily imply rejecting one of the alternative theories. As Mundell himself taught us long ago, economists must rely on a "reservoir of models" in order to select the one most fit to solve the problem in relation to the specific state of the world.[1] In general, the complexity of economics allows for several modelling strategies, bringing about a plurality of hypotheses, mostly non-excludable (Cesarano 2006a); even in a given historical setting, several theories can be advanced. In a sense, rather than to the 'true' model of the economy, we should resort to the best available model contingent on the state of the world. This especially applies to the policymaker who, with respect to the theorist, must consider many additional aspects in making decisions.[2]

This brief methodological digression helps to convey the message of this paper. Compared to theory, economic policy involves a lower level of abstraction. The policymaker analyses the problem he faces, weighing its manifold nature from a specific perspective. With regard to optimum currency areas, both the traditional approach and the equilibrium approach, though hinging on distinct hypotheses, can be useful to answer diverse questions – e.g., the expected net benefit of joining a monetary union, the implications of this decision at different time horizons and the role of economic policies in a currency area.

The purpose of this paper is to discuss the significance of these alternative views in relation to some specific policy issues. A library of models provides for distinct planes of analysis, helping the policymaker's decision-making process. Comparing the two approaches to the subject, this paper shows their antithetical properties (section 1) and their usefulness for solving different policy problems (section 2).

---

[1] "Thus it is helpful to have on hand depression models even though the world is in a state of inflation, or growth models even if the world is retrogressing" (Mundell 1971, p. 77).

[2] As Mundell noted: "The applied theorist seeks usable theory to adapt to practical problems. Adaptation implies transformation of the theoretical form to suit the problem and specification of the data upon which policy makers have to act. The first activity gives the theoretical form relevance, while the second is an inherent component of the communications transmission mechanism. To take a journey a driver must not only have a car that works, he also needs instructions on how it runs and a road map" (1971, p. 78).

1. Alternative approaches to optimum currency areas

Researchers groping for the solution to a controversial issue sometimes serendipitously hit on a new idea about another topic. This is the case of the theory of optimum currency areas. While writing his dissertation on international trade under James Meade, Mundell strove for a critique of flexible exchange rates, which eventually led him to develop the concept of currency area optimality.[3] The starting point of his classic paper is in fact the possible failure of exchange rate flexibility to maintain internal balance in a two-country world. Following a demand shift, either unemployment could be eliminated in the deficit regions through monetary expansion or inflation in the surplus regions through monetary restriction, but not both. The solution is to redraw the countries' borders, grouping the regions where labour is mobile. It is arrived at by constructing a case which, given downward price and wage rigidity and other restrictive assumptions, is impervious to domestic adjustment.

Mundell's seminal article stimulated the introduction of other optimality criteria, but this blurred the analysis rather than clarifying it, prompting Harry Johnson to remark that "the optimum currency area problem has proved to be something of a dead-end problem" (1969, p. 395). In the 1970s, the crisis of Keynesian economics did not substantially affect the received view and the subject remained in limbo. The focus shifted to the introduction of common currencies and their viability, a more tenuous notion than optimality (Cesarano 1985). Some new arguments buttressing the case for monetary union were also put forward (Mundell 1973; see McKinnon 2004), but there was no major change in the state of the art.

Subsequent contributions based on the time consistency literature found smaller costs of forsaking monetary policy autonomy and greater benefits from enhanced inflation credibility, thus reinforcing the case for monetary integration. However, more than three decades after Mundell's pioneering paper, the traditional approach still held

---

[3] See his own detailed reconstruction, a fascinating account of scientific discovery (Mundell 1997). After the war, flexible exchange rates, championed by Friedman and Meade, gained favour as the solution to the latent difficulty of reconciling fixed parities with the quest for full employment, a major weakness of the Bretton Woods monetary order.

sway.[4] The search for further optimality criteria actually boiled down to a case-by-case analysis. Since each of these criteria potentially is a sufficient condition for optimality, though none of them is a necessary condition, hunting for new optimality criteria in order to reach a definitive solution proved to be a mirage, producing a theoretical stalemate, a sort of doctrinal hysteresis. Although the new classical macroeconomics held sway, the theory of optimum currency areas remained grounded in a Keynesian-inspired disequilibrium analysis.

The contrast between classics and Keynesians essentially springs from a different assessment of the self-adjusting property of the economy.[5] The classical model, characterized by the absence of frictions and little room for stabilization policy, leads to a straightforward solution: the optimum currency area is the world. As Mundell (1961, p. 662) observed, the classics considered the stabilization argument for full employment quite irrelevant and the multiplication of currency areas as weakening the functions of money. Hume's specie-flow mechanism, underlying the classical solution, sees to the adjustment of imbalances and the international distribution of money. Obstacles such as the great distance dividing Europe from Asia may hamper adjustment[6] but, nonetheless, self-interest drives towards equilibrium inside a country and even in an extensive empire.

> "We need not have recourse to a physical attraction, in order to explain the necessity of this operation [of international money flows]. There is a moral attraction, arising from the interests and passions of men, which is full as potent and infallible.

---

[4] Useful surveys are Ishiyama (1975), Tower and Willett (1976), Kaway (1987) and Tavlas (1993). For a comprehensive review including recent developments, see Mongelli (2005).

[5] In a radio broadcast anticipating the message of the *General Theory*, Keynes (1934, p. 487) answered negatively to the rhetorical question "Poverty in plenty: is the economic system self-adjusting?", countering the classical viewpoint epitomized by Lionel Robbins. "Professor Robbins [...] stresses the effect of business mistakes under the influence of the uncertainty and the false expectations due to the faults of post-war monetary systems. These authorities do not, of course, believe that the system is automatically or immediately self-adjusting. But they do believe that it has an inherent tendency towards self-adjustment, if it is not interfered with and if the action of change and chance is not too rapid".

[6] "[A]s any body of water may be raised above the level of the surrounding element, if the former has no communication with the latter; so in money, if the communication be cut off, by any material or physical impediment, (for all laws alone are ineffectual) there may, in such a case, be a very great inequality of money" (Hume 1752, p. 64).

How is the balance kept in the provinces of every kingdom among themselves, but by the force of this principle, which makes it impossible for money to lose its level, and either to rise or sink beyond the proportion of the labour and commodities which are in each province? [...] What happens in small portions of mankind, must take place in greater. The provinces of the Roman empire, no doubt, kept their balance with each other, and with Italy, independent of the legislature; as much as the several counties of Great Britain, or the several parishes of each county. And any man who travels over Europe at this day, may see, by the prices of commodities, that money, in spite of the absurd jealousy of princes and states, has brought itself nearly to a level; and that the difference between one kingdom and another is not greater in this respect, than it is often between different provinces of the same kingdom" (Hume 1752, pp. 65-66).[7]

The success of Keynesian economics cast serious doubt on the equilibrium hypothesis and overshadowed the classical view of international adjustment. The malfunctioning gold standard, widely thought to have intensified and propagated the Great Depression, was then regarded as a rigid monetary rule bringing about disequilibrium and unemployment. Mundell (1961, p. 660), likening interregional adjustment to the gold standard, stressed the emergence of domestic imbalances unyielding to adjustment forces. The re-establishment of equilibrium thus required a policy measure, i.e. redesigning currency areas. This result and the classical recipe of a world money are polar solutions, reflecting the extreme assumptions of virtually nil and very high adjustment capacity.

The present discussion is not a mere exercise in doctrinal history but seeks to show that conflicting conceptions of currency area optimality basically depend on the acceptance or not of the equilibrium hypothesis and the related properties of the adjustment mechanism. The modern equilibrium approach is in line with the classical view. Equilibrium forces, grounded in rational behaviour, foster those features defining the optimality criteria that, far from being exogenous characteristics, emerge from the operation of a currency area and are therefore en-

---

[7] In the second paragraph of this quotation Hume, contrary to the standard interpretation of his theory, abides by the law of one price. For a detailed analysis, see Cesarano (1998).

dogenous.[8] However, as distance was deemed by Hume an impediment to adjustment, other kinds of obstructions, chiefly the national border, should likewise be considered. The effectiveness of the self-adjusting properties of the economy is conditional on the absence of obstructions. The equilibrium approach, when appropriately interpreted, is therefore distinct from either a frictionless or a quite rigid world underlying the classical and the Keynesian paradigm respectively.

The countries' border should be thought of not as a mere physical obstacle, but as a basic characteristic of the economy having three main implications. First, inside the country the agents' information set is relatively larger, which heightens the effectiveness of the adjustment mechanism (Cesarano 1997 and 2006c). Considering labour mobility, for instance, people assess the decision about domestic migration more swiftly and with less uncertainty, given the greater availability of information. This principle extends to the mobility of goods and other factors of production between regions and industries. Hence, equilibrium forces do not simply alleviate temporary imbalances, but efficaciously tackle the problem of resource allocation on which long-run adjustment turns. As Friedman noted in his classic paper on flexible exchange rates (1953, p. 182):

> "The ultimate adjustment to a change in external circumstances will consist of a change in the allocation of productive resources and in the composition of the goods available for consumption and investment".

Second, parallel to these theoretical aspects, a common legal and institutional framework also enhances optimal resource allocation. Following Douglass North, a competitive market economy does not function *in vacuo* but needs a set of institutions, which are of course uniform inside national borders. This factor too entails an increase in information, albeit indirectly, thus influencing economic decisions. For instance, direct investment in a foreign country becomes domestic investment after that country joins a politically integrated currency area, with obvious implications for investors' choices. This is but one example among many of how a common institutional setting enhances the decision-making process underlying resource allocation.

---

[8] For a recent analysis of the notion of endogeneity, see de Grauwe and Mongelli (2005).

Third, since we do not live in a world of complete information, various kinds of friction and rigidities hamper instantaneous adjustment, heightening the role of economic policy. Fiscal and regional development policies, in particular, have been invoked to smooth transition from one equilibrium to another, tackling both temporary and structural imbalances.

The significance of the border is therefore manifold, bearing on theoretical, institutional and policy facets of currency areas. The modern approach points out the effectiveness of adjustment within a country, putting currency area optimality back in the sphere of equilibrium theory. The traditional approach, instead, analysed a number of optimality criteria, each related to a specific adjustment channel, but none of them providing for a general hypothesis. The multiplicity of different yet equally plausible criteria not only poses the problem of choosing between them, but can give rise to paradoxical results. As Frankel noted (1999, p. 26), if trade integration induced countries to specialize more in production, incomes would be less correlated. The pursuit of diversification would then spur the design of ever larger currency areas, eventually leading to a world money. If, on the contrary, individual regions were not sufficiently diversified, they would be prompted to split into smaller units which, however, would be even less diversified, leading to ever smaller units. Yet this paradox contrasts with both formal empirical findings, corroborating the hypothesis that income correlation positively depends on trade integration (Frankel and Rose 1998), and casual empiricism which rules out corner solutions. In fact, as a world currency is not a reality in a fiat money context, a minute fragmentation of national currencies is not observed either: tiny countries – Liechtenstein, Monaco and the like – always form a monetary union with a larger neighbour because the costs of setting up their own currency are not matched by the benefits of an independent monetary policy or any other advantages.

The difficulty of modelling an interior solution actually stems from the very notion of optimum currency area as theorized by the traditional approach, in that the static analysis of potentially conflicting optimality criteria resolves into a will-o'-the-wisp. The modern approach instead builds on an equilibrium model, stressing the endogeneity of optimality criteria. The impact of the countries' border on agents' behaviour, institutions and economic policies bears heavily on the notion of optimum currency areas. This does not mean that the observed political geography defines the optimum, but rather that, once borders are set, it is hard to move away from equilibrium. There is a clear analogy with the reluctance to abandon the circulating money, even in periods of hyperinflation (Friedman and Schwartz 1986, p. 44). In both cases, the costs of forsaking the existing monetary mechanism are immediately perceived and are not offset by the uncertain, prospective benefits. Thus, the prevalence of the 'one country, one money' configuration is no mere political accident, but is accounted for by economic theory. In fact, Jeffrey Frankel's acute remark (1999, p. 16),

> "It is striking that, although in theory, the boundaries of political units and optimal currency areas need not coincide, in practice, they almost always do",

is actually explained by the equilibrium approach.

2. A policy view

Frankel's graphic observation recalls the neglected post-war literature on monetary unions which, though failing to develop a fully-fledged analysis of optimality, anticipated Mundell's hypothesis and tackled several policy issues that are still debated today. The analysis of monetary unions is the dual of the theory of optimum currency areas: while in the latter the objective is to find out the criteria for optimally re-drawing the borders of currency areas, in the former the extension of the monetary area is given and the question is whether it squares with the optimality criteria. Beginning in the early 1950s, the efforts towards European economic integration stimulated the theoretical debate on monetary unification. Meade and Scitovsky probed the subject in depth. Contrasting the smoothness of interregional adjustment with the cumbersome international adjustment process, they pointed out several factors – goods and factor mobility, fiscal and monetary policies, regional development measures, an integrated capital market and a common banking system (Meade 1953, pp. 41-43; 1957, pp. 385-87; Scitovsky 1957, pp. 19-21 and 24-31; 1958, pp. 97-99) – that explained the negligible impact of money flows on output and employment within a country compared with the costly adjustment between countries under the gold standard.[9]

Interestingly, though they shared the same theoretical apparatus, Meade and Scitovsky suggested opposite solutions for implementing European monetary unification. Both argued that making all the above-mentioned adjustment factors operative in a monetary union was tantamount to establishing a supranational government. But, while Meade considered such a change unfeasible in the short run and suggested a gradual strategy, Scitovsky viewed the early circulation of a common currency as a means to accelerate economic integration.[10] In his classic paper, Mundell (1961, section IV) discussed the issue, concluding that the dispute could be reduced to an empirical question, i.e. whether or not there was a high degree of factor mobility in Western Europe.

In contrast with Mundell, the equilibrium approach considers the optimality criteria as endogenous, not as inborn features of the economy. Thus, the modern approach is, at a certain remove, related to the early post-war literature, which accounts for the effectiveness of domestic adjustment by the integration of goods and factor markets and the presence of an economic policy authority. Both these features originate in the existence of borders. The point may seem obvious, but as shown in section 1, it carries momentous implications for the theory of optimum currency areas.

The development of diverse approaches does not necessarily compel us to accept only one of them and reject the others. Depending on the nature of the problem and the institutional setting, the adjustment properties of the economy can fit the theoretical benchmark of the equilibrium hypothesis more or less closely. Different assumptions reflecting those properties therefore suggest different modelling strategies. To take a striking example, it is a commonplace that within a country the effects of money flows are inescapable but, while for Mundell (1961, p. 660) this heightens domestic imbalances, for other economists – Lerner (1944, pp. 375-77), Friedman (1953, p. 193, n. 16),

---

[9] The origins of the literature on optimum currency areas can be traced back to Lerner (1944 and 1947). For a close examination, see Cesarano (2006b).

[10] In the 1970s, the same contraposition reappeared under the improperly defined division between 'economists' and 'monetarists'. The recent introduction of the euro reflects the latter's view and, ultimately, the strategy of using the fulcrum of the common currency for political unification in Europe.

Meade (1957) and Scitovsky (1958) – it makes interregional adjustment highly effective. That these clashing results are derived from the same hypothesis, the specie-flow mechanism, seems puzzling. But weighing the alternative interpretations of a crucial assumption, i.e. the presence of obstructions to adjustment, solves the puzzle: Mundell considers regions located in different countries, thus severed by the border, a condition that hampers adjustment and requires redrawing currency areas to achieve internal balance, while Lerner *et al.* focus on regions within a country, arguing that the effectiveness of equilibrium forces inside the border eases adjustment and does away with domestic imbalances.

The usefulness of different theoretical frameworks emerges especially in connection with policy issues raised by the introduction and the viability of a common currency. In this respect, two main distinctions can be drawn between, on the one hand, the transition to monetary union and its full operation and, on the other, a currency area composed of sovereign countries and a common money circulating in a politically unified territory – or, in short, between monetary union and political union.

The transition stage involves a once-and-for-all adjustment from one equilibrium to another. Extending the functions of money to a larger area generates benefits that are non-rival in consumption, a characteristic of public goods stemming from the nature of money (Hamada 1977, pp. 16-17). Yet each country loses the monetary policy instrument and experiences a temporary deceleration or acceleration of monetary aggregates. In general, while benefits are spread over all participants, costs fall unevenly on each of them.

The outcome of transition depends on the initial conditions: the economies involved may be more or less divergent. The traditional approach to optimum currency areas, by focusing on the optimality criteria *ex ante*, is suitable to appraise such conditions. The evaluation of goods and factor mobility, variability of inflation rates and other criteria helps to assess the starting point of the integration process as well as the costs of transition. This proposition has been corroborated by de Grauwe's (1992) empirical findings contrasting German monetary unification with the Polish experience. While East Germany suffered a sharp fall in output, Poland, which maintained its own currency, smoothed the process of economic liberalization by using the exchange rate. This is precisely the recipe prescribed by Meade (1957) in order to arrive at monetary unification gradually, without suffering unemployment and income losses. Limited to the short-run transition stage, therefore, Mundell's suggestion to estimate the degree of labour mobility is appropriate. *Ex ante*, the closer are the monetary union's economies to the optimality criteria, the smaller will be the adjustment costs of the introduction of the common currency.

This general principle applies to various aspects of the transition stage, each linked to an optimality criterion. Hence, strong integration of goods and factor markets enhances price equalization in the currency area and flexibility in resource allocation, accelerating the process of economic convergence. Market integration also affects trade between member countries, which, given the positive relationship between trade integration and cyclical correlation, strongly affects the smoothness of the transition to monetary union. Moreover, lack of segmentation in financial markets heightens risk-sharing. A final point concerns economic policy, and particularly fiscal policy, which can play a key role, witness the recent experience in Germany, where the fall in income in the East was offset by large budgetary transfers (de Grauwe 1992, p. 449).[11]

The last aspect brings us to the second distinction between monetary union and political union, which reflects the actual origins of common currencies. With the exception of tiny countries, currency areas are brought into being either by the deliberate choice of a group of nations or by political unification, Europe's EMU and German monetary unification being the main recent examples respectively. On the basis of historical evidence, Bordo (2004) contends that only the latter survive while the former inevitably collapse. To account for this stylized fact, it should be emphasized that the difference between monetary union and political union is a difference in kind, not in degree. Just as a fixed exchange rate regime is quite distinct from a monetary union, the latter is quite distinct from fully-fledged political unification. In these cases, the diverse features characterizing the monetary order increasingly approximate an equilibrium model.

---

[11] In this connection, Scitovsky's call for the immediate establishment of monetary union, in opposition to Meade's gradual strategy, rests on the assumption that a common currency facilitates the integration of the real and financial sectors. Nevertheless, in line with the then-dominant Keynesian paradigm, Scitovsky (1957, pp. 35-36) calls for a supranational authority to implement fiscal policy aimed at full employment.

The viability of monetary union presumes a frictionless world, in which information is so largely available that the arrangement mimics the properties of an equilibrium model, swiftly solving any eventual disequilibria. Viewed in a historical perspective, these assumptions are even stricter than those underlying the gold standard, whose rules allowed the temporary suspension of convertibility in case of large imbalances. At the same time, the obligation to return to the gold parity enhanced credibility, which decisively contributed to the long life of the gold standard, spanning almost half a century. In a monetary union, even the gold standard's limited leeway is disposed of. Thus, monetary union is a stiff and yet fragile construction because it exacerbates the adjustment problem inside the currency area and lacks an economic policy authority. Absent political unification, if market rigidities and national regulations prevail, the real and financial sectors will not respond to the need for integration, thus hindering convergence to the optimality criteria.[12]

The long-run effects of monetary unification are best analysed by the modern equilibrium approach, emphasizing the endogeneity of optimality criteria. However, the maintenance of national borders hampers the adjustment mechanism in various ways, substantially affecting agents' behaviour, the legal and institutional framework and the scope of economic policies, thus undermining currency area optimality. The prudent conclusion "of moderate optimism" reached by de Grauwe and Mongelli (2005, p. 29) about the endogeneity of four optimality criteria in the euro area – integration of prices and trade, financial integration, symmetry of shocks and product and labour market flexibility – may be ascribed to the maintenance of national borders. Certainly, the optimum currency area criteria have to be appraised *ex post*, but the integration process requires a considerable span of time, measured

---

[12] With regard to the pernicious effects of national regulations in Europe, a recent story in *The Economist* (2006) is quite telling. In order to slash the price of cross-border mobile calls, which yield margins above 90%, a EU commissioner proposed a "home pricing" scheme, which would abolish charges for incoming calls and compensate for the loss of roaming fees by raising prices everywhere. Yet, this scheme would induce consumers to sign contracts abroad at lower prices and bring them back home. Also, it would have the perverse effect of reducing prices for international business travellers while increasing them for most consumers. This story graphically shows how considerable the border effects can be. Moreover, it is ironic that the suggested solution to the negative impact of these effects on optimal resource allocation is the call for other regulations, which further distort resource allocation.

in decades, not years.[13] Hence, the impact of monetary union on the economies of the member countries may be substantial even in the presence of political unification, witness the recent German experience, buttressing the relevance of Mundell's analysis.

As argued in section 1, the antithesis between the traditional approach and the modern approach ultimately depends on whether the equilibrium hypothesis is rejected or not. These contrasting theoretical views are always considered as mutually exclusive. Yet, from an economic policy standpoint, both theories can be useful to tackle different problems in different states of the world. This is not unusual in economics, a discipline characterized by the non-excludability of most hypotheses (Cesarano 2006a). Theories that had been disparaged or discarded have later been revived, like Keynes's liquidity trap to account for monetary developments in Japan during the past decade.

Upon establishing a currency area, the initial response and the pace of integration depend on the actual characteristics of the participating economies relative to the optimality criteria. In this respect, the traditional approach, based on the static, disequilibrium model of Keynesian economics, is most suitable. On the other hand, the analysis of the long-run viability of a common currency, especially in the case of political unification, should be grounded in the dynamic, equilibrium model of the modern approach akin to classical economics. In this case, the lack of obstructions enhances long-run equilibrium, bringing about the emergence of the optimality criteria. By removing national borders, political unification naturally heightens the effectiveness of equilibrium forces through the abundant availability of information, the common institutional framework and the substantial powers of the economic policy authority.

3. Conclusions

Robert Mundell's seminal contribution stimulated the introduction of several optimality criteria which, though shedding light on the subject, eventually made the analysis more elusive. To paraphrase the title of

---

[13] With regard to the trade-creating effects of monetary union, Rose (2004) suggests a period of about 15-20 years.

Pirandello's famous play, optimum currency areas became a "character in search of an author". In the past decade, an alternative view emphasized the effectiveness of adjustment within a currency area, considering the optimality criteria as endogenous. In the economist's box of tools, however, there is place for both theories to analyse different situations and policy issues. Going to extremes, if agents' information set is very small and adjustment capacity quite limited, the traditional approach should be resorted to; *mutatis mutandis*, the equilibrium approach should be followed.

In general, all equilibrium propositions hinge on simplifying assumptions. For instance, the Modigliani-Miller theorem assumes no taxes and transaction costs and a large information set. The latter is especially essential to the validity of equilibrium models: the more we move away from it, the less relevant equilibrium propositions become. Equilibrium hypotheses therefore provide a theoretical benchmark against which the actual features of the economy must be evaluated, in order to arrive at the most appropriate model.

The subject of optimum currency areas is a case in point. The impact of establishing a common currency may be substantial, depending on the initial conditions of the participating economies. The transition to and the stability of the new equilibrium essentially depend on the area's capacity for adjustment, whose speed and effectiveness are influenced by several factors and hindered by various kinds of obstructions. The positive appraisal of EMU, boosted by the spread of the new classical macroeconomics, should therefore be tempered in view of the implications of maintaining national borders, an important obstacle to the emergence of the optimality criteria. A certain degree of eclecticism is thus needed to select the model yielding correct predictions, between the poles of Mundell's pathbreaking paper and the modern equilibrium approach.

REFERENCES

BORDO, M.D. (2004), "The United States as a monetary union and the euro: a historical perspective", *Cato Journal*, vol. 24, nos. 1-2, pp. 163-70.

CESARANO, F. (1985), "On the viability of monetary unions", *Journal of International Economics*, vol. 19, nos. 3-4, pp. 367-74.

CESARANO, F. (1997), "Currency areas and equilibrium", *Open Economies Review*, vol. 8, no. 1, pp. 51-59.

CESARANO, F. (1998), "Hume's specie-flow mechanism and classical monetary theory: an alternative interpretation", *Journal of International Economics*, vol. 45, no. 1, pp. 173-86.

CESARANO, F. (2006a), "Economic history and economic theory", *Journal of Economic Methodology*, vol. 13, no. 4, pp. 447-67.

CESARANO, F. (2006b), "The origins of the theory of optimum currency areas", *History of Political Economy*, vol. 38, no. 4, pp. 711-31.

CESARANO, F. (2006c), "The equilibrium approach to optimum currency areas", *Banca Nazionale del Lavoro Quarterly Review*, vol. 59, no. 237, pp. 193-209.

DE GRAUWE, P. (1992), "German monetary unification", *European Economic Review*, vol. 36, nos. 2-3, pp. 445-53.

DE GRAUWE, P. and F.P. MONGELLI (2005), "Endogeneities of optimum currency areas. What brings countries sharing a single currency closer together?", *Working Paper Series*, no. 468, European Central Bank.

THE ECONOMIST (2006), "Roaming holiday", vol. 379, April 15th, p. 62.

FRANKEL, J.A. (1999), *No Single Currency Regime Is Right for All Countries or at All Times*, Essays in International Finance, no. 215, Princeton University, International Finance Section, Princeton.

FRANKEL, J.A. and A.K. ROSE (1998), "The endogeneity of the optimum currency area criteria", *Economic Journal*, vol. 108, no. 449, pp. 1009-25.

FRIEDMAN, M. (1953), "The case for flexible exchange rates", in *Essays in Positive Economics*, The University of Chicago Press, Chicago, pp. 157-203.

FRIEDMAN, M. and A.J. SCHWARTZ (1986), "Has government any role in money?", *Journal of Monetary Economics*, vol. 17, no. 1, pp. 37-62.

HAMADA, K. (1977), "On the political economy of monetary integration: a public economics approach", in R.Z. Aliber ed., *The Political Economy of Monetary Reform*, Macmillan, London, pp. 13-31.

HUME, D. (1752), "Of the balance of trade", reprinted in D. Hume, *Writings on Economics*, ed. by E. Rotwein, The University of Wisconsin Press, Madison, 1970, pp. 60-77.

ISHIYAMA, Y. (1975), "The theory of optimum currency areas: a survey", *IMF Staff Papers*, vol. 22, no. 2, pp. 344-83.

JOHNSON, H.G. (1969), "The 'problems' approach to international monetary reform", in R.A. Mundell and A.K. Swoboda eds, *Monetary Problems of the International Economy*, The University of Chicago Press, Chicago, pp. 393-99.

KAWAY, M. (1987), "Optimum currency areas", in J. Eatwell, M. Milgate and P. Newman eds, *The New Palgrave: A Dictionary of Economics*, vol. 3, Macmillan, London, pp. 740-43.

KEYNES, J.M. [1934] (1973), "Poverty in plenty: is the economic system self-adjusting?", reprinted in *The Collected Writings of John Maynard Keynes*, vol. 13, ed. by D. Moggridge, Macmillan, London, pp. 485-92.

LERNER, A.P. (1944), *The Economics of Control: Principles of Welfare Economics*, Macmillan, New York.

LERNER, A.P. (1947), "Discussion of 'International Monetary Policy and the Search for Economic Stability' by Ragnar Nurkse", *American Economic Review: Papers and Proceedings*, vol. 37, no. 2, pp. 592-94.

McKINNON, R.I. (2004), "Optimum currency areas and key currencies: Mundell I versus Mundell II", *Journal of Common Market Studies*, vol. 42, no. 4, pp. 689-715.

MEADE, J.E. (1953), *Problems of Economic Union*, George Allen and Unwin, London.

MEADE, J.E. (1957), "The balance-of-payments problems of a European free-trade area", *Economic Journal*, vol. 67, no. 267, pp. 379-96.

MONGELLI, F.P. (2005), "What is European economic and monetary union telling us about the properties of optimum currency areas?", *Journal of Common Market Studies*, vol. 43, no. 3, pp. 607-35.

MUNDELL, R.A. (1961), "A theory of optimum currency areas", *American Economic Review*, vol. 51, no. 4, pp. 657-65.

MUNDELL, R.A. (1971), *Monetary Theory: Inflation, Interest, and Growth in the World Economy*, Goodyear, Pacific Palisades.

MUNDELL, R.A. (1973), "Uncommon arguments for common currencies", in H.G. Johnson and A.K. Swoboda eds, *The Economics of Common Currencies*, Harvard University Press, Cambridge, Mass., pp. 114-32.

MUNDELL, R.A. (1997), "Updating the agenda for monetary union", in M.I. Blejer, J.A. Frenkel, L. Leiderman and A. Razin eds, in cooperation with D.M. Cheney, *Optimum Currency Areas: New Analytical and Policy Developments*, International Monetary Fund, Washington, pp. 29-48.

ROSE, A.K. (2004), "A meta-analysis of the effect of common currencies on international trade", *Working Paper*, no. 10373, National Bureau of Economic Research.

SCITOVSKY, T. (1957), "The theory of the balance of payments and the problem of a common European currency", *Kyklos*, vol. 10, no. 1, pp. 18-44.

SCITOVSKY, T. (1958), *Economic Theory and Western European Integration*, George Allen and Unwin, London.

TAVLAS, G.S. (1993), "The 'new' theory of optimum currency areas", *The World Economy*, vol. 16, no. 6, pp. 663-85.

TOWER, E. and T.D. WILLETT (1976), *The Theory of Optimum Currency Areas and Exchange Rate Flexibility*, Special Papers in International Economics, no. 11, Princeton University, International Finance Section, Princeton.

PART V

ECONOMICS AS A SOCIAL SCIENCE

Journal of Economic Methodology 13:4, 447–467 December 2006

Economic history and economic theory

Filippo Cesarano

Abstract Since the mid-1950s the spread of formal models and econometric method has greatly improved the study of the past, giving rise to the 'new' economic history; at the same time, the influence of economic history on economists and economics has markedly declined. This paper argues that the contribution of history to the advancement of economics is still paramount, as is evident from the evolution of monetary theory and institutions.

JEL classification: NO1, A12

Keywords: economic history, economic theory

1 INTRODUCTION

In the past fifty years the advanced tools of economic theory have been deployed in the study of the past, giving rise to the new economic history. Increasing the rigor and consistency of historical inquiry, the new approach has brought substantial progress and a pervasive impact that has reshaped the state of the art. Parallel to these developments, however, economists have steadily lost interest in the subject (McCloskey 1976: 435–7), considering economic history as an applied field confined to specialists, like urban or labor economics, and far removed from the heights of theory.

However, while economic history was improving in terms of rigorous analysis, construction of statistical data and sophisticated econometric techniques, the profession generally disregarded these achievements.[1] As a result, the separation between economists and economic historians was accentuated. This paper inquires into this widening gulf, focusing not on the usefulness of economic theory for historical research (pioneered by Heckscher (1929 [1953]) and now a given in the field) but on the more elusive, less thoroughly studied inverse relationship. In this regard, Robert Gordon remarked: 'The feature of the "new economic history" is its use of modern theoretical and statistical tools. But so far as economic theory is concerned, we are still on a one-way street. The movement is from theory to

Journal of Economic Methodology ISSN 1350-178X print/ISSN 1469-9427 online

© 2006 Taylor & Francis http://www.tandf.co.uk/journals

DOI: 10.1080/13501780601049038

history; there is little if any movement the other way' (1965: 118). There has been little change since and, to retain Gordon's metaphor, the traffic from history to theory has practically disappeared.

Although most scholars keep away from methodological issues,[2] the contemporary fissure between economic history and economic theory demands examination, in that it contrasts with the lively intercourse that prevailed up to World War II. Probing the factors underlying this break is no mere intellectual curiosity: it illuminates the influence of economic history on theory, opening new avenues of economic analysis.

2 IN SEARCH OF A ROLE FOR ECONOMIC HISTORY

The foundations of nineteenth-century classical economics were in apriorism: theories are abstract, deductive constructions whose validity is judged by their coherence with basic postulates not with empirical evidence. Observed reality may well be at odds with economic principles, but this only indicates a violation of the *ceteris paribus* clause, not a falsification of the theory, a concept foreign to the classics.[3] Reacting against this prevailing view, the historical school aimed to challenge and eventually replace classical economics. Its failure was a fatal blow to the role of history in economic analysis (Fogel 1965: 94). Far from being totally disregarded, however, economic history retained a prominent place as part of the long tradition going back to the very beginnings of economics. An outstanding example is Hume, who wrote a monumental *History of England* and whose economic essays (1752 [1970]) are shot through with historical digressions, used both for formulating hypotheses and for testing them.[4]

This two-way relationship has often been noted.[5] Until the mid-twentieth century the influence of economic history on economic theory remained substantial, even after Ricardo's turn towards abstract analytical constructions. As McCloskey remarked: 'Smith, Marx, Mill, Marshall, Keynes, Heckscher, Schumpeter, and Viner, to name a few, were nourished by historical study and nourished it in turn. Gazing down from Valhalla it would seem to them bizarre that their heirs would study economics with the history left out' (1976: 434). McCloskey's list of great economists ends abruptly in the 1950s, just as the new economic history was emerging. This is no coincidence. As shown in the following pages, the very factors that fostered the new approach caused the decline in the economists' interest for history.

Between the Wars, economics underwent a major change in 'language' with the spread of formal models and econometrics, and this accelerated sharply in the decades that followed. Of course, mathematical economics had important precursors, from Cournot to Slutsky, Ramsey and others, whose contributions produced a quantum jump in knowledge, but the mainstream eschewed formal analysis. This attitude is conspicuous in Keynes, himself a trained mathematician but openly opposed to mathematical modeling because it would necessarily restrict the focus to just a few variables, failing to capture the interaction among the many relevant factors and ultimately weakening the analysis.

It is a great fault of symbolic pseudo-mathematical methods of formalising a system of economic analysis ... that they expressly assume strict independence between the factors involved and lose all their cogency and authority if this hypothesis is disallowed; whereas, in ordinary discourse, where we are not blindly manipulating but know all the time what we are doing and what the words mean, we can keep 'at the back of our heads' the necessary reserves and qualifications and the adjustments which we shall have to make later on, in a way in which we cannot keep complicated partial differentials 'at the back' of several pages of algebra which assume that they all vanish. Too large a proportion of recent 'mathematical' economics are mere concoctions, as imprecise as the initial assumptions they rest on, which allow the author to lose sight of the complexities and interdependencies of the real world in a maze of pretentious and unhelpful symbols. (1936 [1964]: 297–8)

That even an innovator like Keynes took this position is indicative of the reluctance to embrace a mathematical approach. The centuries-long predominance of this view made room for the influence of history on economics. After World War II, the revolution in method took hold and, above all, extended to economic history.[6] In their pioneering article, Meyer and Conrad urged economic historians to follow economists and formulate hypotheses with general validity rather than analyze specific episodes.[7] With the benefit of hindsight, however, we can see that Keynes was right; the gain in rigor, precision and consistency came at the cost of narrowing the scope of analysis. A side-effect of the change in techniques was therefore to shrink the place of history in economic theory.

The achievements of the new economic history did not greatly appeal to economists, because they could find scarcely any usefulness in historical analyses that tackled specific problems using their own techniques. They were interested in economic history not as the output of an applied field, but as an input for widening their research perspectives and formulating original hypotheses, which the new historical economics could not deliver.[8] In a sense, the deployment of theoretical models and econometrics, while reviving economic history, actually swallowed up its role in economic theorizing.

The heated debate promoted by these developments touched on the usefulness of economic history for economic theory, but the discussion eventually petered out as the divide between economists and historians widened.[9] The plurality of arguments, and their weakness, shows how hard it was to make a convincing case. In the first place, studying history for its own sake, as a pleasant cultural experience satisfying one's intellectual curiosity, is hardly sufficient justification, since many other activities, cultural and not, could have similar effects. Equally irrelevant, in the context of Friedman's 'positive economics', is the old-fashioned argument that history helps one to make 'realistic' assumptions. Finally, the commonplace that economic history could serve as additional empirical evidence to test theories just extends the quest for corroborating hypotheses to past events and basically concerns the influence of theory on historical inquiry, which is not at issue nowadays. Arrow refers to this interpretation as a '"naïve" view on the role of history' (1986: 17), stimulating the search for other arguments to support the case for economic history.

The answer, then, must be sought elsewhere. The examination of empirical regularities, and especially of anomalies or deviations from stylized facts, is essential to pose puzzles, hint at new hypotheses, build alternative models. Widening the scope of observed reality enhances theoretical work. As Paul Samuelson has put it:

> [Economic history] is much more than an antiquarian's descriptive narrative of what happened in the past relevant to pig iron, sealing wax, inflation and financial panic. To me economic history is any documentation of *empirical experience* – across space and time. Put this way, only a nineteenth century *deductive* economist or a naïve *a prioristic* philosopher could fail to understand that the fruitfulness of any deductive syllogism cannot originate inside itself. Somewhere in the axioms of a relevant paradigm ('model') there must have already been put in relevant (and testable) factual assertions. Garbage in: Garbage out. Tycho Brahe's good astronomical measurements in: Keplerian gold out. (2001: 272)

Economic history is thought to contribute to economic theory in several ways. Noting that history is a unique process that precludes repetition, Supple (1965: 100) describes its usefulness as suggesting the proper analytical approach rather than a set of results. Solow (1986: 22–4), denying the possibility of explaining all economic phenomena with a single theoretical framework, stresses the role played by economic history in enlarging the theorist's range of observation. And Kindleberger (1986: 88) points out that broader knowledge of economic history, not mathematics, provides the intuitions instrumental to original research.

In general, these suggestions are intertwined and hinge essentially on a single argument, namely the historical conditioning of economic analysis, which extends to a spatial dimension. Differences in institutions, culture and legal framework across time and space create a variety of scenarios, revealing hidden aspects that help to produce well-founded solutions. As Nicholas Crafts noted, 'the importance of the past to the economist lies in the information that it was in some respects different from today' (1987: 37). And for McCloskey (1976: 448), in path-breaking contributions the historical conditioning of economic theory is palpable.

History is therefore an efficacious antidote to a narrow approach to inherently complex phenomena; it enriches theory while baring its limitations. In this connection, historians and economists tend to have opposite shortcomings. The former may fail to use rigorous theory because they consider as many aspects as possible, while the latter may lack the wider scope offered by history (Cipolla 1991: 30). Of course, this latter analytical deficiency depends not on the reduced number of variables of economic models, a requisite for any theoretical construction, but on limited and superficial empirical experience. As Schumpeter emphasized, a wanting sense of history precludes a full grasp of economic reality:

> the subject matter of economics is essentially a unique process in historic time. Nobody can hope to understand the economic phenomena of any, including the present, epoch who has not an adequate command of historical *facts* and an adequate amount of historical *sense* or of what may be described as *historical experience*. (1954: 12–13)[10]

In an earlier article, Schumpeter (1947) put the case for economic history to the test, focusing on the role of entrepreneurial activity in economic change. He distinguishes the adaptive response of the economy to an exogenous shock, which can be explained by standard theory, from the creative response, which cannot be predicted because its effects work through other mechanisms that must be investigated in each instance. Anticipating the concept of path dependence, Schumpeter argues that the creative response conditions the course of future developments and can be understood only ex post. Hence, 'creative response is an essential element in the historical process' (1947: 150), not amenable to standard comparative statics.

Besides Paul David's work on path dependence, Schumpeter's insight recalls Douglass North's analysis of the role of transaction costs. These modern contributions undoubtedly appealed to economists, not only as end-products of historical research but also as raw materials of historical experience – statistical, narrative, anecdotal – in which the interest of the theorist at work really lies. Theory and history are complementary; pursuing abstraction and complexity respectively, they have distinct yet mutually integrating objectives: to formulate a precise hypothesis and to draw the broad picture.[11] This diversity of aims is reflected in the analytical armory, i.e. the economist's rigorous formal modeling and the historian's more eclectic approach. Indeed, highly sophisticated techniques in economic history may be unsuitable to capture multifaceted phenomena and eventually prove sterile. This is not to be interpreted as a call for unsystematic story-telling or for going back to sloppy historical investigations unfamiliar with the principles of economics. On the contrary, theory must illuminate historical research as it does any other social science. The point is not 'old' vs. new economic history but rather to recognize that from the economist's angle the usefulness of sundry approaches to history for building novel theories is quite variable. As Samuelson observed: 'Certainly ... cliometrics does fit into one corner of my nominated definition of economic history. But the cliometric slant is by no means a necessary element in valid economic history' (2001: 272).

History can certainly prove interesting to economists when it tackles significant issues from a wide-ranging perspective, not minor topics amenable to applied economics. In recent decades, the increasing specialization of historical studies was paralleled by the steady decrease in economists' demand for economic history. To attract the theorist's attention, the historian should rather focus on sweeping questions and frame them in a comprehensive and far-reaching approach.[12]

3 THE CONTRIBUTION OF ECONOMIC HISTORY TO ECONOMIC THEORY

The study of economic history can widen research perspectives and foster the advancement of economic theory. But its contribution is uneven and depends on the nature of the topic. It is virtually nil in tackling clear-cut abstract problems such as the paradox of value or (to take a less antiquarian question) the existence of equilibrium in the Walrasian economy, whose proof benefited most from the acquaintance with fixed point theorems. At the other end of the spectrum, historical knowledge is most helpful in analyzing multiform, intricate subjects like economic growth. Between these extremes, the usefulness of economic history increases along a wide range of topics.

The impact of economic history on economic theory, therefore, relates to the nature of the subject rather than to the historical setting. Recent happenings can teach the economist much more than past ones if they concern entangled questions that do not lend themselves to straightforward treatment. Hence, a study of the present-day transition of Eastern European countries to the market economy is more instructive than an account of inflation under Diocletian or during the French Revolution because, while those episodes simply point to the established principles of the quantity theory, the former sheds light on an unprecedented situation, suggestive of a variety of novel developments not immediately susceptible to standard modeling.

The case for the importance of history must thus be built on the general concept of complexity of economic phenomena, not just on the historical conditioning of economic analysis. The time dimension is one element of complexity, but not the only one. In constructing a theory, the economist extracts a small subset of variables from the economic universe. Yet several such subsets can be taken; and, more important, a slight change in the assumptions leads to different, often contrasting hypotheses. The research strategy chosen is therefore crucial. By extending the knowledge of temporal and spatial contingencies, history can provide the decisive additional information to study complex topics. With regard to the Eastern European transition, for example, an approach that neglects transaction costs, property rights, and institutions – all issues emphasized in the work of Douglass North – would perform poorly. It would fail to capture the essence of the problem, witness the numerous mistaken predictions about the timing and effects of the transition.

While history *per se* does not immediately contribute to theory, it points to a plurality of features characterizing diverse configurations of the economy. History is not a tool of economic theorizing, as the historical school claimed, and thus plays no direct role in model-building. But its indirect role is important because, besides enriching the data, it suggests other relevant variables and alternative interactions between the factors involved. Presenting different scenarios and showing the conditions under which some hypotheses have been corroborated, history acts as a catalyst, enhancing the modeling strategy and the design of economic policies. To take a striking example, the stock market crash of October 1987 did not have the disastrous consequences of that of October 1929, since that experience had brought a substantial advancement in theory and the application of the right policy.

Certainly, it is the economist's task to weigh the lesson of history relative to other elements in the information set and exploit its potential. Successful results are ultimately rooted in the economist's serendipitous intuition, helping to select the appropriate theoretical approach. Milton Friedman's (1968) classic paper on monetary policy is a case in point. Friedman explicitly recognized the importance of economic history in this article and in his overall theoretical work, stressing, however, the difficulty of describing exactly through which mechanisms.

> I have no doubt that economic history did influence my work on economic theory, but I have great difficulty in saying precisely how or through what channels. ... my presidential address on 'The Role of Monetary Policy' is studded with references to historical developments that either illustrated a point I wanted to make, indicated why a point I was making was significant, or provided historical evidence for a proposition. ... As economists, we can only reason about a world we know something about, and our major source of knowledge about that world comes from economic history. However, it is seldom possible to trace the precise connection between particular historical episodes and specific theoretical propositions. History defines our problems and tests our answers. (2001: 127, 129)

However, economists have increasingly departed from this approach. Economics is often compared to physics but, excepting the analysis of the simplest issues, this is far-fetched. As Arrow observed in discussing the analogy between economics and geology: 'In an ideal theory, perhaps, the whole influence of the past would be summed up in observations on the present. But such a theory cannot be stated in any complex uncontrolled system, not even for the Earth' (1986: 19).

Complex structures do not lend themselves to plain analytical treatment. The large number of variables affecting economic phenomena may give rise to different testable hypotheses, and yet most of them cannot be conclusively rejected. In economics, testability does not ensure excludability. On the one hand, several conjectures are not refuted, leaving the theorist with various modeling alternatives. Hence, the theory of real business cycles, stressing the supply side, coexists with other theories of economic fluctuations focusing on aggregate demand, which have not been rejected. On the other hand, even a rejected hypothesis can be corroborated at a different time and place. Thus, the liquidity trap, a weak point of Keynes's *General Theory* ever devoid of empirical support, has now been revived to analyze the stagnation of the Japanese economy.[13] In both cases, the structural complexity of economics prevents the excludability of most hypotheses. This is what determines the shakiness of economic forecasts which, to a much greater extent than weather forecasts for instance, cannot fully grasp the interplay of a variety of factors underlying non-excludable conjectures.[14] In the physical sciences, instead, a falsified theory can confidently be excluded, so that the coexistence of any such theory with a well-corroborated hypothesis can be ruled out.

To contrast economics with another field, James Watson's (1968) fascinating account of the DNA breakthrough tells of countless attempts to envisage the right structure until the double helix was eventually found. It was hard to intuit the model, but once it had been discovered, the other hypotheses were excluded and DNA provided the keystone for building molecular biology. In the social sciences, however, the concept of 'true' model takes a rather different meaning, as a substantial number of hypotheses cannot be excluded, thus defying a well-founded solution. So where the discovery of the structure of DNA successfully concluded the search for a molecular model to explain the inheritance of genetic traits, no such precise answer could ever be offered to account for, say, unemployment, economic development or the behavior of stock market prices.[15]

In this connection, it is a commonplace to see the distinctive feature of social sciences as the impossibility of controlled experiments,[16] but this is rather an implication of complexity than a distinguishing element. In fact, controlled experiment is impossible in meteorology too, yet satellites have increased information so greatly that weather forecasts have become much more accurate. This could be because of the lesser complexity of the model of the weather (see note 14), whose predictive power was heightened by additional information despite the unfeasibility of controlled experiments. The impossibility of controlled experimentation in economics is therefore just a symptom of the problems of structural complexity and the non-excludability of alternative hypotheses. If, for the sake of the argument, economics could be shorn of these characteristics to the point that models yielded clear-cut solutions and accurate forecasts, there would be no need for experimentation at all. The economy's development path could be as predictable as the evolution of some colonies of ants or bees where social organization is complex but individual behavior is repetitive, unvarying. Such a scenario is patently unrealistic, not for the lack of experimentation but simply because the inherent complexity of economic phenomena[17] gives rise to various hypotheses that cannot usually be excluded. In other words, the main obstacle to building 'the' model in economics is not the impossibility of experiment but simply the very great number of relevant variables and their interactions.

Certainly, excludability is a matter of degree not of kind; yet there is a discontinuity in the social sciences, in that several conjectures coexist and once-neglected theories can successfully explain elusive new issues. Hence, excludability should not be seen as the basis of an absolute dichotomy between the physical and social sciences, so clear-cut as to be tantamount to a criterion of demarcation, but rather as a principle that throws light on the distinctive traits of various branches of knowledge. In this regard, recalling a trite proposition, economics has an in-between position among disciplines as the least imprecise of the social sciences. This view of knowledge running from hard to soft sciences can also be found within economics, which itself displays a sort of continuum of topics with varying degrees of complexity.

The contribution of economic history to economic theory stems from these peculiar features and increases with the complexity of the subject. Hence, simple problems in applied microeconomics have little to gain from historical inquiry, while theoretical and policy issues in macroeconomics do. A finance minister asking about the expected yield of a tax on wine would receive a rather precise answer whose accuracy may approach that of the physical sciences, since in the current state of advancement of microeconomics, rival hypotheses can mostly be excluded. By contrast, complex macroeconomic questions defy excludability. Thus, the welfare effects of a country's membership in a monetary union cannot be determined within any simple, straightforward theoretical framework, as the analysis touches on numerous aspects involving different hypotheses.

In general, excludability varies inversely with complexity; thus, complexity increases the number of alternative models. As Mundell observed, in the course of time good models can become bad models and the selection is made on the basis of empirical relevance and axiomatic consistency.[18] Again, the choice of the modeling strategy ultimately rests with the economist's intuition and critical judgment. By providing additional information, historical knowledge can dispel uncertainty to some extent and substantially enhance the theory's explanatory power.

Finally, there is also feedback from theory to economic history, since hypotheses are tested by subsequent events, which in turn prompt new conjectures.[19] This is a circular process propelled by exogenous shocks that can displace the prevailing paradigm until the next major event engenders another paradigm shift. Thus, the Great Depression led to Keynesian economics and the stagflation of the 1970s spurred the new classical macroeconomics. Moreover, history plays a key role also in ordinary circumstances, helping the theorist to prune the tree of economic knowledge to produce the appropriate model. All in all, regardless of the intricacy and magnitude of the issue, the impact of history on theory is always substantial; by throwing light on the specific aspects of complex problems it enhances both the explanatory power of theory and the policy design.

4 ECONOMICS AND THE SENSE OF HISTORY

Viewed as a unique process in historic time, the subject of economics does not give rise to repetition (Schumpeter 1954: 12; Supple 1965: 100). Hence, one derives from the past not stereotyped patterns but hints about the nature of economic change that may be crucial for understanding the present and forecasting the future. Schumpeter's emphasis on the sense of history reflects this point. A familiarity with history enables the economist to avoid a narrow focus on the subject, which may miss essential assumptions. While economics has progressively departed from this approach,[20] great economists seldom lack the sense of history; escaping the inertia of ingrained modes of thought, they tend to anticipate important developments.

The evolution of the monetary system in the twentieth century provides several cases in point. In the aftermath of World War I, the crisis of the gold standard triggered an epochal transformation of monetary arrangements culminating in the generalized diffusion of fiat money after two and a half millennia of commodity money. Wartime inflation, soaring public debt and the hardships of real adjustment in the belligerent countries made the return to gold, and in particular the restoration rule of imposing prewar parities, virtually impracticable. Nevertheless, the consensus on the gold exchange standard that emerged at the Genoa conference was shared by academic economists, with the notable exception of Keynes, who spotted the momentous change in the properties of the system.

Advocates of the ancient standard do not observe how remote it now is from the spirit and the requirements of the age. A regulated non-metallic standard has slipped in unnoticed. *It exists.* Whilst the economists dozed, the academic dream of a hundred years, doffing its cap and gown, clad in paper rags, has crept into the real world by means of the bad fairies – always so much more potent than the good – the wicked Ministers of Finance. (1923: 173)

In Keynes's view, the hybrid gold exchange standard, which retained the defects of the gold standard without its advantages, was doomed; a prediction grounded in both theory and history that proved correct. As regards theory, Keynes noticed the key role of the restoration rule for the credibility of the gold standard – 'It is of the essence of the argument that the *exact* pre-war parity should be recovered' (1923: 150) – and thus, in case of a sizeable depreciation making the rule impossible to enforce, he called for a policy aimed at price level stability. As regards history, Keynes emphasized the transition from a 'natural' to a 'managed' money and the increasing power of central banks, especially of the US Fed because of its enormous gold reserves,[21] in stabilizing the price level and also output and employment. Keynes caught the crucial historical event of the moment, i.e. the severing of the connection between gold and the money supply, which gave birth to modern monetary policy. He accordingly called for cutting the link with gold outright, a watershed in monetary thought: 'Therefore I make the proposal – which may seem, but should not be, shocking – of separating entirely the gold reserve from the note issue' (1923: 196).

This fertile interplay between history and theory is also found in others of Keynes's works. In the *General Theory* he considers the long-run effects of changes in the quantity of money as 'a question for historical generalisation rather than for pure theory' (1936 [1964]: 306). Since friction in the monetary transmission mechanism is greater downward than upwards, in case of persistent deflationary pressure the preferred solution will always be to change the monetary standard, as is shown by the secular rise in the price level. Keynes's contribution to the post-WWII monetary reconstruction starts from the lesson of past monetary arrangements to contrive a scheme that, correcting their shortcomings, could project the monetary system into the future. The Keynes Plan was designed to remedy the defects of the inter-war gold exchange standard – bilateral trade, competitive devaluations, a volume of international reserves dependent on the gold industry and on the policies of individual countries, asymmetry – and avoid an adjustment mechanism that, based on changes in liquidity, caused sharp variations in output and employment. His proposed Clearing Union would operate through changes in the velocity of circulation rather than in the stock of money (Keynes 1943). Although little of the Keynes Plan survived during the Bretton Woods negotiations, it did provide a kind of blueprint for the European Payments Union, one of the most successful postwar institutions.

These examples drawn from Keynes's writings corroborate the hypothesis of a positive relationship between the influence of economic history on economic analysis and the complexity of the topic. Monetary policy and international monetary reform are complex indeed, involving theory, institutions and politics. A thorough knowledge of history widens one's analytical perspective and helps to devise a research strategy that can produce sound, original results.

The impact of economic history does not relate to the economist's vision. Milton Friedman, who is in this regard antithetic to Keynes, also uses his vast knowledge of monetary history to build hypotheses running against the mainstream, and yet yielding correct predictions. His analysis of Bretton Woods is an excellent example. While the consensus view endorsed the new monetary order as the solution to the severe interwar imbalances, Friedman and a few other critics, like Frank Graham and James Meade, pointed out its inconsistencies – chiefly, the inadequacy of the adjustment mechanism and the adjustable peg – and argued for flexible exchange rates. Friedman also stressed that gold played no role in the monetary system and should therefore be traded in free markets like any other commodity (1953: 192). These propositions anticipated the events of the following decades, but at the time they were considered heretical. In particular, although the actual role of gold had waned, its indirect influence in the form of a strong commitment to fixed exchange rates was still substantial. This attitude revealed a backward-looking and myopic attachment to metallic standards that would eventually contribute to the demise of the Bretton Woods system. Recalling the evolution of international monetary arrangements before and after World War II, Friedman underscored the failure to understand these developments:

> Only a cultural lag leads us still to think of gold as the central element in our monetary system. A more accurate description of the role of gold in U.S. policy is that it is primarily a commodity whose price is supported, like wheat or other agricultural products, rather than the key to our monetary system. (1960: 81)

Friedman's correct forecast shows how the grasp of historical trends helps in building sound economic analysis. In a sense, history enables us to lop off the dead wood of theory and save the healthy branches projecting into the future. This pruning is essential in tackling complex issues, as distinguished from abstract and clear-cut problems. A sense of history helps us to single out the key factors and guides the construction of the model. Of course, since the outcome can be judged only ex post, there is a natural tendency to overrate economists' forecasting ability because wrong predictions are quickly forgotten. Ex ante, the challenge is to select, among various research strategies, the right direction of analysis.

On international monetary arrangements, Friedman and Mundell reach very different conclusions from their reading of economic history. In his Nobel lecture, Robert Mundell (2000) teaches several important lessons, distinguishing three key developments in twentieth-century monetary history: the transformation of the gold standard after World War I and its role in causing the Depression; the contradiction between independent domestic policies and fixed exchange rates stemming from the Tripartite Agreement and sanctioned at Bretton Woods; and the outbreak of inflation and the lack of policy discipline under flexible exchange rates. Looking to the future, he identifies two central unresolved questions now that monetary stability has been regained, namely exchange rate volatility and the absence of an international currency. He proposes some sort of monetary unification of the three main currencies, but is aware of possible obstacles: 'It remains to be seen where leadership will come from and whether a restoration of the international monetary system will be compatible with the power configuration of the world economy' (2000: 339). Mundell supports fixed exchange rates; Friedman unyieldingly called for flexible exchange rates.

International monetary arrangements can also be considered through the evolution of the medium of exchange. This alternative approach underscores the diffusion of fiat money, as a watershed in monetary history. After the demise of commodity money, the very idea of designing an international monetary system may be impracticable. In particular, while fixed parities were a natural feature of the commodity standard, their restoration would be somewhat artificial and lack solid foundations after the spread of fiat money – 'the logical domestic counterpart of flexible exchange rates' (Friedman 1953: 191). Moreover, the transition to fiat money paralleled the implementation of autonomous monetary policy, which would not be sacrificed on the altar of fixed exchange rates. Indeed, even now in the heyday of the new classical macroeconomics, stabilization policies are seen as playing an essential role in the presence of rigidities.[22] Hence, the constraint on domestic policies and the associated macroeconomic costs of short-run adjustment imposed by a rigid exchange rate regime may not be acceptable nowadays. The weighing of a monetary anchor, result of the last century of monetary theory and institutions, may make the return to fixed exchange rates a remote possibility indeed. And the creation of a world currency clashes with the interests of the dominant power; as Mundell (2000: 335, 338–9) recognizes, it would not be practicable.

The foregoing discussion does not aim to suggest which solution will eventually prevail, but to show how one's reading of the past can decisively affect the direction and the outcome of research. Though they both have a thorough knowledge of monetary history, Friedman and Mundell stress different aspects of historical experience and so reach opposite conclusions. Furthermore, even the implausibility of a return to fixed exchange rates may be overturned. In a futuristic scenario, technological progress could eliminate tangible money and perhaps make the idea of discretionary monetary policy obsolete, giving rise to an accounting system of exchange (Black 1970; Fama 1980). In such a system, the Wicksellian problem of price level indeterminacy would require issuing a constant stock of a fiat instrument which, like gold in an advanced gold standard, would not actually circulate but simply anchor the price level. Fixed parities, in this case, could link the instruments issued by the various countries.

5 CONCLUSIONS

The message of this paper could not be conveyed better than by Keynes's celebrated passage elaborating on the skills necessary to the economist.

> The study of economics does not seem to require any specialised gifts of an unusually high order. Is it not, intellectually regarded, a very easy subject compared with the higher branches of philosophy and pure science? Yet good, or even competent, economists are the rarest of birds. An easy subject, at which very few excel! The paradox finds its explanation, perhaps, in that the master-economist must possess a rare *combination* of gifts. He must reach a high standard in several different directions and must combine talents not often found together. He must be mathematician, historian, statesman, philosopher – in some degree. He must understand symbols and speak in words. He must contemplate the particular in terms of the general, and touch abstract and concrete in the same flight of thought. *He must study the present in the light of the past for the purposes of the future.* (1924: 321–2, second italics added)

The simplicity of economics is only apparent; it stems from the intuitive character of the basic axiom of maximizing behavior. Yet most economic problems actually present an inherent structural complexity and can thus be viewed from several perspectives, like the changing images of a hologram; this generates different theories. Hence, in choosing his research strategy, the economist should resort to all sources of information, deploying the combination of abilities emphasized by Keynes. Economic history retained a prominent place until World War II but then faded away. Nowadays, most practitioners would ridicule Schumpeter's statement that 'In principle ... Latin palaeography ... is one of the techniques of economic analysis' (1954: 13). In fact, following the revolution in the 'language' of economics,[23] the rise of the new economic history produced substantial progress, but by transforming economic history into a field of applied economics it marked the decline of the economists' interest in the subject.[24]

A pluralistic approach is certainly to be encouraged. However, the value of the contribution of economic history varies with the complexity of the topic. The Slutsky equation and the Bickerdike condition are analytically elegant solutions to clear-cut, abstract problems, which do not much benefit from historical investigation. On the other hand, in working on entangled and complex issues, the wide-ranging perspective of historical knowledge stimulates intuition and suggests alternative interpretations, helping to build the appropriate model. History is indeed a goldmine of ideas that can provide useful material invaluable for deepening our comprehension of economic reality and guiding our research strategy.

Filippo Cesarano
Banca d'Italia, Rome, Italy
filippo.cesarano@bancaditalia.it

ACKNOWLEDGEMENTS

Thanks are due to Cristina Bicchieri, Stefano Fenoaltea, Jeffrey Williamson and two anonymous referees for their perceptive comments. The usual caveat applies.

NOTES

1 The collection of essays edited by William Parker (1986) was a reaction to this state of affairs. See Parker's preface to the book.
2 As Heckscher observed: 'Controversies regarding method are almost always barren' (1929 [1953]: 421). And Rostow noted: 'I do not much hold with ardent debate about method. A historian's method is as individual – as private – a matter as a novelist's style. ... Moreover, as a practical matter, no good cause is likely to be served by further exhortation to the historian to use more theory or to the theorist to read more history. Progress in this old contentious terrain is made only by meeting a payroll; that is, by demonstrating that something interesting and worth while can be generated by working with historical data within a conscious and orderly theoretical framework, or by adding to the structure of theory through historical generalization' (1957: 509).
3 Mark Blaug clearly describes the classical position: 'Over and over again, in Senior, in Mill, in Cairnes, and even in Jevons, we have found the notion that "verification" is not a testing of economic theories to see whether they are true or false, but only a method of establishing the boundaries of application of theories deemed to be obviously true: one verifies in order to discover whether "disturbing causes" can account for the discrepancies between stubborn facts and theoretically valid reasons; if they do, the theory has been wrongly applied, but the theory itself is still true. The question of whether there is any way of showing a logically consistent theory to be false is never even contemplated' (1992: 71–2).
4 Thus, analogously, Ferdinando Galiani on 'the art of government, less studied than any other ... . The materials with which to depict it are provided by history. History is an unbroken account of the errors and punishments of mankind: it is thus easy, meditating on the past and growing wise from the mistakes of others, to rectify the first and remedy the second. And just as with centuries of astronomical observations the system of the planets' motion proved not difficult to fathom, so too in the science of government' (1751 [1963]: 12, author's translation).
5 Thus Heckscher observed: 'the historical and the theoretical treatment of economic phenomena are not mutually exclusive methods, but ..., on the contrary, theory is needed for the understanding of economic development, and

history for applying theory to the right sort of premisses' (1933 [1967]: 705). And, in his presidential address to the first meeting of the Economic History Association, Edwin Gay stated: 'The tentative generalizations of the economists give foothold and insight to the economic historian, and in turn the perspectives of the economic historian help in the valuations of the economist' (1941 [1953]: 413). See also the closing sentence of Rostow's quotation in note 2 above.

6   Actually, Schumpeter's often quoted dictum – that, of the three fields making up economic analysis, i.e. history, statistics and theory, 'economic history ... is by far the most important' (1954: 12) – did not reflect the state of the art in the early 1950s. He had anticipated this idea a few years earlier. According to Samuelson, 'Joseph Schumpeter astounded a New York 1949 National Bureau of Economic Research Conference by declaring: "Yes, mathematics is important for the economic theorist. But I must assert that wisdom about economic history is even more important"'(2001: 271). I am indebted to a referee for clarifying this point.

7   'As a social scientist with a strong orientation toward public policy problems, the economist seeks to establish theories with at least some generality and timeliness. He is interested therefore in the systematic, repetitive aspects of economic behavior. Consequently, the economic historian should not be surprised if the economist shows little interest in the social competence and family relationships of some nineteenth-century merchants – *unless it is previously or concomitantly established* that social competence and family relationships help to explain the successes or failures of individuals in general. The economic historian, in sum, should seek the limited generalization that is the objective of all science; only if that course is adopted can economic history expect to influence the development of economics' (Meyer and Conrad 1957: 535–6).

8   In this connection, Douglass North remarked: 'It seems to me that we have been ignored by the economists for good reasons. We have simply been taking their traditional tools and applying these mechanically to the past .... If that is all we can do, then we are truly expendable and Economics Departments are quite right in relegating us to a marginal position in their staffing requirements' (1976: 462). And Robert Solow, after censuring the flat application of the standard model to any problem independently of time and place, observed: 'As I inspect some current work in economic history I have the sinking feeling that a lot of it looks exactly like the kind of economic analysis I have just finished caricaturing: the same integrals, the same regressions, the same substitution of t-ratios for thought. Apart from anything else, it is no fun reading the stuff any more. Far from offering the economic theorist a widened range of perceptions, this sort of economic history gives back to the theorist the same routine gruel that the economic theorist gives to the historian. Why should I believe, when it is applied to thin eighteenth-century data, something that carries no conviction when it is done with more ample twentieth-century data?' (1986: 26).

9   Besides the early writings republished in Lane and Riemersma (1953: section III), the main literature dates from the 1950s to the 1980s. In particular, see the contributions to the conference on 'The Integration of Economic Theory and Economic History' in the December 1957 issue of the *Journal of Economic History* and the papers presented at the meeting of the American Economic Association in December 1964. An analogous session was held twenty years later; revised versions of these articles were published, together with other essays, in Parker (1986).

10   Disparaging Ricardo's neglect of history and the consequential 'Ricardian Vice', he also observed: 'The trouble with [Ricardo] is akin to the trouble I have, in this respect, with my American students, who have plenty of historical material pushed down their throats. But it is to no purpose. They lack the historical sense that no amount of factual study can give. This is why it is so much easier to make theorists of them than economists' (Schumpeter 1954: 472, n. 2).

11   As David Landes put it: 'The economist seeks abstraction, the better to order and systematize and build models. He wants sufficient explanation; and as Milton Friedman likes to say, one good reason is enough. The historian on the other hand, revels in complexity, is happy to incorporate new unknowns in his problem (and let the simultaneous equations be damned), and generally follows the law of conservation of evidence. The explanation should try to account for as many pieces of evidence as possible and as are known. Indeed ideally, it should account for the whole story. Two good reasons are better than one, and three are better then two' (1978: 9).

12   The recent book of O'Rourke and Williamson (1999) on globalization represents a notable example of such work.

13   Schumpeter made this point most clearly, contrasting the alternate prevalence of monetary analysis and real analysis in the history of economics: 'the reason for the defeat or rather the collapse of Monetary Analysis in the last decades of the eighteenth century was its weakness. Even if, for the sake of argument, we grant without qualification that the principle of monetary analysis is sound and that the modern development of it is an improvement upon the real analysis of the nineteenth century, it should be clear that the latter was not less superior to the monetary analysis of the eighteenth. Such spirals of advance are, I believe, not uncommon: theories that it is an achievement to displace may return to displace those by which they had been displaced, and both the displacement and the return may benefit that strange thing, scientific knowledge' (1954: 288).

14   In his John Locke Lectures, Hilary Putnam elaborates on the concept of structural complexity in relation to the distinction between physical and social sciences. 'What I maintain ... is that there is a fundamental difference between physics and the social sciences (or better, social *studies*) in this respect. Physics does provide detailed explanatory models of such natural kinds. But we are not, realistically, going to get a detailed explanatory model for the natural kind 'human being'. And the difficulty does not have to do with *mere* complexity. Meteorologists do have a mathematical model of the *weather* (or of many kinds of weather phenomena), although (notoriously) they cannot predict the weather very well in practice because (a) the values of the requisite parameters are not all accurately known; and (b) the computations would be too complex to carry out even if they were known. The reason one can have a fairly simple mathematical model of the natural kind 'weather' is that, although the weather is a mess, it is a relatively unstructured mess. What causes problems for the theorist, as opposed to the engineer, is not complexity *per se*, but highly structured complexity – that is, complexity of structure' (1978: 62).

15   In the opening paragraphs of his classic essay, Louis Bachelier emphasizes the impossibility of predicting stock market prices, given the high number of variables and the interaction between the factors involved. 'The influences which determine fluctuations on the Exchange are innumerable; past, present, and even discounted future events are reflected in market price, but often show

no apparent relation to price changes. Besides the somewhat natural causes of price changes, artificial causes also intervene: The Exchange reacts on itself, and the current fluctuation is a function, not only of previous fluctuations, but also of the orientation of the current state. The determination of these fluctuations depends on an infinite number of factors; it is, therefore, impossible to aspire to mathematical prediction of it. Contradictory opinions concerning these changes diverge so much that at the same instant buyers believe in a price increase and sellers in a price decrease. The calculus of probabilities, doubtless, could never be applied to fluctuations in security quotations, and the dynamics of the Exchange will never be an exact science' (1900 [2000]: 18).

16 There is, of course, a well-developed field of experimental economics, but it is confined to microeconomic behavior and cannot deal with more complex issues, particularly in macroeconomics. As Solow remarked: 'The research [experimental economics] is certainly to be encouraged. In the immediate context I am thinking primarily about macroeconomics, where replicable experimentation is more or less out of the question. How could we replicate in a laboratory a set of memories, beliefs and expectations about the behavior of the Federal Reserve System? How could we even know that experimental subjects believe that the laboratory's monetary policy is really produced by the real Fed? I grant that it is the job of an imaginative experimenter to provide satisfactory answers to or circumventions of such questions or – as Charles Plott has pointed out to me – to reduce them to more elementary questions that are susceptible of experiment. I am all for trying, but I am allowed to be skeptical' (1986: 28).

17 The notion of the greater complexity of economics *vis-à-vis* the physical sciences was explored by John Stuart Mill in the last of his Essays (1844) on the definition and methodology of political economy.

18 'Models can be rejected because they fail to meet the two fundamental tests of economic reliability and relevance: conformity to experience (a matter of history and econometrics), and/or conformity to the axioms on which the science is founded. In economics, the unifying core of theory is the axiom of rational self-interest; belief in the relevance of this axiom is the science's sine qua non' (Mundell 1971: 78).

19 In this connection, Lawrence Summers (1991) emphasizes the importance of establishing stylized facts as a guide to economic theory, arguing that the starting point of many theoretical contributions is the historical investigation of particular events.

20 Even in the analysis of economic growth, the topic deemed to benefit most from historical investigation, there has been little interplay. As Nicholas Crafts observed: 'Sadly, it must be said straightaway that economic history has had little influence upon and has been relatively little affected by growth theory of the postwar variety. More disappointingly and surprisingly, economic history has contributed hardly at all to major questions of applied economics of growth such as the relative decline of the UK economy in the long run' (1987: 40).

21 'For the past two years the United States has *pretended* to maintain a gold standard. *In fact* it has established a dollar standard; and, instead of ensuring that the value of the dollar shall conform to that of gold, it makes provision, at great expense, that the value of gold shall conform to that of the dollar' (Keynes 1923: 198).

22   As Robert Lucas remarked in his presidential address: 'If ... rigidities of some
     kind prevent the economy from reacting efficiently to nominal or real shocks,
     or both, there is a need to design suitable policies and to assess their
     performance. In my opinion, this is the case: I think the stability of monetary
     aggregates and nominal spending in the postwar United States is a major
     reason for the stability of aggregate production and consumption during these
     years, relative to the experience of the interwar period and the contemporary
     experience of other economies. If so, this stability must be seen in part as an
     achievement of the economists, Keynesian and monetarist, who guided
     economic policy over these years' (2003: 11).

23   Of course, a change in language should not be confused with a change in
     knowledge: one can work highly sophisticated models to arrive at silly
     conclusions and use plain English to make a breakthrough in economic
     theory. What matters is not the kind of language used but original ideas that
     advance economic knowledge.

24   The first anticipation of the impact came in the debate on Meyer and Conrad's
     seminal paper, where most participants called for methodological eclecticism
     in order to preserve the contribution of economic history to economic theory.
     Simon Kuznets summarized the discussion as follows: 'in view of the great
     complexity of the problems faced by economic historians in organizing and
     interpreting the data on the course of economic change, allowance must be
     made for various approaches in formulating hypotheses – from selective
     description and interpretation that appeal on the basis of intuitive plausibility
     to the more rigid structure in which quantifiable variables are sharply defined
     and specific assumptions concerning the functions are made to permit the
     combination of the variables in an equation – even when an *e* term to allow for
     random errors is included. In particular, it was suggested that much of the
     value of economic history lies not in testing narrowly defined hypotheses, but
     in providing the basis for formulating them, in other words, in amassing a
     stock of hypotheses that have been suggested by specific complexes of
     historical events (1957: 547).

REFERENCES

Arrow, K. J. (1986) 'History: the view from economics', in William N. Parker (ed.)
    Economic History and the Modern Economist, Oxford: Basil Blackwell, pp. 13–20.
Bachelier, L. [1900] (2000) 'Theory of Speculation', in Paul H. Cootner (ed.) *The
    Random Character of Stock Market Prices*, London: Risk Publications, pp. 18–91.
Black, F. (1970) 'Banking and interest rates in a world without money: the effects of
    uncontrolled banking', *Journal of Bank Research* 1: 9–20.
Blaug, M. (1992) *The Methodology of Economics: Or How Economists Explain*,
    Cambridge: Cambridge University Press.
Cipolla, C. M. (1991) *Between History and Economics: An Introduction to Economic
    History*, Oxford: Basil Blackwell.
Crafts, N. F. R. (1987) 'Economic history', in John Eatwell, Murray Milgate and
    Peter Newman (eds) *The New Palgrave: A Dictionary of Economics*, London:
    Macmillan, pp. 37–42.
Fama, E. F. (1980) 'Banking in the theory of finance', *Journal of Monetary
    Economics* 6: 39–57.
Fogel, R. W. (1965) 'The reunification of economic history with economic theory',
    American Economic Review. Papers and Proceedings 55: 92–8.

466   *Articles*

Friedman, M. (1953) 'The case for flexible exchange rates', in Milton Friedman, *Essays in Positive Economics*, Chicago: The University of Chicago Press, pp. 157–203.

Friedman, M. (1960) *A Program for Monetary Stability*, New York: Fordham University Press.

Friedman, M. (1968) 'The role of monetary policy', *American Economic Review* 58: 1–17.

Friedman, M. (2001) 'Friedman on Friedman', *Rivista di Storia Economica* 17: 127–30.

Galiani, F. [1751] (1963) *Della Moneta*, Milano: Feltrinelli.

Gay, E. F. [1941] (1953) 'The tasks of economic history', *Journal of Economic History*, Supplement, 1: 9–16, reprinted in Frederic C. Lane and Jelle C. Riemersma (eds) *Enterprise and Secular Change: Readings in Economic History*, London: George Allen and Unwin, pp. 407–14.

Gordon, R. A. (1965) 'Discussion', *American Economic Review: Papers and Proceedings* 55: 116–8.

Heckscher, E. F. [1929] (1953) 'A plea for theory in economic history', *Economic Journal*, Supplement, 1: 525–34, reprinted in Frederic C. Lane and Jelle C. Riemersma (eds.) *Enterprise and Secular Change: Readings in Economic History*, London: George Allen and Unwin, pp. 421–30.

Heckscher, E. F. [1933] (1967) 'The aspects of economic history', in *Economic Essays in Honour of Gustav Cassel. October 20th 1933*, London: Frank Cass, pp. 705–20.

Hume, D. [1752] (1970) *Writings on Economics*, ed. Eugene Rotwein, Madison: The University of Wisconsin Press.

Keynes, J. M. (1923) *A Tract on Monetary Reform*, London: Macmillan.

Keynes, J. M. (1924) 'Alfred Marshall, 1842–1924', *Economic Journal* 34: 311–72.

Keynes, J. M. [1936] (1964) *The General Theory of Employment, Interest and Money*, London: Macmillan.

Keynes, J. M. (1943) 'The objective of international price stability', *Economic Journal* 53: 185–7.

Kindleberger, C. P. (1986) 'A further comment', in William N. Parker (ed.) *Economic History and the Modern Economist*, Oxford: Basil Blackwell, pp. 83–92.

Kuznets, S. (1957) 'Summary of discussion and postscript', *Journal of Economic History* 17: 545–53.

Landes, D. S. (1978) 'On avoiding Babel', *Journal of Economic History* 38: 3–12.

Lane, F. C. and Riemersma, J. C. (eds) (1953) *Enterprise and Secular Change: Readings in Economic History*, London: George Allen and Unwin.

Lucas, R. E. (2003) 'Macroeconomic priorities', *American Economic Review* 93: 1–14.

McCloskey, D. N. (1976) 'Does the past have useful economics?', *Journal of Economic Literature* 14: 434–61.

Meyer, J. R. and Conrad, A. H. (1957) 'Economic theory, statistical inference, and economic history', *Journal of Economic History* 17: 524–44.

Mill, J. S. (1844) *Essays on Some Unsettled Questions in Political Economy*, London: Parker.

Mundell, R. A. (1971) *Monetary Theory: Inflation, Interest, and Growth in the World Economy*, Pacific Palisades, CA: Goodyear Publishing Company.

Mundell, R. A. (2000) 'A reconsideration of the twentieth century', *American Economic Review* 90: 327–40.

North, D. C. (1976) 'The place of economic history in the discipline of economics', *Economic Inquiry* 14: 461–5.

O'Rourke, K. H. and Williamson, J. G. (1999) *Globalization and History: The Evolution of a Nineteenth-Century Atlantic Economy*, Cambridge, MA: The MIT Press.

Parker, W. N. (ed.) (1986) *Economic History and the Modern Economist*, Oxford: Basil Blackwell.

Putnam, H. (1978) 'Meaning and knowledge', in Hilary Putnam *Meaning and the Moral Sciences*, London: Routledge & Kegan Paul, pp. 7–80.

Rostow, W. W. (1957) 'The interrelation of theory and economic history', *Journal of Economic History* 17: 509–23.

Samuelson, P. A. (2001) 'Economic history and mainstream economic analysis', *Rivista di storia economica* 17: 271–7.

Schumpeter, J. A. (1947) 'The creative response in economic history', *Journal of Economic History* 7: 149–59.

Schumpeter, J. A. (1954) *History of Economic Analysis*, Oxford: Oxford University Press.

Solow, R. E. (1986) 'Economics: is something missing?', in William N. Parker (ed.) *Economic History and the Modern Economist*, Oxford: Basil Blackwell, pp. 21–9.

Summers, L. H. (1991) 'The scientific illusion in empirical macroeconomics', *Scandinavian Journal of Economics* 93: 129–48.

Supple, B. E. (1965) 'Has the early history of developed countries any current relevance?', *American Economic Review. Papers and Proceedings* 55: 99–103.

Watson, J. D. (1968) *The Double Helix*, New York: Atheneum.

Name index

Mises, L., von 84, 85, 122, 125, 126
Mlynarsky, F. 129
Moggridge, D. 131, 132
Mongelli, F.P. 173, 193, 195, 201
Mott, T. 42
Mundell, R.A. 5, 81, 107, 109, 118–19, 137,
  144, 146, 151, 153, 154, 155, 157–8,
  165, 166, 167, 168, 173–80, 184,
  190–4, 197–200, 202, 217, 220–1, 226

Niehans, J. 2, 5, 45, 55, 56, 66, 74, 96, 97,
  100, 110, 111, 151, 158, 171, 179
North, D. 195, 213, 214, 224
Nurkse, R. 121

O'Rourke, K.H. 225
Obstfeld, M. 108, 130
Offenbacker, E. 25
Oh, S. 57
Ostroy, J.M. 2, 3, 45, 46, 56, 57, 66, 68, 73,
  98, 100, 102, 153
Oswald, J., of Dunnikier 120

Pagano, M. 154
Pantaleoni, M. 20, 151
Parker, W. 223, 224
Patinkin, D. 14, 24, 25, 26, 35, 48, 63, 72,
  89, 90, 100, 112
Pearce, D.K. 19, 21
Pesek, B.P. 24
Pigou, A.C. 122, 126, 156
Ploeg, F., van der 114
Plosser, C.I. 45
Prachowny, M.F.J. 119
Putnam, H. 225

Redish, A. 4, 87, 103
Ricardo, D. 210, 225
Richter, R. 62
Riemersma, J.C. 224
Robbins, L. 193
Robertson, D.H. 13, 55, 57, 68, 122, 123
Rogers, C.A. 154, 157
Rogers, J.H. 182, 185
Rogoff, K. 108, 114
Roper, D.E. 147
Rose, A.K. 181, 196, 202
Rostow, W.W. 223
Rotwein, E. 120
Rush, M. 21

Sachs, J. 155, 159
Sala-i-Martin, X. 155, 159
Salant, W.S. 143
Samuelson, P.A. 212, 214, 224

Santomero, A.M. 23, 30
Sargent, T.J. 111
Saving, T.R. 24
Say, J.-B. 82
Scadding, J.L. 34
Schacht, H.H.G. 133
Schumpeter, J.A. 1, 43, 52, 73, 74, 80, 106,
  120, 151, 155, 156, 213, 218, 222, 224,
  225
Schwartz, A.J. 11, 14, 20, 21, 24, 28, 30, 36,
  44, 47, 53, 54, 55, 57, 68, 88, 107, 197
Scitovsky, T. 143, 151, 159, 176–7, 178,
  180, 197, 198, 199, 200
Selgin, G.A. 54
Shaw, E.S. 19, 21, 28
Shell, K. 30, 35, 36
Shubik, M. 89
Sichel, D.E. 34, 37
Simon, H.A. 143, 145, 146, 158
Smith, A. 43, 44, 56, 66, 102
Solow, R.E. 212, 224, 226
Spaventa, L. 26
Spencer, D.E. 34
Spindt, P. 25
Spinelli, F. 25
Sprenkle, C.M. 25
Starr, R.M. 3, 45, 46, 57, 66, 68, 73, 98, 100,
  102, 153
Starrett, D. 46
Stigler, G.J. 151, 157
Summers, L.H. 226
Sumner, S. 52, 62
Supple, B.E. 212, 218
Swoboda, A.K. 143

Taub, B. 54
Tavlas, G.S. 179, 180, 193
Taylor, A.M. 130
Thornton, D.L. 34
Tinbergen, J. 110, 165, 178
Tobin, J. 12, 45, 63, 73
Tower, E. 109, 166, 171, 179, 193
Triffin, R. 159
Tsiang, S.C. 71, 96, 111
Tucker, D.P. 28
Tullock, G. 81, 93
Turnovsky, S.J. 147

Ulph, A.M. 25, 46
Ulph, D.T. 25, 46

Vaciago, G. 25
Vanhaverbeke, W. 183
Verga, G. 25, 26
Vicarelli, F. 25